D1797318

FrontPage 97
Made Simple

COMPUTING MADE SIMPLE

AT ONLY £7.99 • 160 PAGES • PAPERBACK

Booksellers and customers agree, this is the best liked and most user friendly series of Computer books for PC users.

The original and the best. These books sell fast!

These books explain the basics of software packages and computer topics in a clear and simple manner, providing just enough information to get started. For users who want an insight into software packages and computers without being overwhelmed by technical terminology they are ideal.

- **Easy to Follow**
- **Task Based**
- **Jargon Free**
- **Easy Steps**
- **Practical**
- **Excellent Value**

ALL YOU NEED TO GET STARTED

BESTSELLER

Works for Windows 3.1 (Version 3)
P. K. McBride
0 7506 2065 X   1994

Lotus 1-2-3 (2.4 DOS Version)
Ian Robertson
0 7506 2066 8   1994

WordPerfect (DOS 6.0)
Stephen Copestake
0 7506 2068 4   1994

BESTSELLER

MS DOS (Up To Version 6.22)
Ian Sinclair
0 7506 2069 2   1994

BESTSELLER

Excel For Windows 3.1 (Version 5)
Stephen Morris
0 7506 2070 6   1994

BESTSELLER

Word For Windows 3.1 (Version 6)
Keith Brindley
0 7506 2071 4   1994

BESTSELLER

Windows 3.1
P. K. McBride
0 7506 2072 2   1994

BESTSELLER

Windows 95
P. K. McBride
0 7506 2306 3   1995

Lotus 1-2-3 for Windows 3.1 (Version 5)
Stephen Morris
0 7506 2307 1   1995

BESTSELLER

Access For Windows 3.1 (Version 2)
Moira Stephen
0 7506 2309 8   1995

BESTSELLER

Internet for Windows 3.1
P. K. McBride
0 7506 2311 X   1995

Pageplus for Windows 3.1 (Version 3)
Ian Sinclair
0 7506 2312 8   1995

Hard Drives
Ian Sinclair
0 7506 2313 6   1995

BESTSELLER

Multimedia for Windows 3.1
Simon Collin
0 7506 2314 4   1995

Powerpoint for Windows 3.1 (Version 4.0)
Moira Stephen
0 7506 2420 5   1995

Office 95
P. K. McBride
0 7506 2625 9   1995

Word Pro for Windows 3.1 (Version 4.0)
Moira Stephen
0 7506 2626 7   1995

BESTSELLER

Word for Windows 95 (Version 7)
Keith Brindley
0 7506 2815 4   1996

BESTSELLER

Excel for Windows 95 (Version 7)
Stephen Morris
0 7506 2816 2   1996

Powerpoint for Windows 95 (Version 7)
Moira Stephen
0 7506 2817 0   1996

BESTSELLER

Access for Windows 95 (Version 7)
Moira Stephen
0 7506 2818 9   1996

BESTSELLER

Internet for Windows 95
P. K. McBride
0 7506 2835 9   1996

Internet Resources
P. K. McBride
0 7506 2836 7   1996

Microsoft Networking
P. K. McBride
0 7506 2837 5   1996

Designing Internet Home Pages
Lilian Hobbs
0 7506 2941 X   1996

BESTSELLER

Works for Windows 95 (Version 4.0)
P. K. McBride
0 7506 3396 4   1996

NEW

Windows NT (Version 4.0)
Lilian Hobbs
0 7506 3511 8   1997

NEW

Compuserve
Keith Brindley
0 7506 3512 6   1997

NEW

Microsoft Internet Explorer
Sam Kennington
0 7506 3513 4   1997

NEW

Netscape Navigator
Sam Kennington
0 7506 3514 2   1997

NEW

Searching The Internet
Sam Kennington
0 7506 3794 3   1997

NEW

The Internet for Windows 3.1 (Second Edition)
P. K. McBride
0 7506 3795 1   1997

NEW

The Internet for Windows 95 (Second Edition)
P. K. McBride
0 7506 3846 X   1997

NEW

Office 97 for Windows
P. K. McBride
0 7506 3798 6   1997

NEW

Powerpoint 97 For Windows
Moira Stephen
0 7506 3799 4   1997

NEW

Access 97 For Windows
Moira Stephen
0 7506 3800 1   1997

NEW

Word 97 For Windows
Keith Brindley
0 7506 3801 X   1997

NEW

Excel 97 For Windows
Stephen Morris
0 7506 3802 8   1997

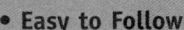

NEW MADE SIMPLE SERIES

PROGRAMMING MADE SIMPLE

AT ONLY £9.99 • 200 PAGES • PAPERBACK

If you're a student or home enthusiast, taking your first steps in programming or an experienced programmer who wants to quickly know the essentials of a new language then the Made Simple programming books are for you.

- Easy to Follow
- Jargon Free
- Task Based
- Practical Exercises

By a combination of tutorial approach, with tasks to do and easy steps, the MADE SIMPLE series of Computer Books from Butterworth-Heinemann stands above all others.

Thousands of people have already discovered that the MADE SIMPLE series gives them what they want fast! Many delighted readers have written, telephoned and e-mailed us about the Made Simple Series of computer books. Comments have included:

- 'Clear, concise and well laid out.'
- 'Ideal for the first time user.'
- 'Clear, accurate, well presented, jargon free, well targeted.'
- 'Easy to follow to perform a task.'
- 'Illustrations are excellent.'
- 'I haven't found any other books worth recommending until these.'

This best selling series is in your local bookshop now, or in case of difficulty, contact:
Heinemann Publishers, Oxford, P.O. Box 381, Oxford OX2 8EJ.
Tel: 01865 314300
Fax: 01865 314091
Credit card sales: 01865 314627
Visit us on the World Wide Web at: http://www.bh.com

NEW		
Java		
P. K. McBride		
0 7506 3241 0		1997
NEW		
Java Script		
P. K. McBride		
0 7506 3797 8		1997
NEW		
Pascal		
P. K. McBride		
0 7506 3242 9		1997
NEW		
C++ Programming		
Conor Sexton		
0 7506 3243 7		1997
NEW		
C Programming		
Conor Sexton		
0 7506 3244 5		1997
NEW		
Visual Basic		
Stephen Morris		
0 7506 3245 3		1997
NEW		
Delphi		
Stephen Morris		
0 7506 3246 1		1997
NEW		
Visual C++		
Stephen Morris		
0 7506 3570 3		1997
NEW		
Unix		
P. K. McBride		
0 7506 3571 1		1997
NEW		
Windows 95 Programming		
Stephen Morris		
0 7506 3572 X		1997
NEW		
Cobol Programming		
(for the year 2000)		
Conor Sexton		
0 7506 3834 6		1997

FrontPage 97
Made Simple

Nat McBride

MADE SIMPLE
BOOKS

Made Simple
An imprint of Butterworth-Heinemann
Linacre House, Jordan Hill, Oxford OX2 8DP
A division of Reed Educational and Professional Publishing Ltd

    A member of the Reed Elsevier plc group

OXFORD   BOSTON   JOHANNESBURG
MELBOURNE   NEW DELHI   SINGAPORE

First published 1998

© Nat McBride, 1998

All rights reserved. No part of this publication
may be reproduced in any material form (including
photocopying or storing in any medium by electronic
means and whether or not transiently or incidentally
to some other use of this publication) without the
written permission of the copyright holder except in
accordance with the provisions of the Copyright,
Design and Patents Act 1988 or under the terms of a
licence issued by the Copyright Licensing Agency Ltd,
90 Tottenham Court Road, London, England W1P 9HE.
Applications for the copyright holder's written permission
to reproduce any part of this publication should be addressed
to the publishers.

TRADEMARKS/REGISTERED TRADEMARKS
Computer hardware and software brand names mentioned in this book are protected
by their respective trademarks and are acknowledged.

British Library Cataloguing in Publication Data
A catalogue record for this book is available from the British Library

ISBN 0 7506 3941 5

Typeset by P.K.McBride, Southampton

Archtype, Bash Casual, Cotswold and Gravity fonts from Advanced Graphics Ltd
Icons designed by Sarah Ward © 1994
Printed and bound in Great Britain by
Scotprint Ltd, Musselburgh, Scotland.

Contents

Preface IX

1   Getting started   1

What is a web? 2
The Explorer window 4
The Editor window 6
Working with pages 8
Page properties 11
Previewing pages 14
Keeping track of your work 16
Summary 18

2   Text and graphics   19

Text 20
Fonts 22
Alignment and lists 24
Placing images 26
Image properties 29
Alternative representations 31
Background sounds 33
Summary 34

3   MS Image Composer   35

MS Image Composer 36
Sprites 38
Shaped sprites 40
Layering sprites 41
Art effects, warps and filters 42

Grouping and flattening 44

Patterns and Fills 45

Erasing 46

Summary 48

4   Active content   49

Active sorcery 50

AVI video clips 51

Other video formats 53

Marquees 54

Animated GIFs 56

Java, ActiveX and JavaScript 59

Summary 60

5   Tables   61

Creating a table 62

Table properties 64

Merging cells 66

Editing cells 69

Importing table data 70

Tables in page design 71

Complex designs 72

Filling in the table 74

Troubleshooting 75

Summary 76

6   Bookmarks and links   77

Using Bookmarks 78

Links to other pages 80

Links to Web pages 83

Using images as links 84

Recalculating Hyperlinks 87

Checking your hyperlinks 88

Summary 90

7   Frames   91

What are frames? 92

Working with frames.. 93

Creating a Frame Set 94

Editing frames 96

Custom grids 98

Target frames 100

Summary.. 102

8   Forms and feedback   103

What are forms? 104

Names and values... 105

Handling form data 106

Creating a form 108

Setting out your form 109

Text boxes 110

Text box validation 111

Push buttons 113

Radio buttons 114

Check boxes 115

Drop-down menus 116

Summary.. 118

9 WebBot Components   119

WebBot components 120
Table of contents 121
Substitutions 122
FrontPage Extensions 124
Scheduled components 125
Timestamps 126
Search 127
Confirmation fields 128
Further components 130
Summary 132

10 Publishing your web   133

Publishing your web 134
Updating a web 135
Network connections 136
Web Publishing Wizard 138
Troubleshooting 140
Summary 142

Links and resources   143

Index   145

Preface

HTML – HyperText Markup Language – is the language used to construct pages on the World Wide Web. These pages, and also different parts of the same page, are connected by hypertext links, which guide Web browsers such as Netscape and Explorer through the Internet.

HTML is not a complicated programming language, but it still takes a while to learn, and even experienced users will admit that it is slow and fiddly to work with at times. Since most computer users are not programmers, but are familiar with systems like Microsoft Windows or the Macintosh Operating System, it made sense for the software companies to develop programs which act as HTML translators. You tell the program what you want, using its toolbar and menu commands, and it translates that into HTML so that Web browsers can read it.

There are a number of HTML editing packages available now, all of which do the same sort of job, but some of which do it much better than others. FrontPage 97 is the latest version from Microsoft and it is probably the most powerful package you can get at the moment. It is comfortable to use, and very thorough – you can chop and change things as much as you like, and FrontPage will run around after you, tidying up all the loose ends.

FrontPage also makes use of a number of mini-programs called 'WebBot Components' which allow you to equip your website with facilities which would normally require the help of an experienced programmer. The WebBot Components not only save time when constructing your site, but also make it easy to collect and organise feedback from your visitors; you can even add a search function to help visitors find what they want.

You don't need to know any HTML or have any technical experience to create a professional-looking website using FrontPage – it is far more a question of letting your creative side loose on the machine! It is useful to have some knowledge of how computer networks work, if you want to set up a complicated site with password-restricted areas, for example, but other than that, all you need is a copy of FrontPage, a little imagination – and this book!

The first few pages will give you a general idea of how FrontPage works, and show you around the screen layout; after that you can jump straight into constructing a website. The following chapters will explain what you can do with FrontPage, and more importantly, how to do it with a minimum of fussing, head-scratching and hair-tearing! Finally, I have included a 'Links and resources' page to point you in the direction of some helpful sources of tips and advice. Keep an eye out when you're surfing the Web, too – there's a whole world of ideas out there, and often, people who have used FrontPage to construct their sites will display a FrontPage icon somewhere.

So, put on your construction hat and read on – the World Wide Web is your oyster!

1 Getting started

What is a web? 2

The Explorer window 4

The Editor window 6

Working with pages 8

Page properties 11

Previewing pages 14

Keeping track of your work 16

Summary 18

What is a web?

Most HTML editors help you create Web pages which can then be linked together into a Web site. FrontPage 97 takes a more interconnected approach by prompting you to create fully linked sets of pages called 'webs'.

At its most basic, a web could be a single page, to which you might add a couple of hyperlinks to your favourite Web sites. The upper limit on the size of a web is determined only by the amount of space you have on your Web server, and might include hundreds of pages. Most webs will fall somewhere comfortably between the two – the FrontPage Web Templates give a fair idea of typical webs.

Creating a new Web

When you open FrontPage Explorer, the **Getting Started** dialog box is shown. For the moment, we'll use one of the FrontPage Templates so that you can see what a web with several pages looks like.

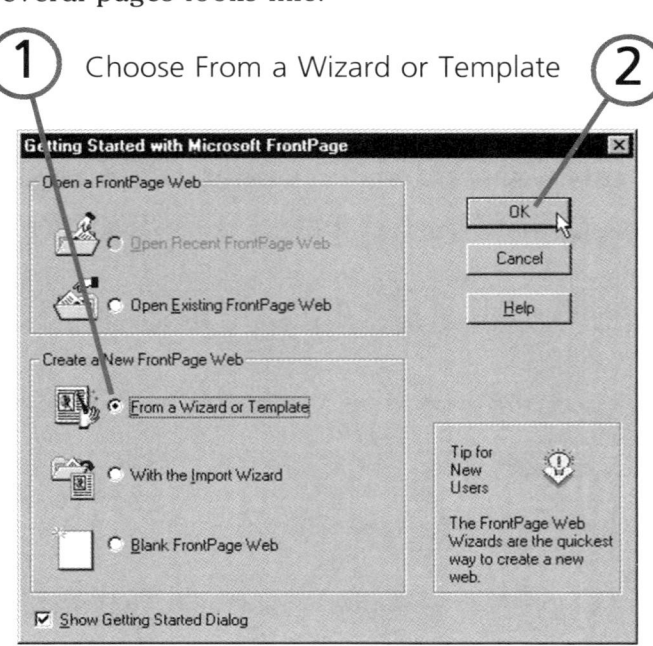

Choose From a Wizard or Template ② Click OK

1 In the **Create a New FrontPage Web** area, choose **From a Wizard or Template**.

2 Click **OK**.

3 Select **Personal Web**.

4 Click **OK**.

5 Type a name for your web.

6 Click **OK**.

Installation

If you have not already installed FrontPage, run setup.exe from the CD to start the installation program. When prompted to install a Personal Web Server, select Yes; this allows webs to run on your machine as they would on the World Wide Web.

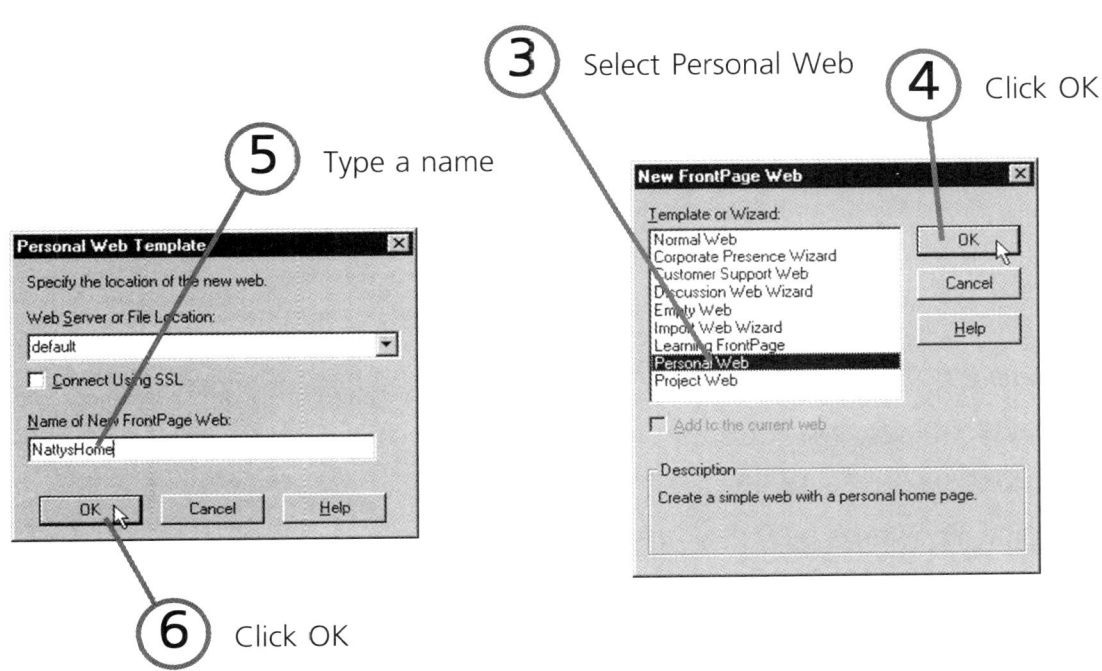

③ Select Personal Web

④ Click OK

⑤ Type a name

⑥ Click OK

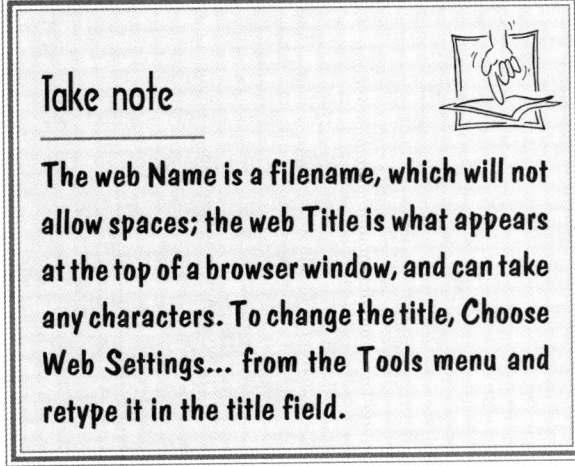

Take note

The web Name is a filename, which will not allow spaces; the web Title is what appears at the top of a browser window, and can take any characters. To change the title, Choose Web Settings... from the Tools menu and retype it in the title field.

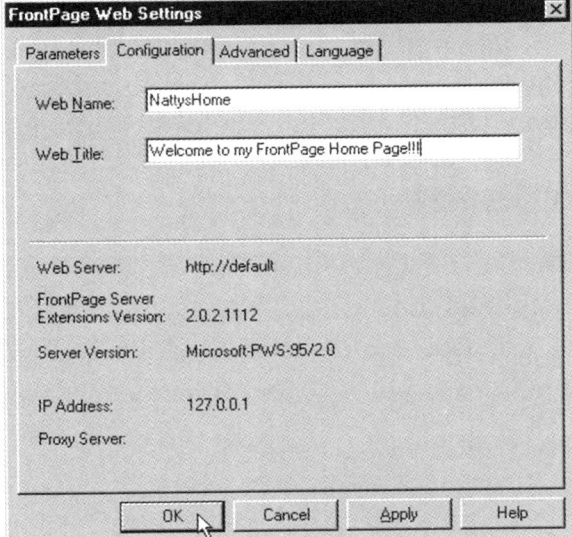

The Explorer window

This window is for working with whole webs. Use it to:

- Create new webs
- Publish existing webs
- Control who can browse or edit pages in a web
- Run spelling checks
- Check the hyperlinks within your web and to sites on the World Wide Web
- Organise the files in your web.

The Explorer window opens in Hyperlink view. This is useful for getting an idea of how a web 'looks'.

The left frame shows the hyperlink structure of your web in the same way that Windows Explorer shows the folder structure of your drives. The *home page*, where visitors to your site will usually arrive, is called 'default.htm' or 'index.htm' by FrontPage, and marked by a house icon.

The right frame shows the hyperlink structure of different parts of your web. When you click on a page in the left frame, that page is shown in the centre of the right frame, along with the hyperlinks leading into and out of it.

Folder view

If you have a lot of pages on your web, and particularly if each page has a <u>navigation bar</u> (page 98), the hyperlink view can get quite cluttered and difficult to follow, in which case you will find the Folder view more helpful.

The Folder view lists the files and folders in your web just as Windows Explorer does. This is useful for finding a particular page or image file – by clicking on the **Name** heading, files can be arranged in alphabetical order.

Tip

Click on the plus and minus signs to follow the links through the web and find out if any pages come to a dead end, or have links to somewhere they shouldn't.

Take note

You can also move, copy and rename files in the same way as in Windows Explorer – right-click on a file to bring up a context menu. When you do so, FrontPage automatically checks and updates any hyperlinks which need to be changed.

Hyperlink view

Editor window (page 6)

Hyperlink view

'To Do' List (page 16)

Image Composer (Chapter 3)

Menu bar

Toolbar

Folder view

Click here to arrange by Name

⊞ shows the page has hyperlinks

Folder view

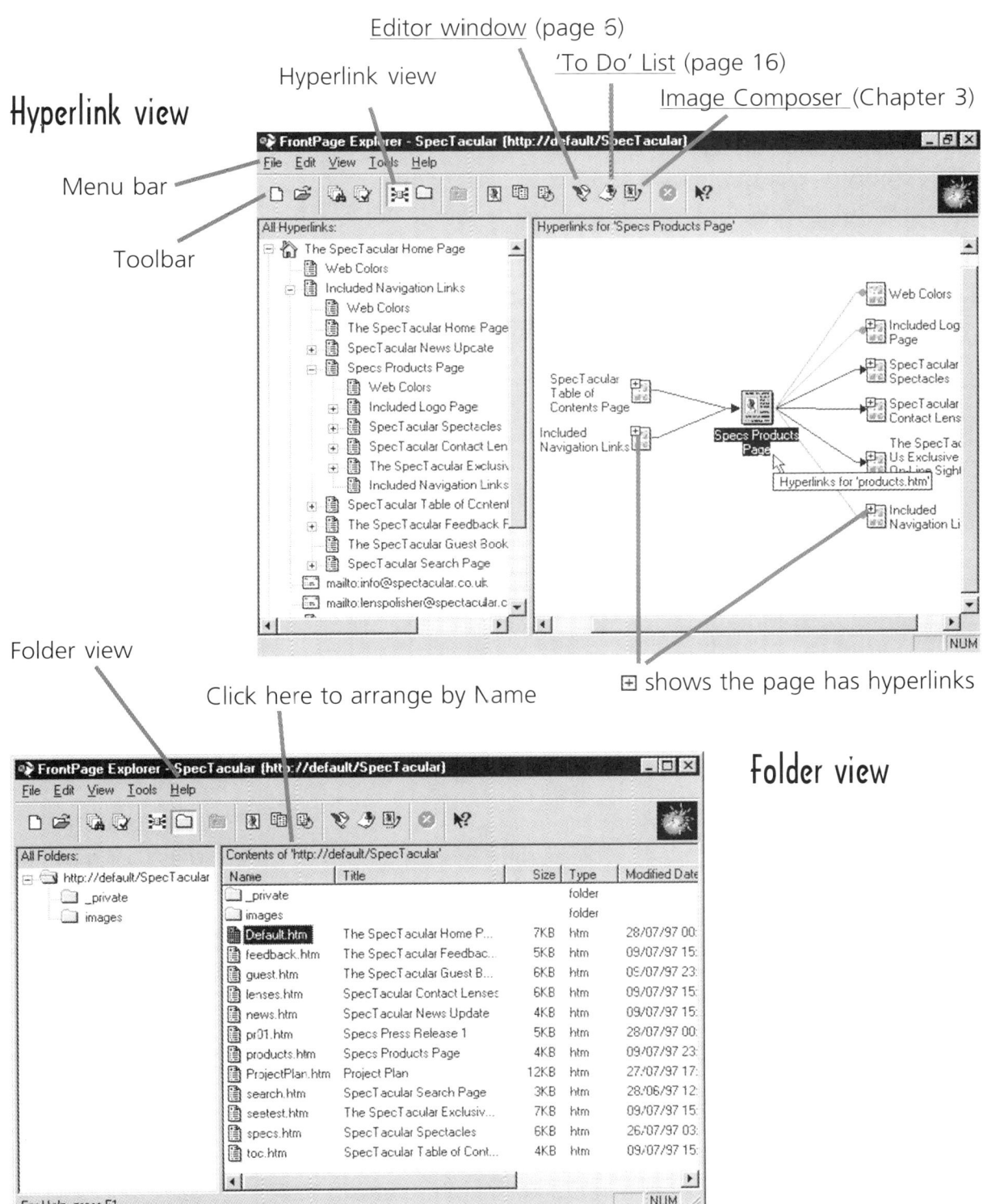

The Editor window

The Editor window is where you will work most of the time, creating and editing pages for your Webs. FrontPage is a WYSIWYG (What You See Is What You Get!) editor – it shows the page you are working on as it would look through a normal Web browser.

The Toolbars have buttons for the most commonly used commands. The Standard and Formatting toolbars are normally open at the start of a session.

You can find all FrontPage's commands on the Menu bar, including the ones on the Toolbar.

The two drop-down menus on the bottom of the Toolbar are used to select the **font** and **style** of your text.

The standard tools

Switch to the Explorer window.

Switch to the 'To Do' List.

Insert a WebBot component.

Insert a table

Insert an image

Create or edit a hyperlink

Increase font size

Decrease font size

Change the text colour

Text styles

Text fonts

Menu bar

Standard Toolbar

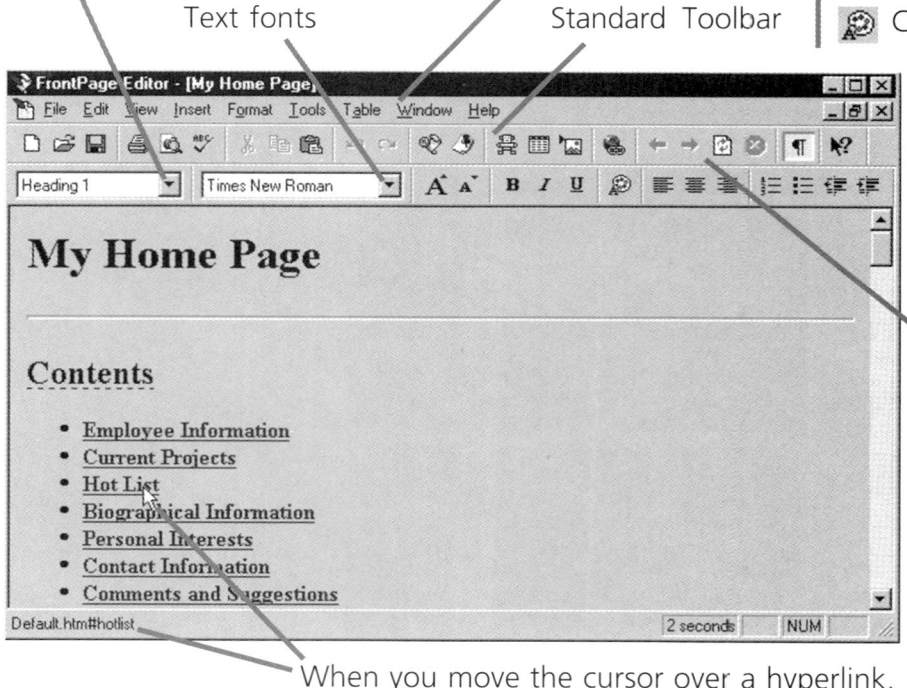

Browser controls – use these for moving between the pages you are editing, as you would in a normal browser

When you move the cursor over a hyperlink, its destination is shown in the status bar.

Basic steps

1 Click on **View** on the Menu bar.

2 Click on a Toolbar to turn its display on – or click to turn off if not wanted.

❑ Visible toolbars have a tick beside them.

The toolbars

There are also three small toolbars which are hidden by default:

● The **Image** toolbar, which pops up if you select an image – see pages 32 and 84.

● ` The **Forms** toolbar, which contains commands for collecting information from visitors to your site – see page 108.

● The **Advanced** toolbar, which is used to insert custom-made HTML and other non-HTML elements such as a Java applet or Active-X control – see page 59.

If you want to display these as well, choose **View** from the menu bar and click on the one you want. If a toolbar is displayed, it will have a tick (✓) next to it.

① Open the View menu

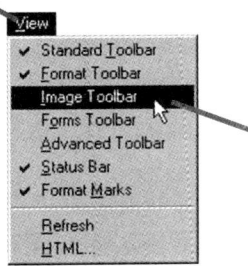

② Click to turn on or off

7

Working with pages

Once you are in the Editor window, you will be working with individual pages rather than the whole web structure. You can edit pages which you've already created, or which are set up in the template webs, or even download a page from the World Wide Web. You can also create new pages – from scratch, or from a further selection of templates. Several pages can be open at once – each one has its own window – and you can move between them as you work.

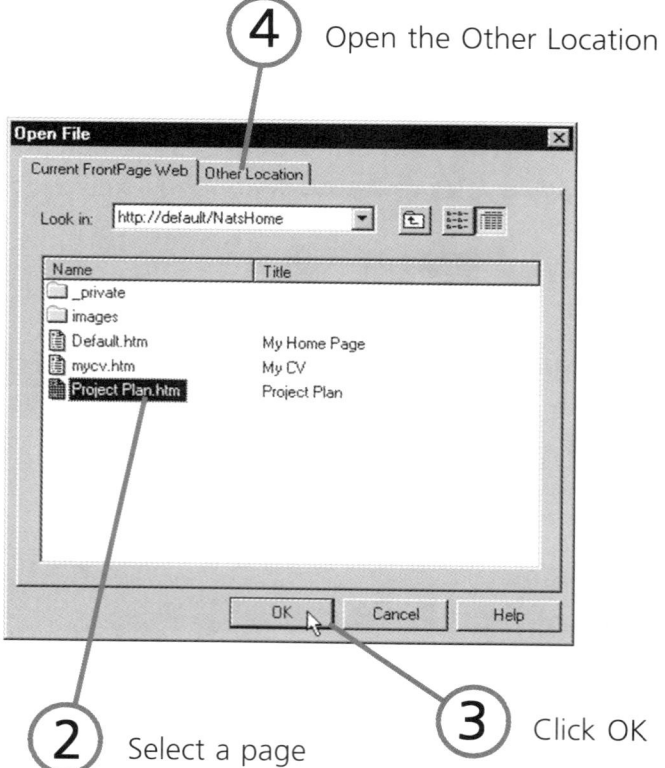

④ Open the Other Location panel

② Select a page

③ Click OK

To open a page:

1 Choose **File** then **Open...** or click 📂 the **Open File** button on the Toolbar.

2 If you have a Web open in the Explorer window, you can select a page from the **Current FrontPage Web**.

3 Click **OK**.

4 If the file is elsewhere on your computer, select the **Other Location** panel in the **Open File** dialog box.

Tip

You can also open pages from the Explorer window – just double click on the page in the right-hand frame (in either view).

Either

5 Choose **Browse...** to find the file.

6 Select it and click **Open**.

or

7 To edit a file from the World Wide Web, choose **From Location**.

8 Type the URL of the page.

9 Click **OK**.

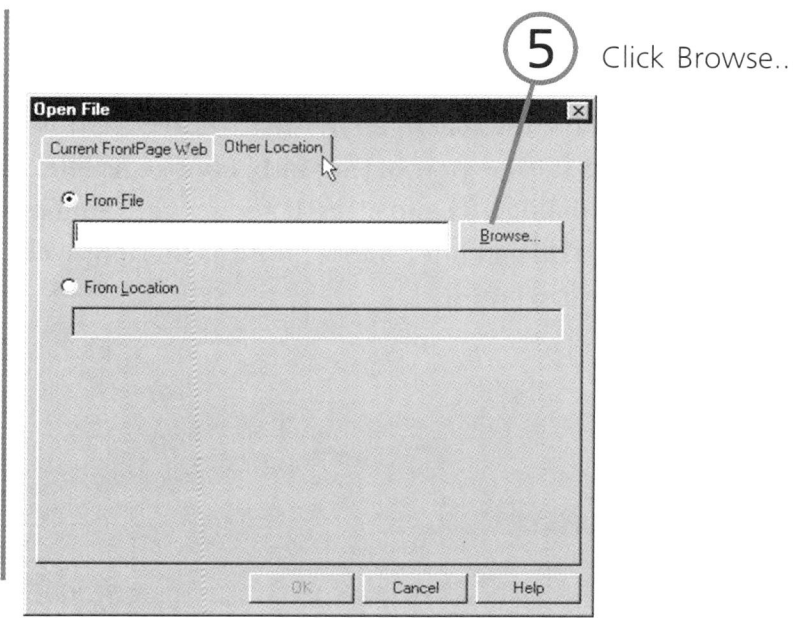

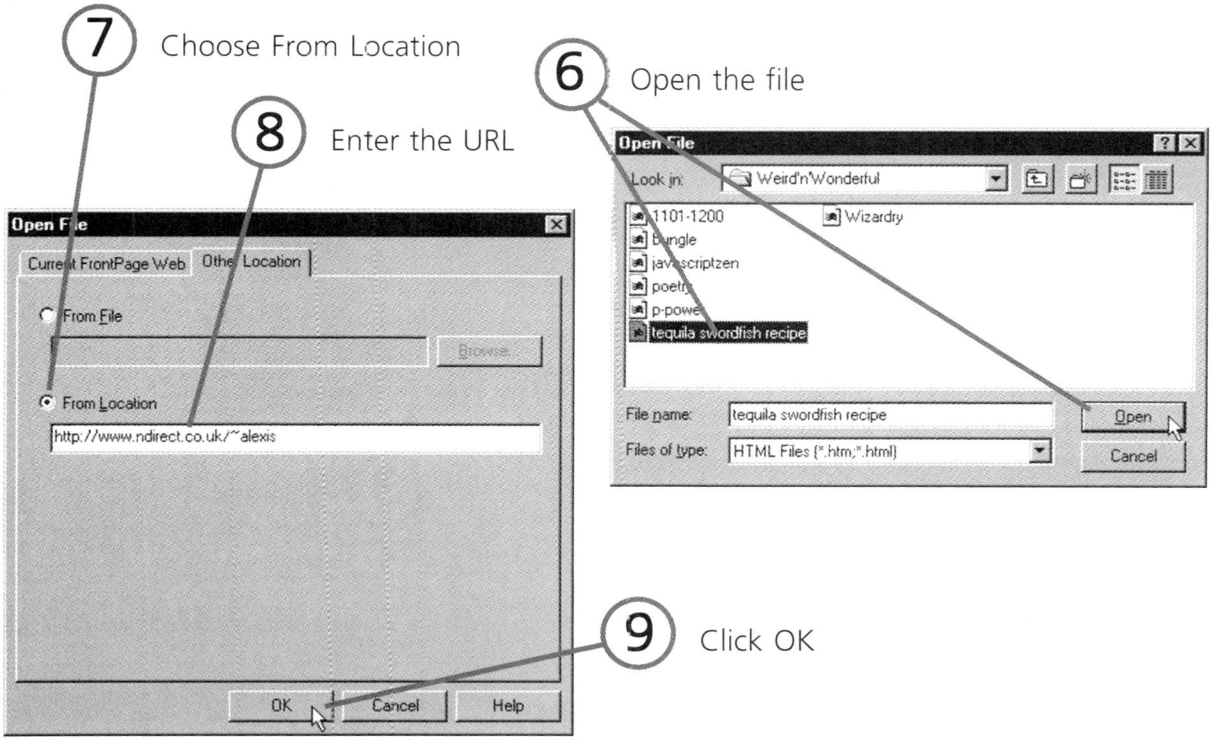

⑤ Click Browse...

⑦ Choose From Location

⑧ Enter the URL

⑥ Open the file

⑨ Click OK

To save pages

Though you can open a page from anywhere and work on it, you can only save it as a Web page to the **Current FrontPage Web**, i.e. the one open in the Explorer window. If you don't want it to be part of that web, choose **As File...** in the **Save as...** dialog box and store it somewhere safe as a separate file. You can later import it into the right web from the Explorer window.

1 Choose **Save As...** from the **File** menu.

2 Type a title into the box, or accept the one FrontPage suggests.

3 Click **OK**.

4 To save all the pages you have been editing to the same Web, click **Save All** from the **File** menu.

5 FrontPage will ask you if you want to save any files or images you may have imported while editing to the web. Choose **Yes to All**.

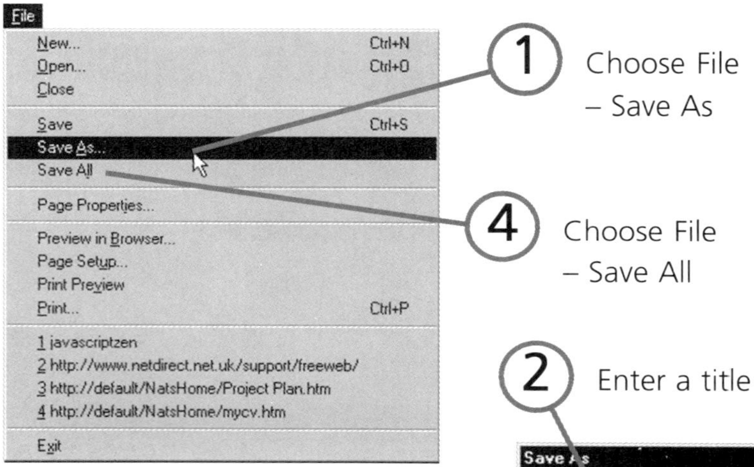

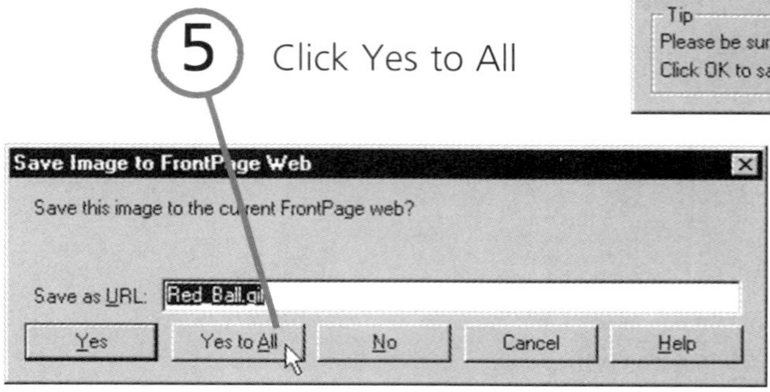

File

New...	Ctrl+N
Open...	Ctrl+O
Close	
Save	Ctrl+S
Save As...	
Save All	
Page Properties...	
Preview in Browser...	
Page Setup...	
Print Preview	
Print...	Ctrl+P
1 javascriptzen	
2 http://www.netdirect.net.uk/support/freeweb/	
3 http://default/NatsHome/Project Plan.htm	
4 http://default/NatsHome/mycv.htm	
Exit	

(1) Choose File – Save As

(4) Choose File – Save All

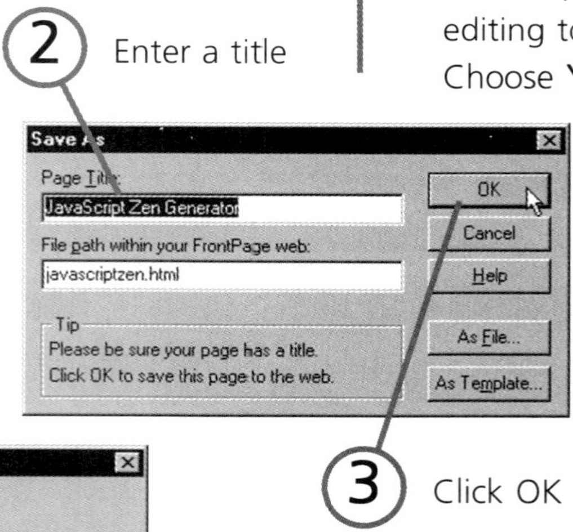

(2) Enter a title

Save As

Page Title:
JavaScript Zen Generator

File path within your FrontPage web:
javascriptzen.html

Tip
Please be sure your page has a title.
Click OK to save this page to the web.

OK | Cancel | Help | As File... | As Template...

(5) Click Yes to All

Save Image to FrontPage Web

Save this image to the current FrontPage web?

Save as URL: Red_Ball.gif

Yes | Yes to All | No | Cancel | Help

(3) Click OK

Basic steps

1 From the **File** menu on the menu bar, choose **Page properties...**

2 Click on the **Background** tab.

3 Click and hold the down arrow ▾ next to a colour setting for a list of colours.

4 Select a colour and release the mouse button.

5 Repeat for the other settings and click OK.

Page properties

From the **Page properties...** dialog box, you can set a colour scheme for your page, choose a background image, set margins, or link a sound file to it (see page 33).

Setting colours

● **Background** – The default 'paper' colour.

● Normal **Text** – Selected text can be recoloured later.

● **Hyperlink** – The initial colour for links.

● **Visited Hyperlink** – The colour of a link which you have already followed.

● **Active Hyperlink** – Selects the colour that the link turns as you click on it.

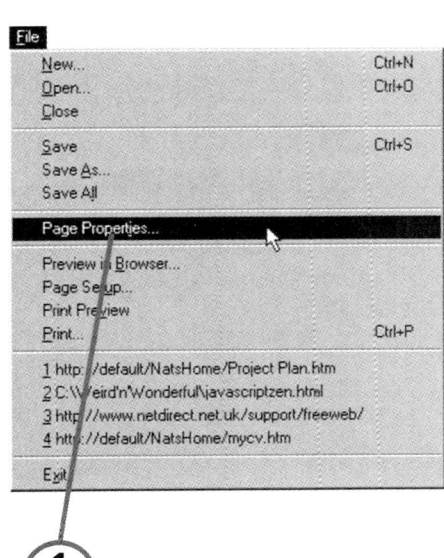

Choose File –
Page Properties

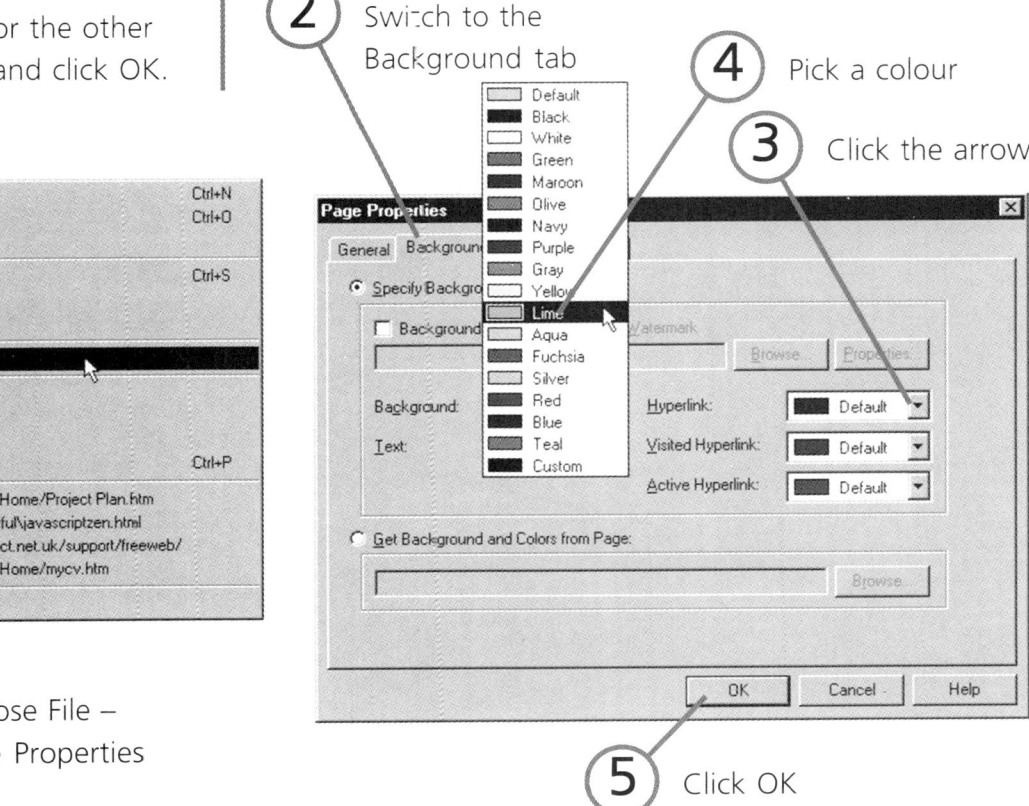

② Switch to the Background tab

④ Pick a colour

③ Click the arrow

⑤ Click OK

Background images and watermarks

A background image can be screen-sized, or small and repeated to give a wallpaper effect. Small ones are often better as they download faster, and don't get in the way of the page's text. The Clip Art panel has a few good examples.

Watermarks only run on Microsoft Explorer at present. When you view the page, the background stays still and the rest of the page moves over it as you scroll up and down.

Basic steps

1 On the **Background** panel, first choose **Background Image**.

2 If you want the image to be a **Watermark**, check this box.

3 Click **Browse…**

4 Select the **Clip Art** panel (or **Other Location** if the image is saved elsewhere).

5 Choose **Backgrounds** from the list.

6 Select a background and click **OK**.

Choose Background Image   Watermark?

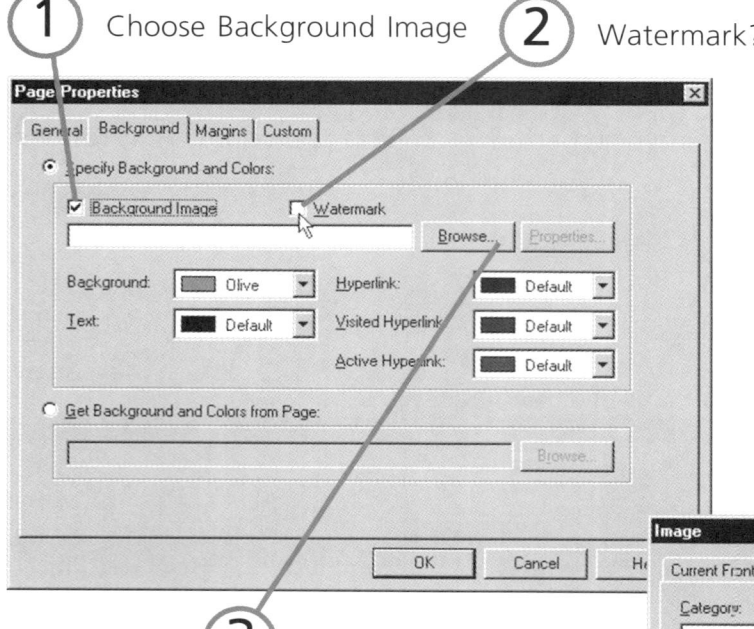

Click Browse

Choose Backgrounds

Select and click OK

Select Clip Art

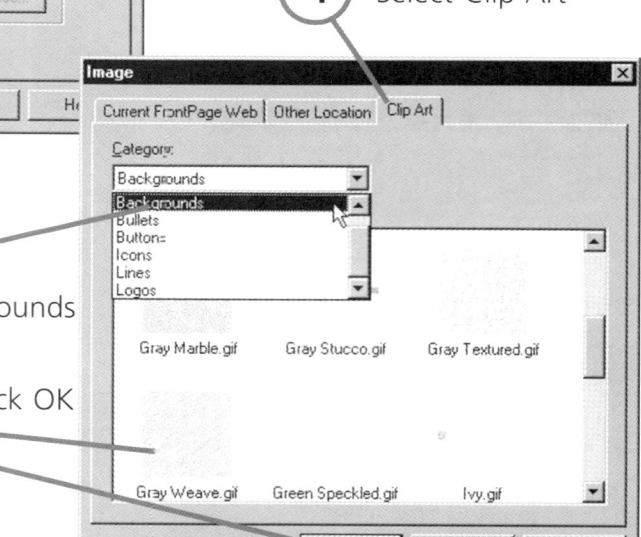

Basic steps

1 Select the **Background** panel in the dialog box.

2 Check the **Get Background and Colors from Page** box.

3 Click **Browse...**

4 Select a page.

5 Click **OK**.

Setting margins

In the **Margins** panel of the dialog box, you can set the depth of the margins at the top and on the left of your page. The background colour or image will extend into the margins, while text and graphics are constrained.

Style pages

Instead of setting up the page properties individually for every single page in a web, you can tell the browser to pick up colour and background settings from a reference page.

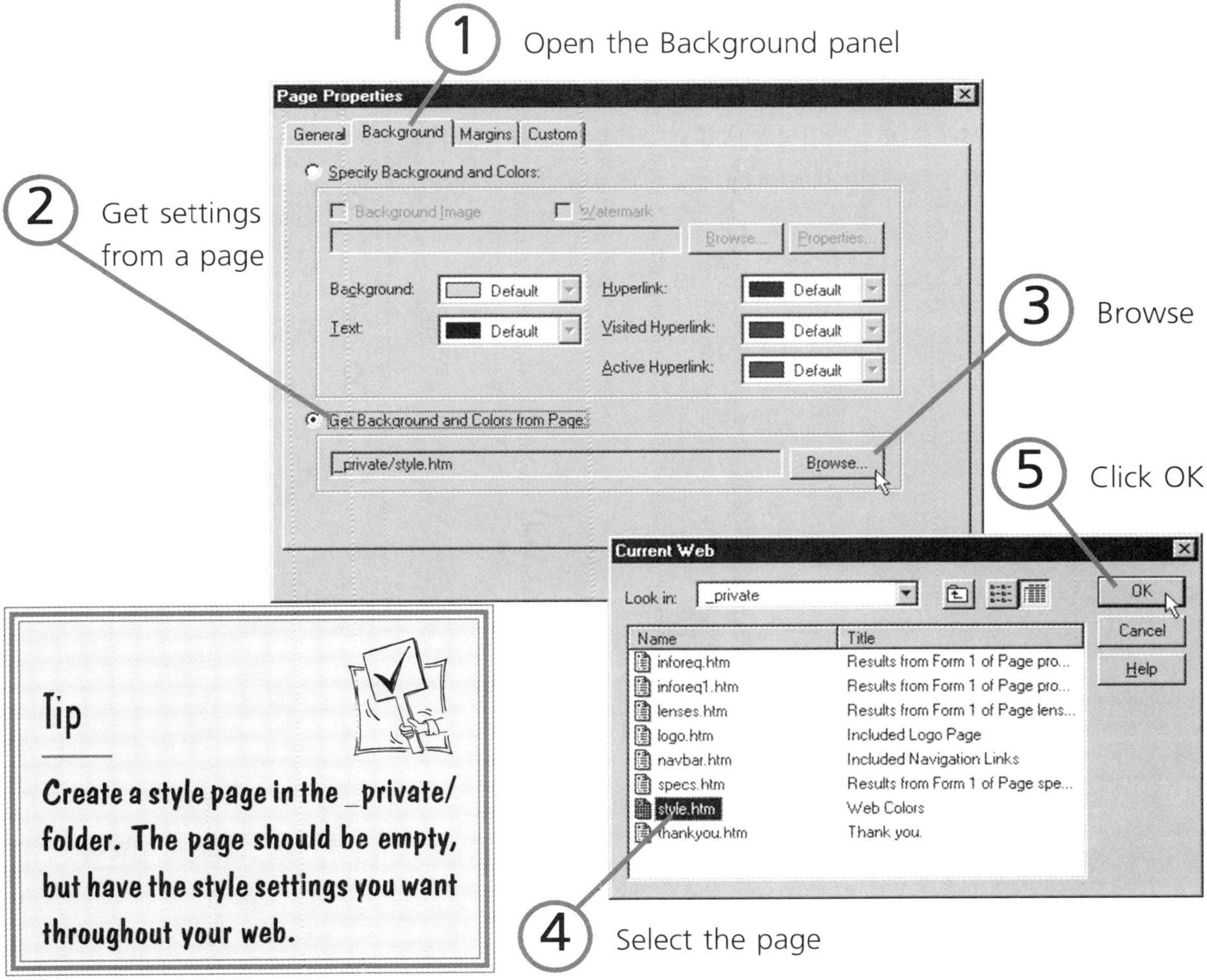

(1) Open the Background panel

Page Properties

General | Background | Margins | Custom |

◯ Specify Background and Colors:

☐ Background Image ☐ Watermark

Browse... Properties...

Background: [Default ▾] Hyperlink: [███ Default ▾]

Text: [███ Default ▾] Visited Hyperlink: [███ Default ▾]

Active Hyperlink: [███ Default ▾]

(2) Get settings from a page

◉ Get Background and Colors from Page:

_private/style.htm Browse...

(3) Browse

(5) Click OK

Current Web

Look in: _private ▾ [↑] [⊞] [▥]

Name	Title
inforeq.htm	Results from Form 1 of Page pro...
inforeq1.htm	Results from Form 1 of Page pro...
lenses.htm	Results from Form 1 of Page lens...
logo.htm	Included Logo Page
navbar.htm	Included Navigation Links
specs.htm	Results from Form 1 of Page spe...
style.htm	Web Colors
thankyou.htm	Thank you.

OK Cancel Help

(4) Select the page

Tip

Create a style page in the _private/ folder. The page should be empty, but have the style settings you want throughout your web.

13

Previewing pages

FrontPage shows pages pretty much as they will appear in a browser window, but as browsers vary a little, you may want to check the appearance of your pages in a normal browser. When you first choose Preview in browser..., you will have to add the browser(s) you use to FrontPage's list of browsers; after that, you can just click the one you want to use.

Window Size

If your pages are going to viewed on the World Wide Web, remember that not everyone has the same type of monitor. Pages that work well on your 1024 x 768 screen may look terrible when viewed on a 640 x 480! If you have any doubts about the layout, preview it in each of the screen sizes.

Basic steps

1 Choose **Preview in browser...** from the **File** menu.

❑ **Adding a browser**

2 Click **Add...**

3 Type a name to identify the browser.

4 Click **Browse...**

5 Find the program command file (probably in the *Program Files* folder).

6 Click **OK**.

❑ **Previewing**

7 Select a browser.

8 Choose a Window Size.

9 Click **Preview**.

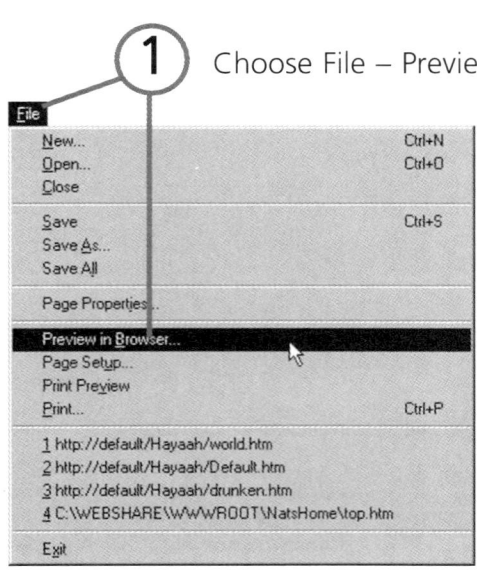

Choose File – Preview in browser ...

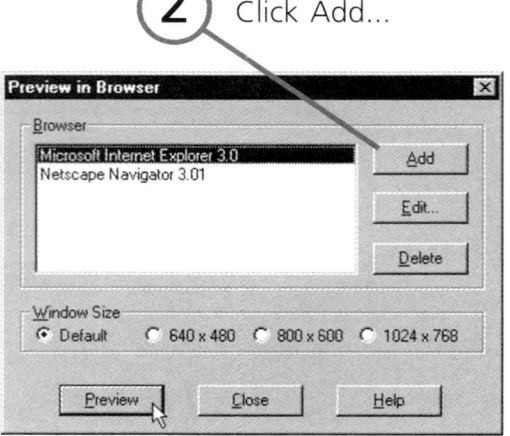

Click Add...

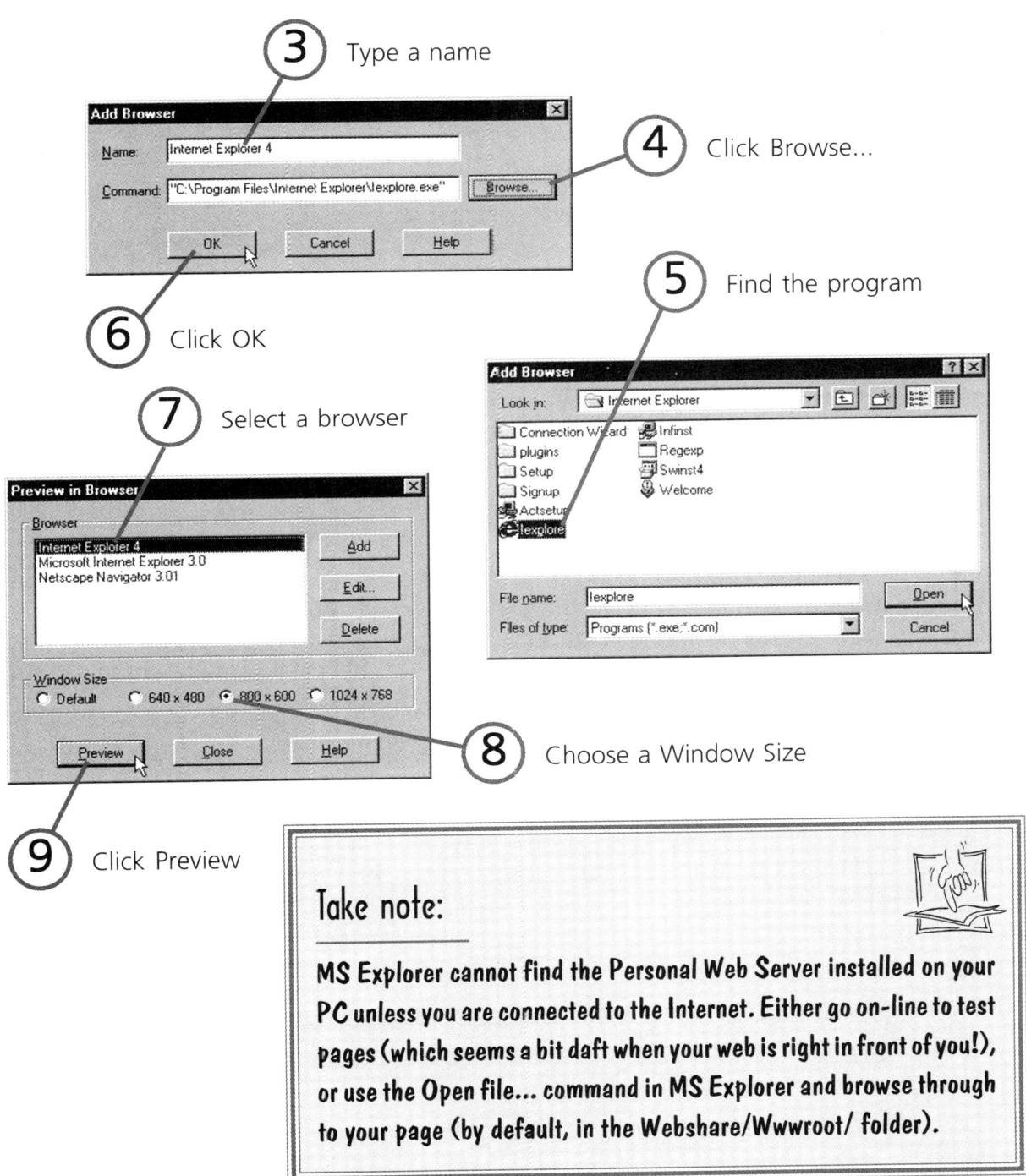

③ Type a name

Add Browser

Name: Internet Explorer 4

Command: "C:\Program Files\Internet Explorer\Iexplore.exe"   Browse...

④ Click Browse...

OK   Cancel   Help

⑥ Click OK

⑤ Find the program

Add Browser

Look in: Internet Explorer

Connection Wizard   Infinst
plugins   Regexp
Setup   Swinst4
Signup   Welcome
Actsetup
Iexplore

File name: Iexplore   Open

Files of type: Programs (*.exe;*.com)   Cancel

⑦ Select a browser

Preview in Browser

Browser
Internet Explorer 4
Microsoft Internet Explorer 3.0
Netscape Navigator 3.01

Add
Edit...
Delete

Window Size
○ Default   ○ 640 x 480   ◉ 800 x 600   ○ 1024 x 768

Preview   Close   Help

⑧ Choose a Window Size

⑨ Click Preview

Take note:

MS Explorer cannot find the Personal Web Server installed on your PC unless you are connected to the Internet. Either go on-line to test pages (which seems a bit daft when your web is right in front of you!), or use the Open file... command in MS Explorer and browse through to your page (by default, in the Webshare/Wwwroot/ folder).

Keeping track of your work

Unless you sit down and construct an entire web in one sitting, the **To Do List** can be very useful. It shows a list of tasks which need to be carried out on your web, along with information about them.

In the **To Do List** window, you can:

● add and remove reminders to do certain tasks;

● assign the task to a certain person if there are several people working on the web;

● set a priority rating for each task;

● make a note of any details needed in the **Comments** field.

Completed tasks are stored in a **History** folder which you can review by checking the **Show History** box. Some of the FrontPage Wizards automatically create a few tasks on the **To Do List** when they create your Web template. These are linked to the page which needs editing so that you can go straight to it by clicking on the **Do Task** button.

❑ **To add a task**

1 In either the Editor or Explorer window, click on the **Show To Do List** button.

2 Click **Add...**

3 Type a brief reminder of the job in the **Task Name** field.

4 Click on a radio button to assign the task a priority.

5 Assign the task to someone.

6 Enter any relevant **Comments**.

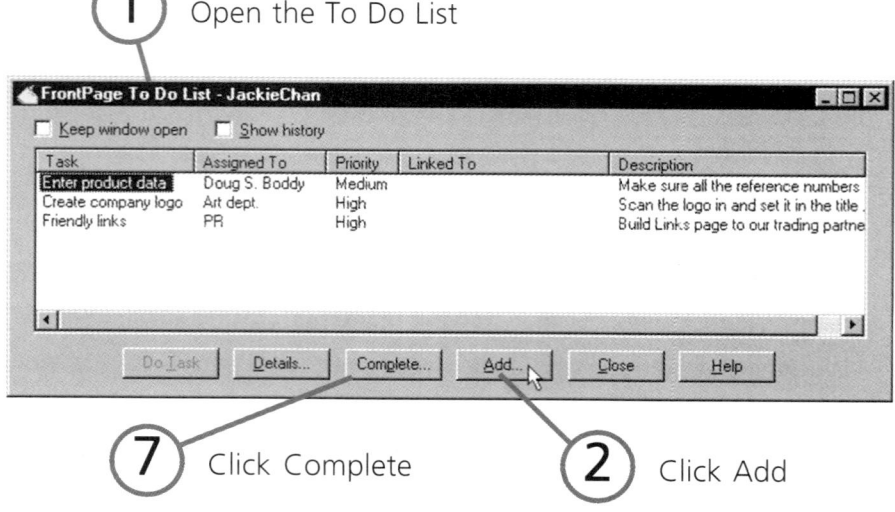

① Open the To Do List

⑦ Click Complete

② Click Add

16

❏ **To remove a task**

7 On the To Do List window, click the **Complete...** button.

8 Mark the task as completed and click **OK**.

Or

9 Delete this task if you do not need a record of it in the To Do History.

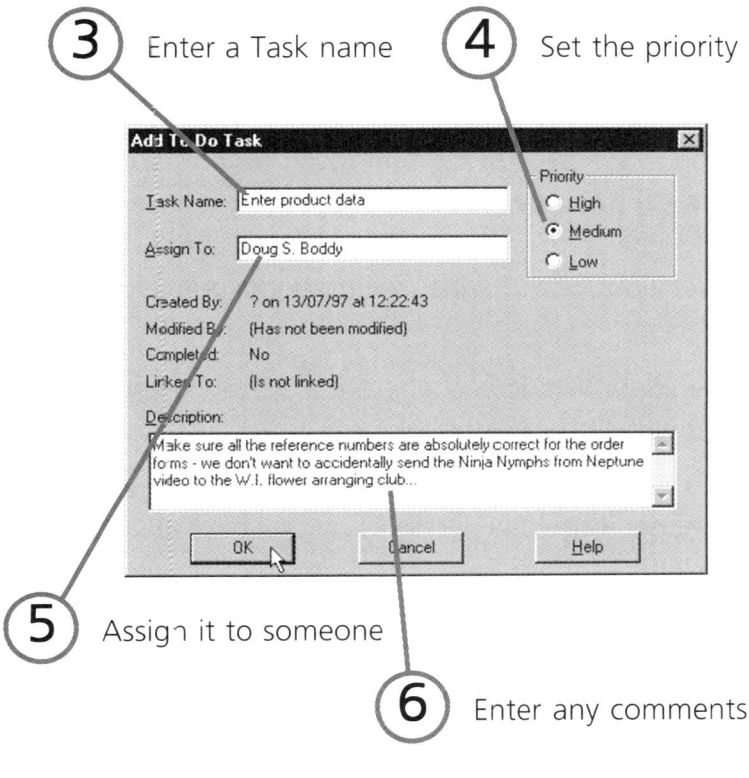

③ Enter a Task name

④ Set the priority

⑤ Assign it to someone

⑥ Enter any comments

⑧ Mark as complete...

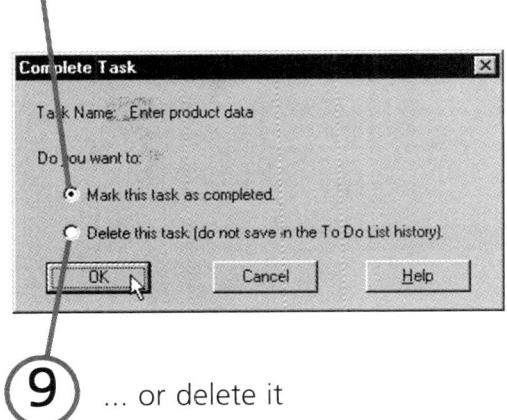

⑨ ... or delete it

Take note

The To Do List window displays the tasks outstanding *for the Web open in FrontPage Explorer*, regardless of what page or web you are working on in the Editor window.

Summary

- [ ] A **web** is a set of HTML pages organised into a navigable system using hypertext links.

- [ ] The **Explorer Window** is where you can view and change the file structure of a web (using the Folder view) and the hypertext links between its pages (using the Hypertext view). You can also set access restrictions from here and publish the web on the Internet.

- [ ] The **Editor Window** is where the actual construction and editing of web pages takes place.

- [ ] You can **work on several pages at once** in the Editor Window, but you have to have a web open in the Explorer window to save pages to it.

- [ ] Use the **Page Properties** dialog box to set basic characteristics for a page, such as background and default text colours.

- [ ] Check the appearance of your page by **previewing it in a browser**, trying different Window Size settings if you have a layout that may not work well at all sizes.

- [ ] The **To Do List** is a set of reminders for keeping track of the construction of your web.

2 Text and graphics

Text 20

Fonts 22

Text alignment 24

Placing images 26

Image properties 29

Alternative representations 31

Background sounds 33

Summary .34

Text

Using text in FrontPage is a similar process to Microscft Word in many basic respects. The Toolbar buttons and keystrokes for common commands are the same – opening, and saving files, printing, checking spelling, undo and redo, cut, copy and paste highlighted text and graphics, **bold**, *italic* and <u>underlined</u> text, etc.

Some things which are determined by HTML conventions are different, though – for instance, only one space can be put between words. Also, when you press [**Enter**], a blank line is inserted before the next paragraph. To avoid this extra line, hold down [**Shift**] and press [**Enter**].

Basic steps

1 Position the cursor anywhere in a line of text.

2 Click on the down arrow next to the **Style** menu field.

3 Select a heading size.

Or

4 Highlight a selection of text.

5 Click on the **Increase** **A** or **Decrease Font Size** **A** buttons.

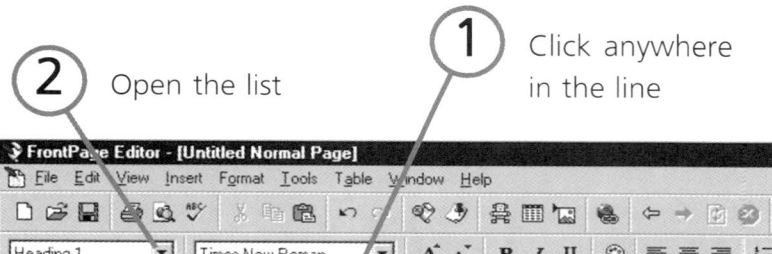

② Open the list   ① Click anywhere in the line

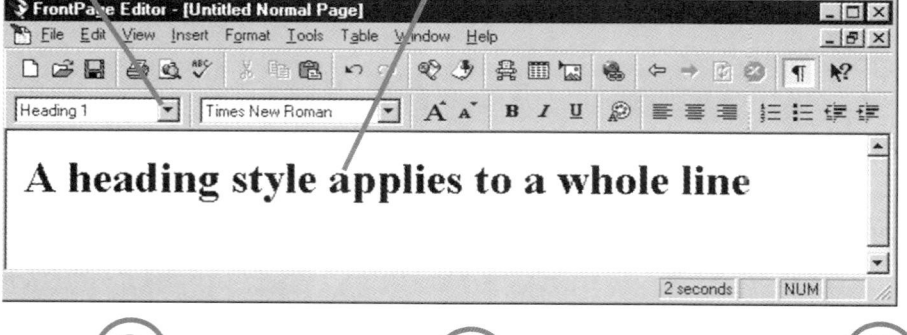

③ Select a style   ④ Highlight the text   ⑤ Adjust the size

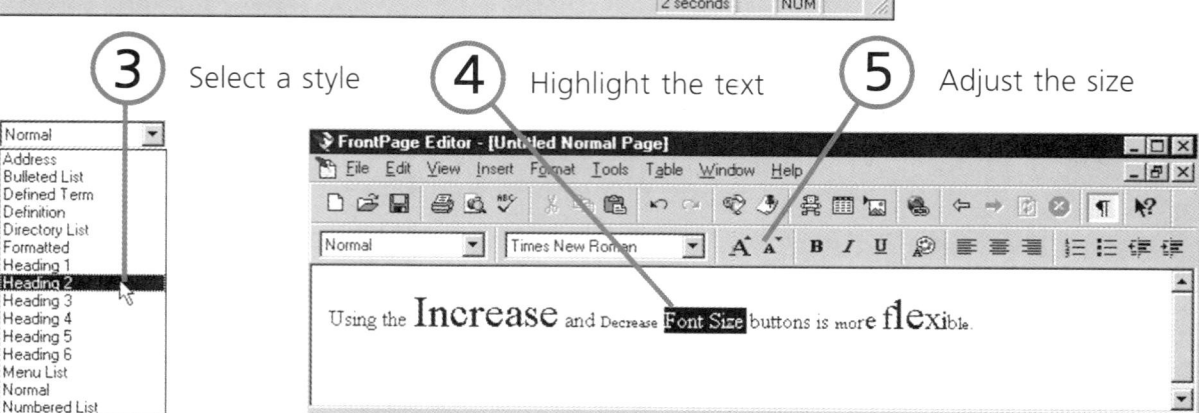

Headings and font size

FrontPage has seven font sizes – one for **normal** text, four larger sizes and two smaller.

The six **Headings** styles are a quick way of setting the size of a line of text; they are all set in **bold type**, and with a blank line below the text.

Tip

To highlight text, point to the start of it, hold down the left mouse button and drag to the end.

Heading 1 is the second largest font size, set in bold, and Heading 6 is the smallest.

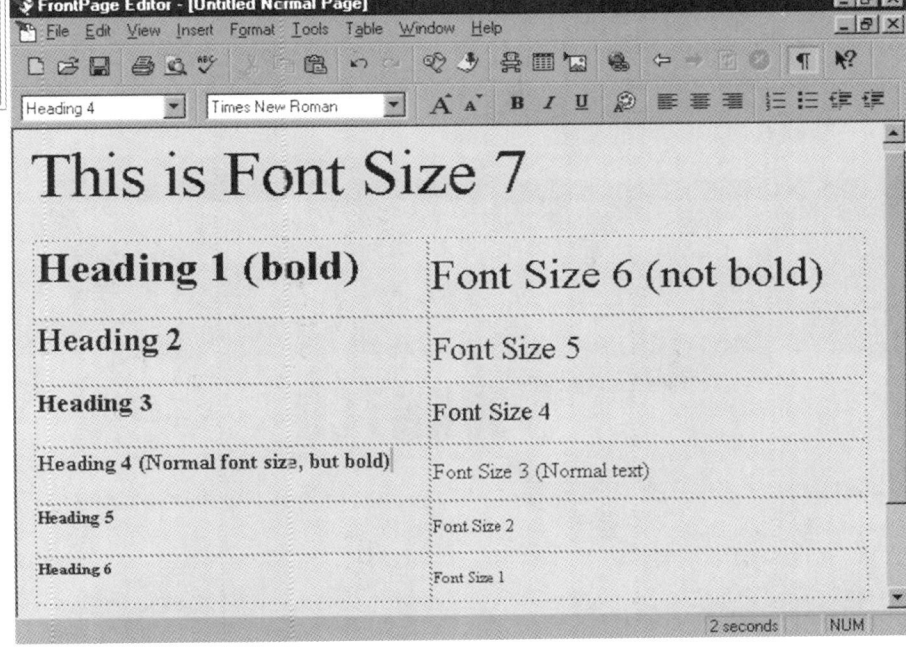

Tip

If you find that changing the Heading size in the Style menu is having no effect on the text you want to change, try Removing the text's formatting (choose this command from the Format menu).

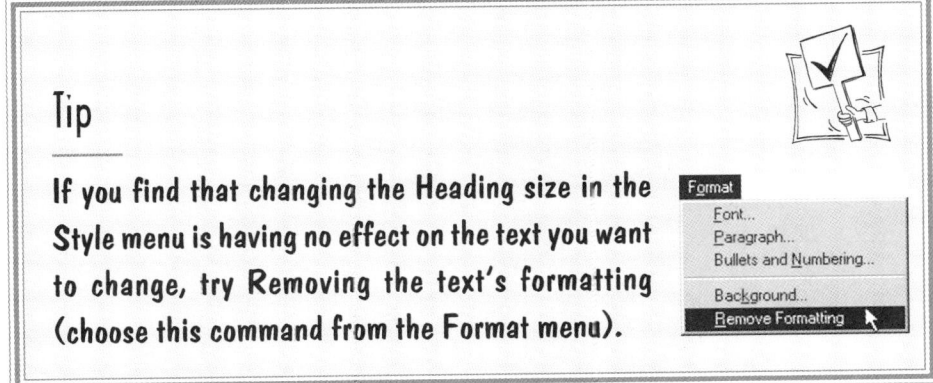

Fonts

The standard font used in HTML is Times New Roman, but you can choose to use other styles of font from the drop-down menu. Note that some fonts, such as Small fonts or System, cannot be set in different sizes.

Font colour

Any section of text – be it a paragraph, a word or a letter – can be changed to a different colour from whatever you set as the default.

Basic steps

1 Highlight a section of text.

2 Click the down arrow next to the Fonts field.

3 Choose a font from the list

4 Click on the Font colour 🎨 button.

5 Pick a colour from the palette and click OK.

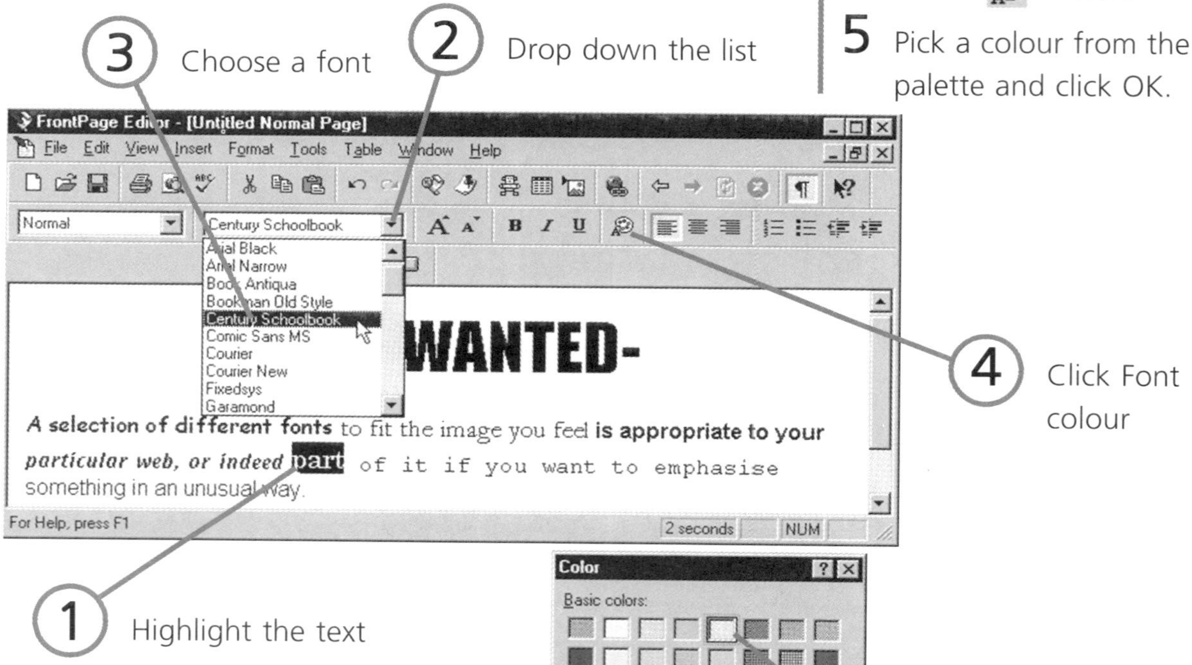

③ Choose a font

② Drop down the list

④ Click Font colour

① Highlight the text

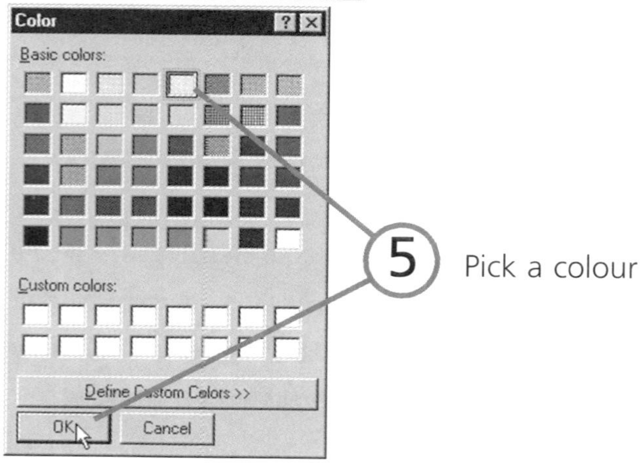

⑤ Pick a colour

Tip

Click Define Custom Color if you want to blend your own colour.

22

Basic steps

1 Highlight a section of text.

2 Select **Font...** from the **Format** menu.

3 Click on the **Special Styles** tab.

4 Check the box next to an option to apply the effect.

❑ **Subscript/Superscript**

5 Click on the Down arrow next to the **Vertical Position** field.

6 Select **Subscript** or **Superscript**.

7 Set the size of the offset (at least 1 for **Superscript** and −1 for **Subscript**).

8 Click **Apply** and then **OK**.

Special font styles

If you highlight a section of text and choose Font... from the Format menu, a dialog box appears which gives you various options such as Strikethrough (rules a line through the text). From the Special Styles panel you can set text to flash (Blink), or offset it as Subscript or Superscript.

(2) Select Font – Format

Format
Font...
Paragraph...
Bullets and Numbering...
Background...
Remove Formatting

(4) Set an option

(3) Go to Special Styles

(5) Open the Vertical Position list

Font

Font | Special Styles

☐ Citation (<cite>)   ☑ Blink (<blink>)   ☐ Bold (<b>)
☐ Sample (<samp>)   ☐ Code (<code>)   ☐ Italic (<i>)
☐ Definition (<dfn>)   ☐ Variable (<var>)   ☐ Keyboard (<kbd>)

Vertical Position: Superscript   By: 1

Sample

AaBbYyGgLLj

OK   Cancel   Apply   Help

(6) Subscript or Superscript?

(8) Apply the settings

(7) Set the offset

23

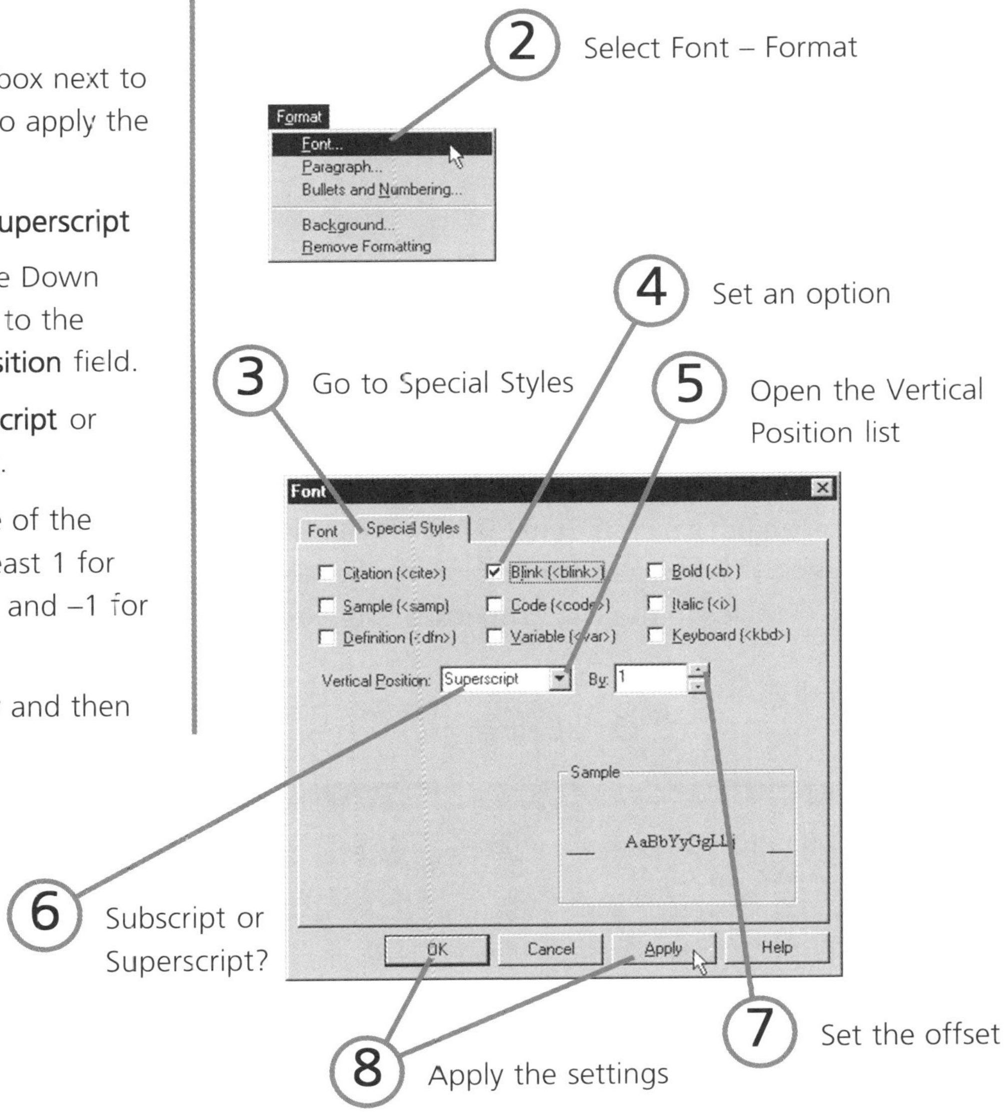

Alignment and lists

Aligning text

Position the cursor anywhere in a paragraph and click on a **text alignment** button ≡ ≡ ≡ to justify the text left, centre or right.

Lists

Lists can present information quickly and clearly on screen – wading through huge passages of text on screen is quite hard on the eyes. The bullets and numbers can be selected from a range of styles in the **List Properties...** dialog box.

Basic steps

1 Click the **Bulleted** or the **Numbered List** button.

2 Type the first item and hit **[Enter]**. A bullet appears ready for the next item. After the last, there will be an unwanted one – press **[←]** to get rid of it.

❑ **Changing the style**

3 Position the cursor over the list and click the right mouse button.

4 Choose **List Properties...**

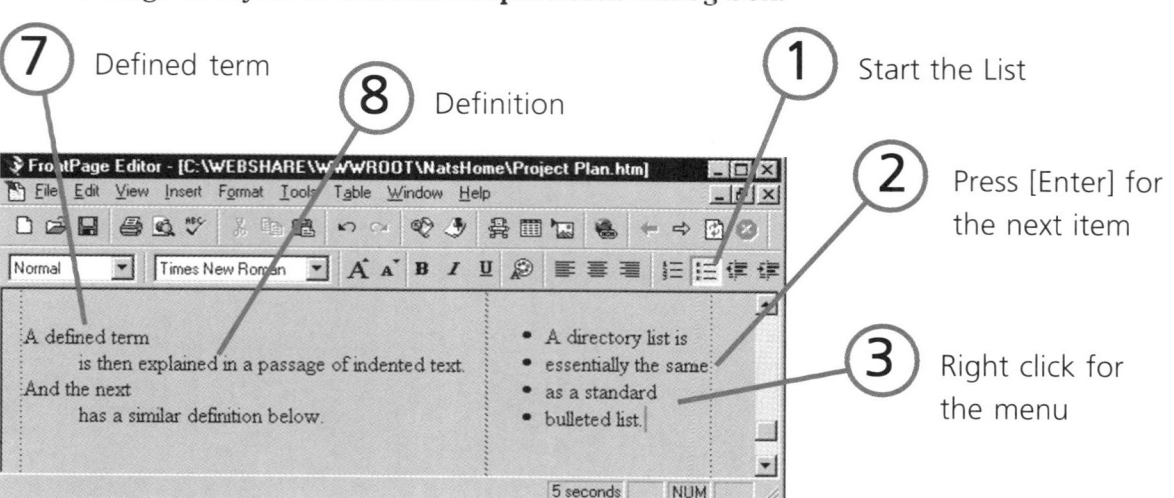

⑦ Defined term

⑧ Definition

① Start the List

② Press [Enter] for the next item

③ Right click for the menu

5 Select a different style from the **Bulleted** or **Numbered** panel.

Or

6 From the **Style** menu, choose **Defined Term**.

7 Type the term to be defined and press [Enter].

8 Type a description of the term and press [Enter].

Repeat steps 7 and 8 for the next terms.

9 After the last definition, choose **Normal** from the **Style** menu.

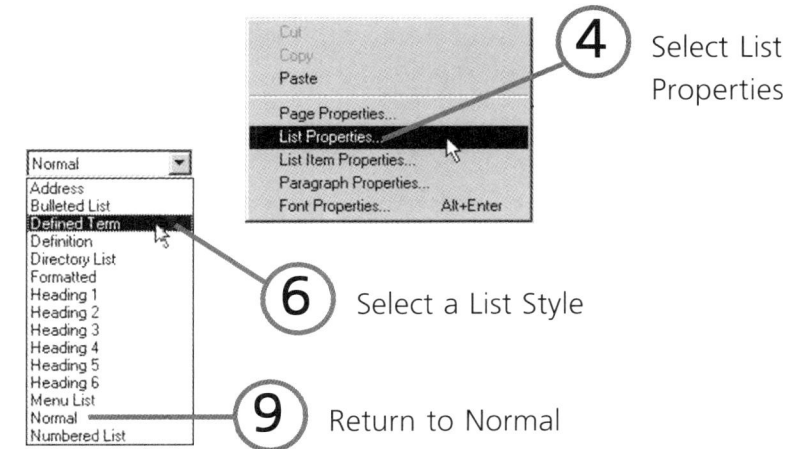

Select List Properties

Select a List Style

Return to Normal

Other lists

A **Definition List** is a two-level list, which is used for a list of terms, each of which has its own definition indented below it. FrontPage arranges the list in pairs of **Defined Terms** and **Definitions**.

A **Directory List** is basically a simple bulleted list, intended for use with a number of short items. As some browsers do not recognise this kind of list you are better off with an ordinary bulleted list.

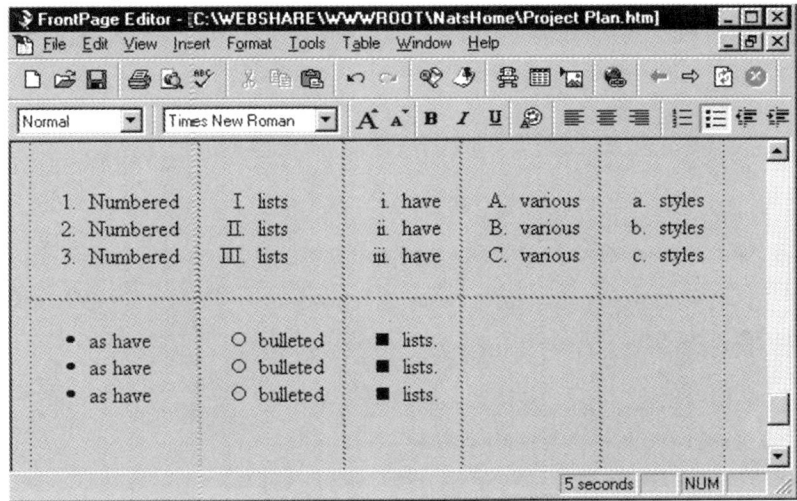

Placing images

You will no doubt want some pictures on your pages to make them more attractive - though you should be careful about the amount of time large images take to download. Images can be imported from other pages on the Web, from a folder on your hard drive, or even from a World Wide Web location.

Animated GIF images can be very effective - have a look under **Animations** in the **Clip Art** panel of the **Insert Image** dialog box.

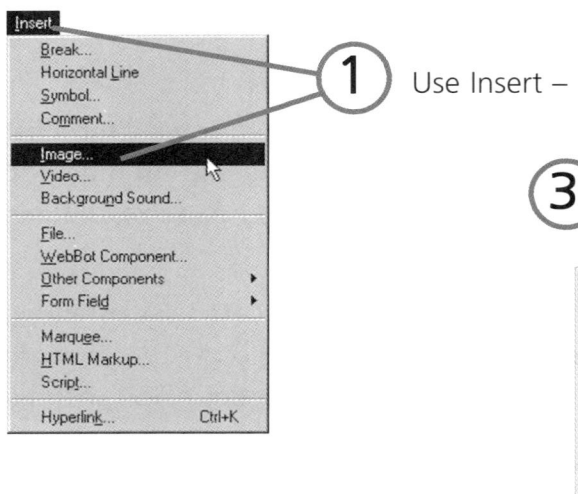

Use Insert – Image

Basic steps

1 From the **Insert** Menu, choose **Image**...

or

2 Click on the **Insert Image** button 🖼.

3 Choose where you want to get the file from.

❑ From the **Current FrontPage Web**:

4 Select the file and click **OK** or **Open**.

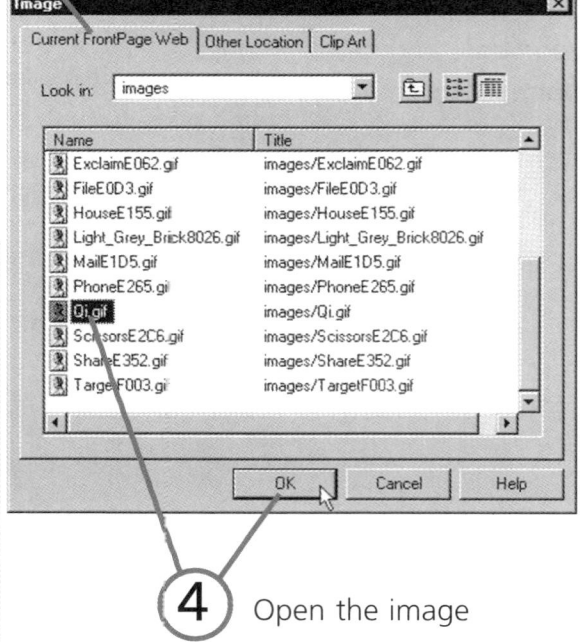

③ Select a panel

④ Open the image

Tip

When arranging text on a page, remember that your visitors may have been browsing for a while before they even get to your page, so you will want to grab their attention with a simple, clear style.

□ *From the **Other Location** panel:*

5 Click **Browse...** to find a file on your hard drive.

or

6 Click **From Location** to download a picture from the Internet.

7 Enter the full URL of the file and click **OK**.

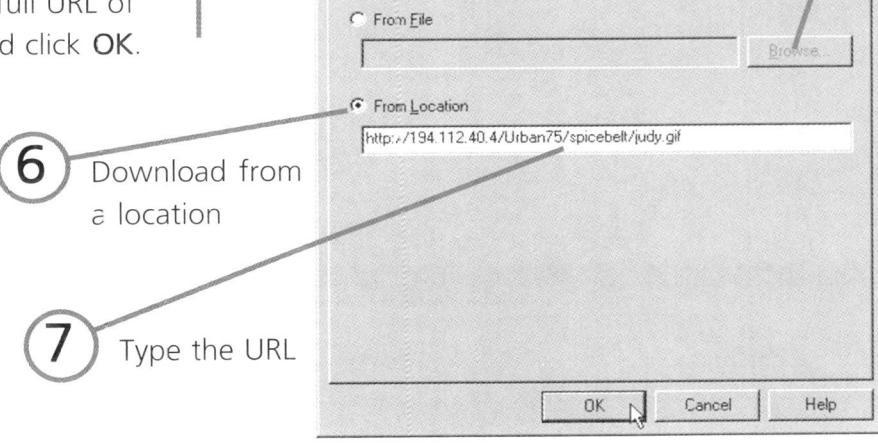

⑤ Find a file

⑥ Download from a location

⑦ Type the URL

Copy and Paste images

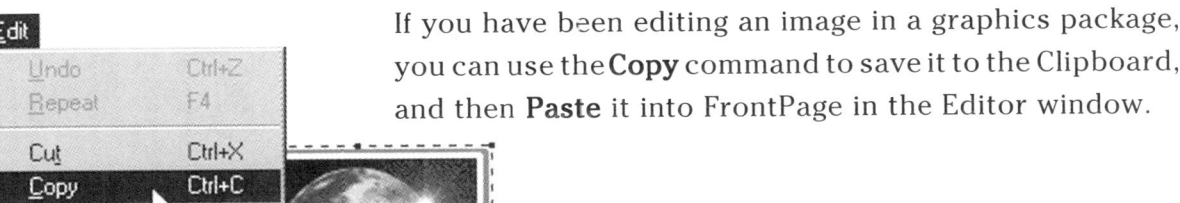

If you have been editing an image in a graphics package, you can use the **Copy** command to save it to the Clipboard, and then **Paste** it into FrontPage in the Editor window.

Select the image and click Copy – in any Windows application

Drag and drop images

A neat feature of FrontPage allows you to hunt for a file using the Windows Explorer or Find File tool and then drag it onto the page you are working on.

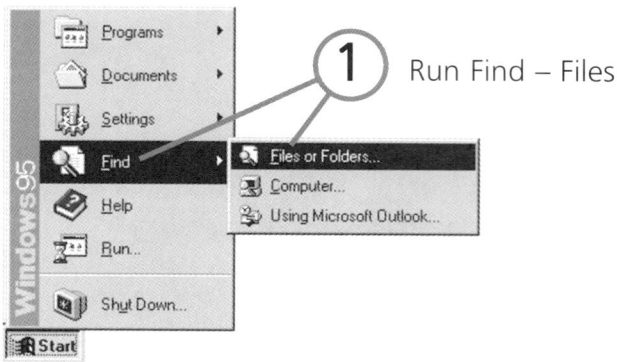

Run Find – Files

1 Run **Find – Files** from the **Start** menu or from **Windows Explorer**.

2 Find the file you want.

3 Resize the window so that you can see where to put the image.

4 Click on the file name and hold the mouse button down.

5 Drag the cursor where you want the image on the Web page.

6 Release the mouse button.

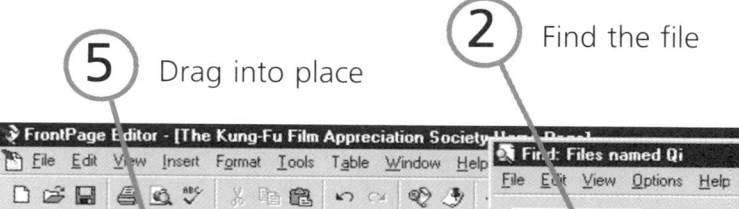

Find the file

Drag into place

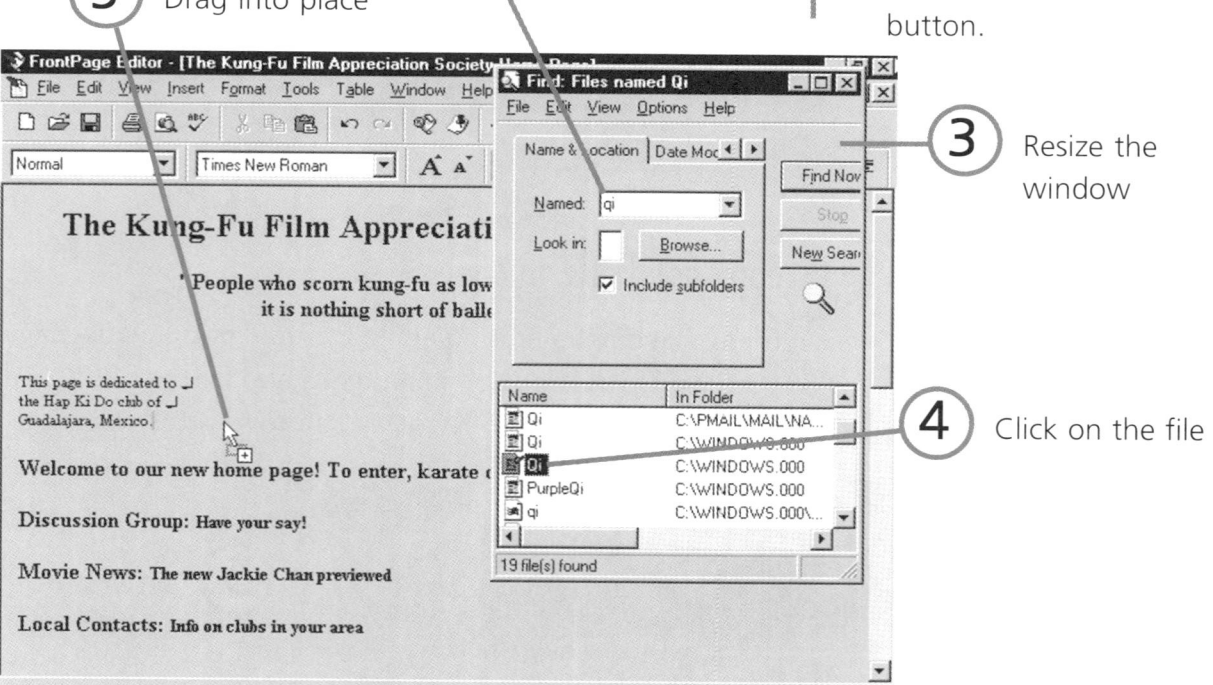

Resize the window

Click on the file

Basic steps

1 Right-click an image to open its context menu.

2 Select **Image properties…**

3 Click on the **Appearance** tab.

4 Turn on **Specify Size**.

5 Set the **Width** and **Height** by entering values and choosing **in Pixels** or **in Percent**.

6 If you want a border, set its **Thickness**.

Image properties

Once an image is placed on a page, there are various properties you can set or change. Some of these alter the appearance of the image itself — its **Size** and **Border**, while others determine its relation to the accompanying text — the **Alignment**, **Horizontal** and **Vertical Spacing**.

● **Size** can be set in pixels, or as a percentage of the browser window it appears in. A percentage is safer for larger images, as you can be sure then that they won't run off the edge of a viewer's screen.

● **Border Thickness** is set in pixels. A value of 4 will give you a reasonably thick line.

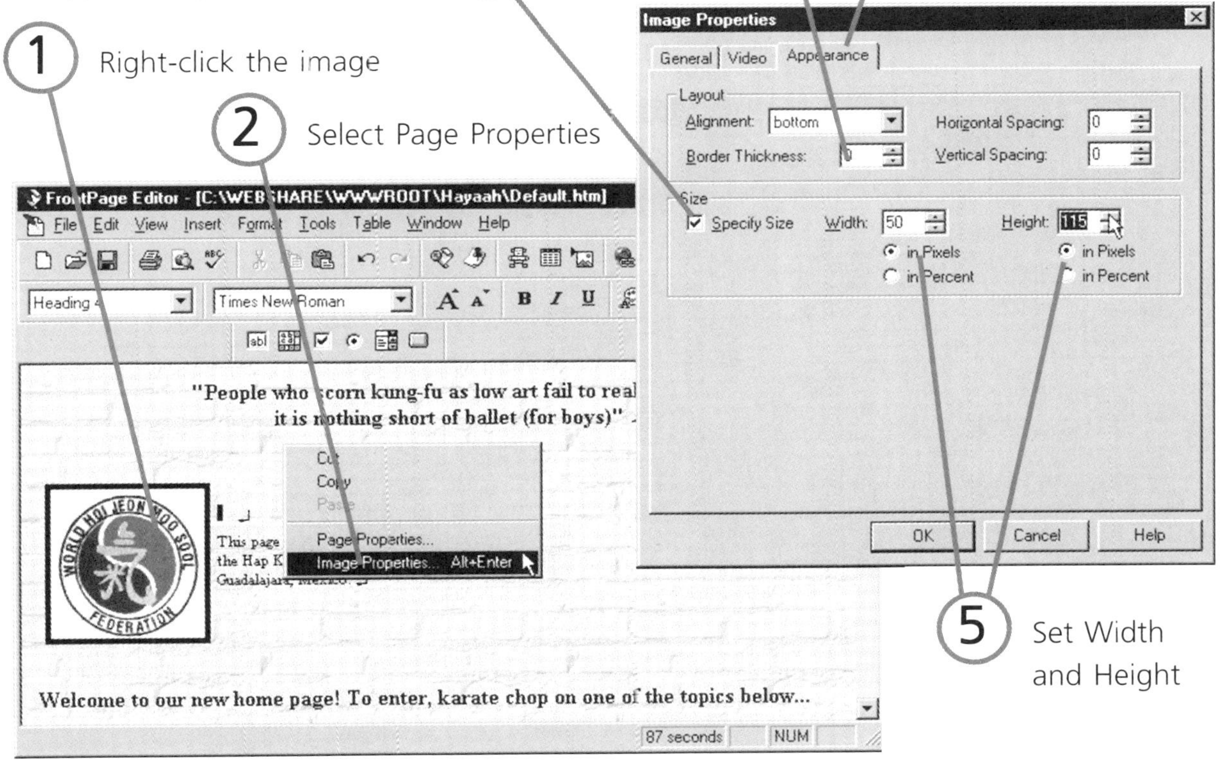

⑥ Set Border Thickness

④ Tick Specify Size   ③ Choose Appearance

① Right-click the image

② Select Page Properties

⑤ Set Width and Height

29

Image alignment

- **Horizontal** and **Vertical Spacing** is also set in pixels, and refers to the distance between the edge of the picture and any surrounding text.

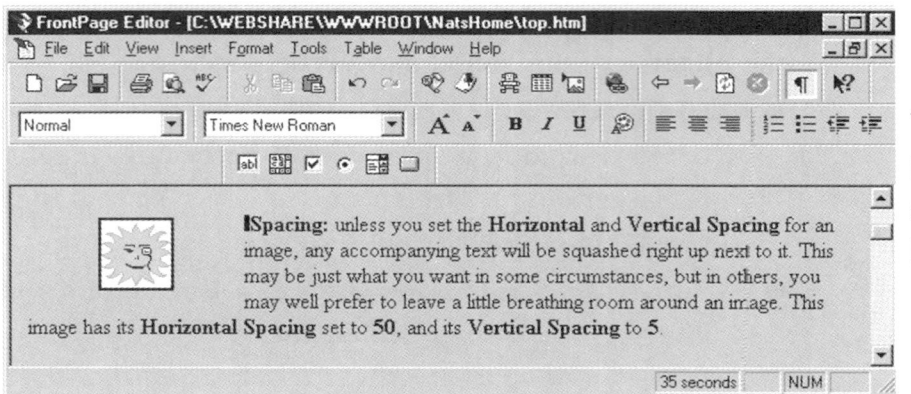

The Vertical distance is also affected by the spacing between the lines of text

- **Alignment** determines how text is arranged around the image. The most useful options on the menu are **Top, Middle** and **Bottom** for captions, and **Left** and **Right** when the image is embedded in text.

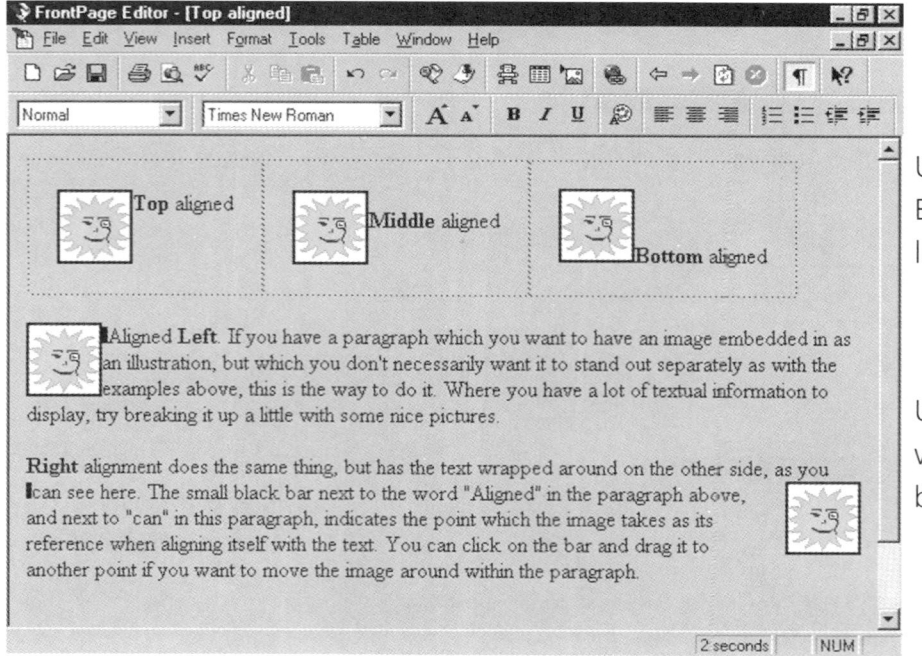

Use Top, Middle or Bottom with a single line of text

Use Left or Right when the image is beside a block of text

Alternative representations

1 Click on the **General** tab.

2 At the **Text** field, enter a title or descriptive message.

3 Click the **Browse** button to find a thumbnail image, if you created one.

4 Click **OK**.

As some people turn off the **View Images** option on their browser so that pages download faster, it is good practice to have a text label which appears in place of your images. Also, a small **Low-res**olution version of a large image gives people an idea of what they are waiting for, rather than making them sit around twiddling their thumbs for ages.

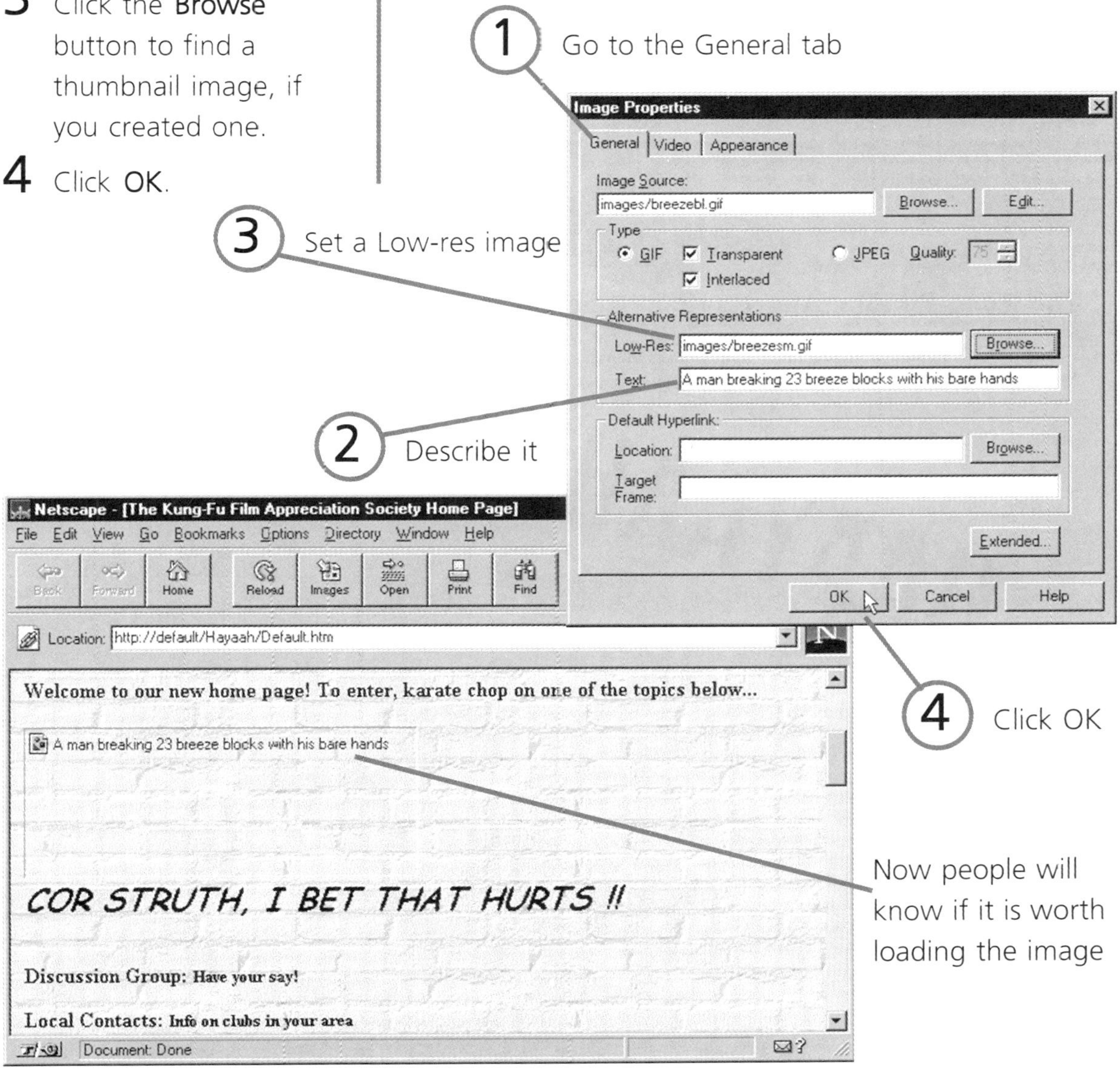

1 Go to the General tab

Image Properties

General | Video | Appearance

Image Source:
images/breezebl.gif   Browse...   Edit...

Type
◉ GIF ☑ Transparent   ○ JPEG Quality: 75
       ☑ Interlaced

3 Set a Low-res image

Alternative Representations

Low-Res: images/breezesm.gif   Browse...

Text: A man breaking 23 breeze blocks with his bare hands

2 Describe it

Default Hyperlink:

Location: Browse...

Target Frame:

Extended...

OK   Cancel   Help

4 Click OK

Netscape - [The Kung-Fu Film Appreciation Society Home Page]

File Edit View Go Bookmarks Options Directory Window Help

Back Forward Home Reload Images Open Print Find

Location: http://default/Hayaah/Default.htm

Welcome to our new home page! To enter, karate chop on one of the topics below...

A man breaking 23 breeze blocks with his bare hands

COR STRUTH, I BET THAT HURTS !!

Discussion Group: Have your say!

Local Contacts: Info on clubs in your area

Document: Done

Now people will know if it is worth loading the image

Transparent colours

The background colour of an image can be set to be transparent, allowing the background colour of the page to show through. This breaks up the monotony of having all the pictures enclosed in rectangular boxes, and is especially useful for stylised text.

1 Click once on an image to select it.

2 Click the **Make transparent** button.

3 Click anywhere on the background colour to make it transparent.

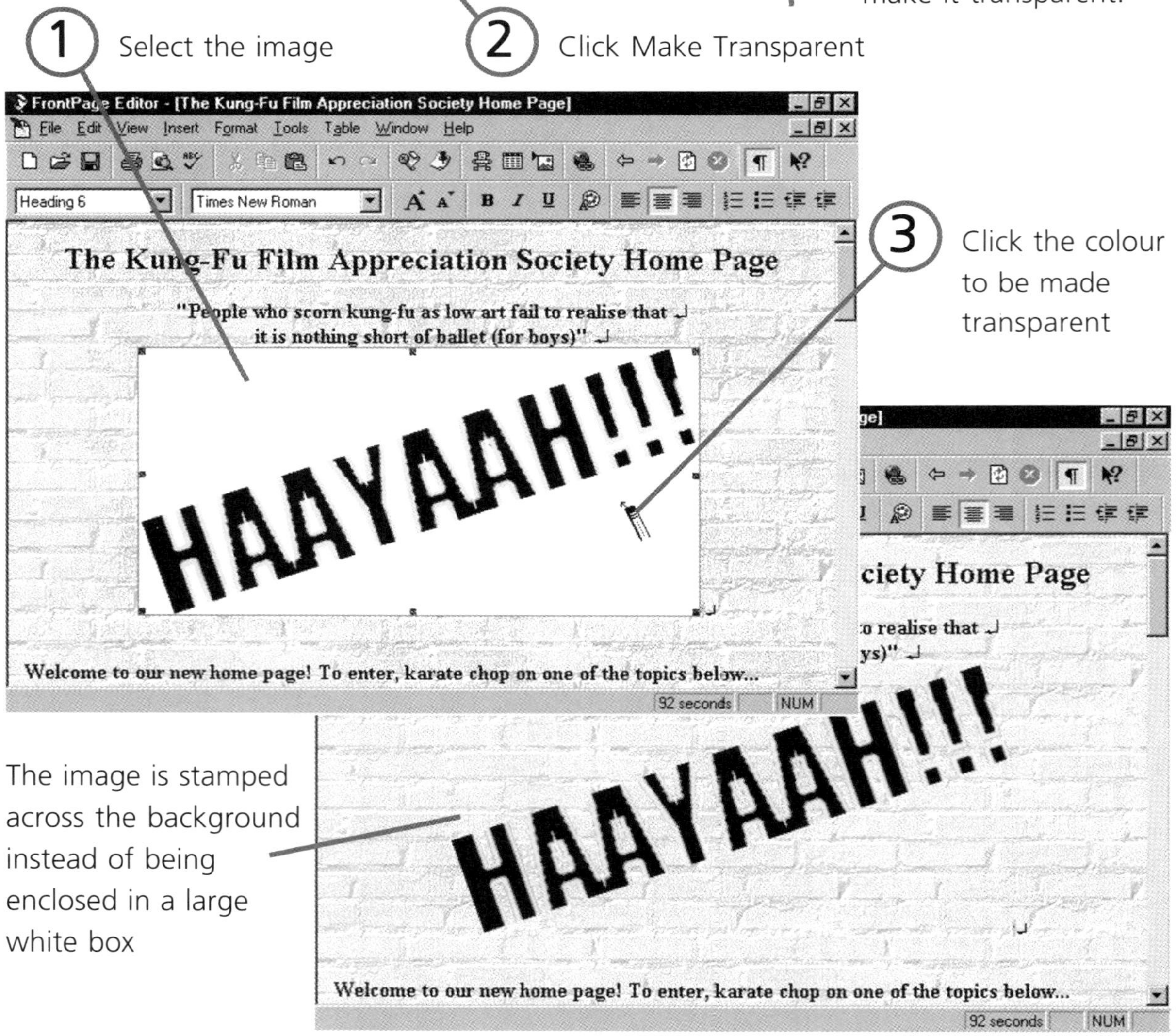

① Select the image ② Click Make Transparent

The Kung-Fu Film Appreciation Society Home Page

"People who scorn kung-fu as low art fail to realise that it is nothing short of ballet (for boys)"

HAAYAAH!!!

Welcome to our new home page! To enter, karate chop on one of the topics below...

③ Click the colour to be made transparent

The image is stamped across the background instead of being enclosed in a large white box

HAAYAAH!!!

Welcome to our new home page! To enter, karate chop on one of the topics below...

32

Basic steps

1 Open the **Insert** menu and select **Background Sound**.

2 Use the **Current Web Page** or **Location** panel to find the sound file.

3 Click **OK**.

Background sounds

If you have a sound file – a spoken message or some music – it can be attached to a page to play in the background when the page is opened.

Whether or not people will be able to hear your file depends upon their hardware and software, and the format of your file. The file extension identifies the format.

AU   Sun's audio format – can be handled directly by Internet Explorer and by Netscape's LiveAudio plug-in. Most people should be able to hear these.

AIFF The Apple sound format.

MID MIDI sequence, played on Windows systems by MPlayer – normally linked to the browser.

WAV Wave format, played by Windows' sound software.

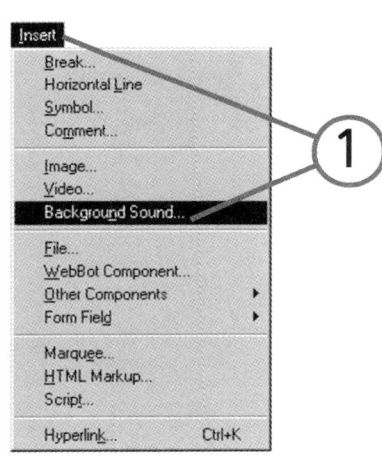

Select Insert – Background Sound

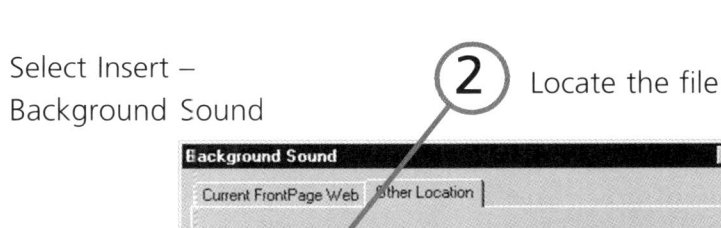

Locate the file

Click OK

Take note

You can also set up a hyperlink to a sound file from an image or text. It will then be played when the visitor clicks on the link.

Summary

- ❏ Set the size of text using the **Increase** and **Decrease Font Size** buttons, or the **Style** drop-down menu.

- ❏ Change text colour by highlighting it and clicking the **Font Color** button to bring up a colour palette.

- ❏ Use **Lists** to make information more visually accessible.

- ❏ You can **Insert** an **image** from the **Current FrontPage Web**, your computer, or from a **Location** on the World Wide Web.

- ❏ You can also **Drag** an image from the **Windows Explorer** or **Find File** and **Drop** it into the page, or **Copy** one from an image editor and **Paste** it in.

- ❏ Change an image's size, alignment and relation to surrounding text, or give it a border from the **Image properties...** dialog box.

- ❏ Give an image **Alternative** text or a thumbnail image to be displayed so that visitors don't have to wait around for pictures which they then find they don't want to see.

- ❏ You can add a **Background Sound** that will play when the page is opened.

3 MS Image Composer

MS Image Composer 36

Sprites 38

Shaped sprites 40

Layering sprites 41

Art effects, warps and filters 42

Grouping and flattening 44

Patterns and Fills 45

Erasing 46

Summary .48

MS Image Composer

To explain fully the entire range of effects which can be achieved with MS Image Composer would take a book in itself, but in fact, most are best understood by playing with them. All you really need is a few pointers to be able to explore them comfortably yourself.

When you are working in the Editor window, double-clicking on an image will, by default, launch MS Image Composer and open the image so that you can edit it. However, you can configure FrontPage to open another graphics application instead, if you prefer.

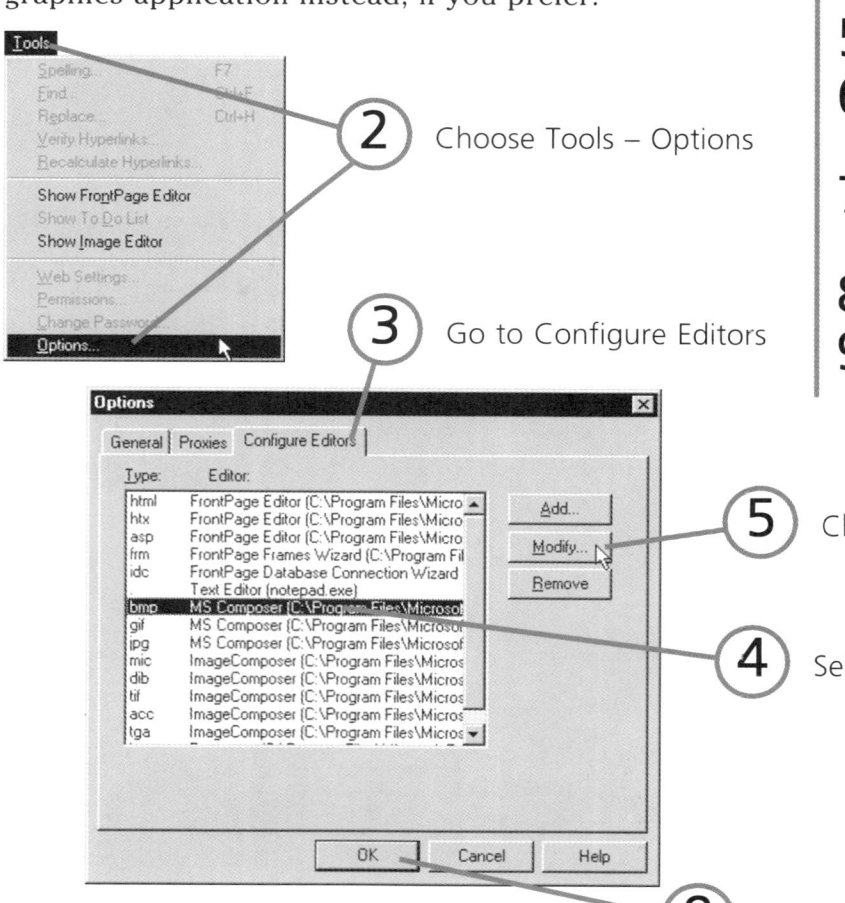

Choose Tools – Options

Go to Configure Editors

Click Modify

Select the file type

Click OK

1 Open the Explorer window.

2 Choose **Options...** from the **Tools** menu.

3 Click the **Configure Editors** tab.

4 Select a file type to associate with another program.

5 Click **Modify...**

6 Type the name of the application.

7 **Browse...** for the program (**Command**).

8 Click **OK.**

9 Click **OK** on the main panel.

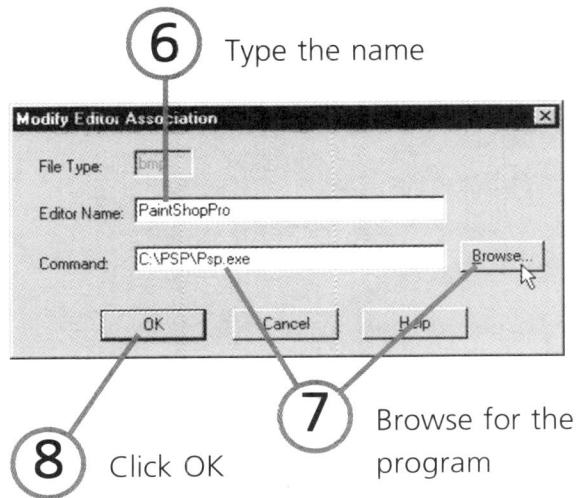

(6) Type the name

(7) Browse for the program

(8) Click OK

Modify Editor Association

File Type: bmp

Editor Name: PaintShopPro

Command: C:\PSP\Psp.exe   Browse...

OK   Cancel   Help

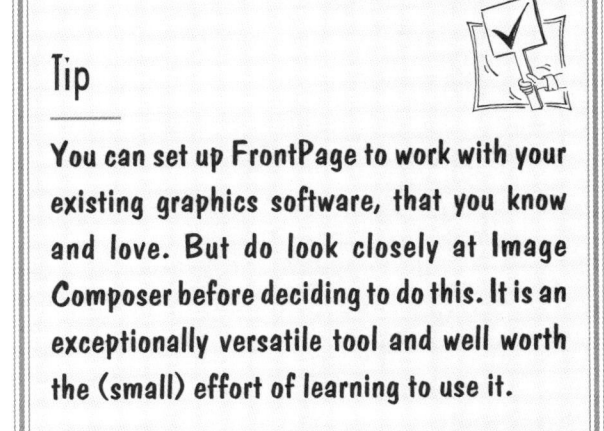

Tip

You can set up FrontPage to work with your existing graphics software, that you know and love. But do look closely at Image Composer before deciding to do this. It is an exceptionally versatile tool and well worth the (small) effort of learning to use it.

The Composer window

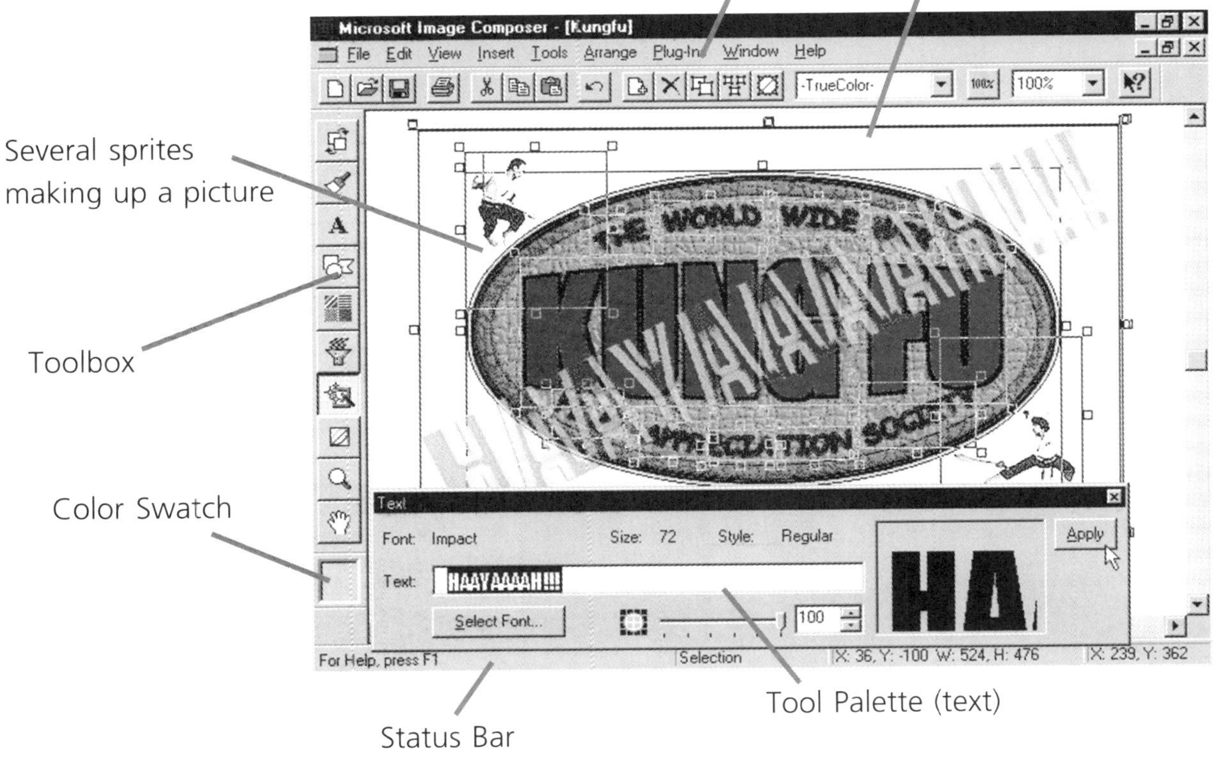

Toolbar

Desktop

Several sprites making up a picture

Toolbox

Color Swatch

Microsoft Image Composer - [Kungfu]

File Edit View Insert Tools Arrange Plug-Ins Window Help

TrueColor   100x 100%

THE WORLD WIDE
KUNGFU
APPRECIATION SOCIETY

Text

Font: Impact   Size: 72   Style: Regular   Apply

Text: HAAYAAAAH!!!

Select Font...   100

HA

For Help, press F1   Selection   X: 36, Y: -100 W: 524, H: 476   X: 239, Y: 362

Tool Palette (text)

Status Bar

37

Sprites

Most standard image editing applications are the digital equivalent of drawing or painting – you have a selection of tools which produce various effects on a piece of paper. Microsoft Image Composer is more akin to making a collage, where each part of a picture – the background, some lettering, an emblem, etc. – is treated as a separate entity.

These are called **sprites**. Individual sprites can be created and edited as you would in an ordinary image editor, and are then arranged together to form a complete picture.

Creating a new sprite

If you are starting from scratch, you will need to create a blank sprite as a working area – you cannot just paint onto the workspace.

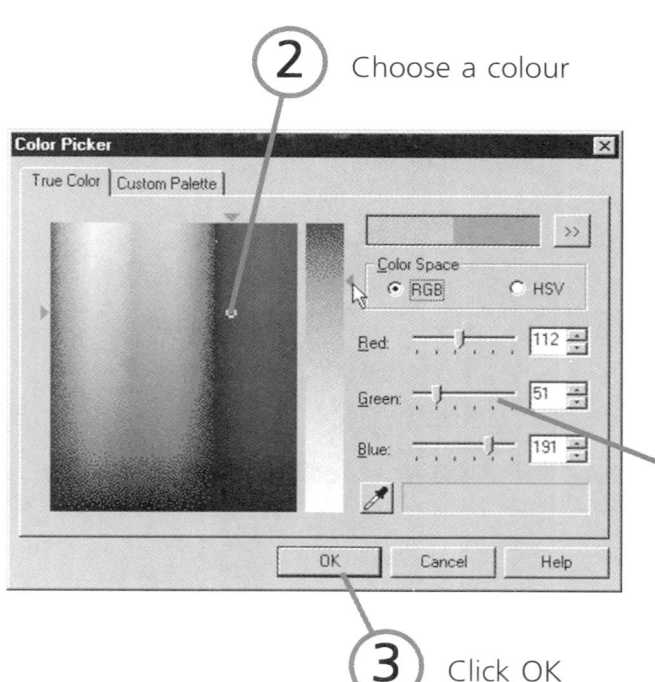

2 Choose a colour

3 Click OK

1 Click the **Color Swatch** box ▓ under the Toolbox.

2 Choose a colour from the palette.

3 Click **OK**.

4 Click the Shapes button ▧ on the Toolbox.

5 Click the **Rectangle** or **Oval** button.

6 On the desktop the working area – click and drag to create an area large enough to work in.

7 If you want to change the Opacity – the density of the colour – do it now.

8 Click **Render**.

If you prefer, you can define the colour by setting its Red/Green/Blue values

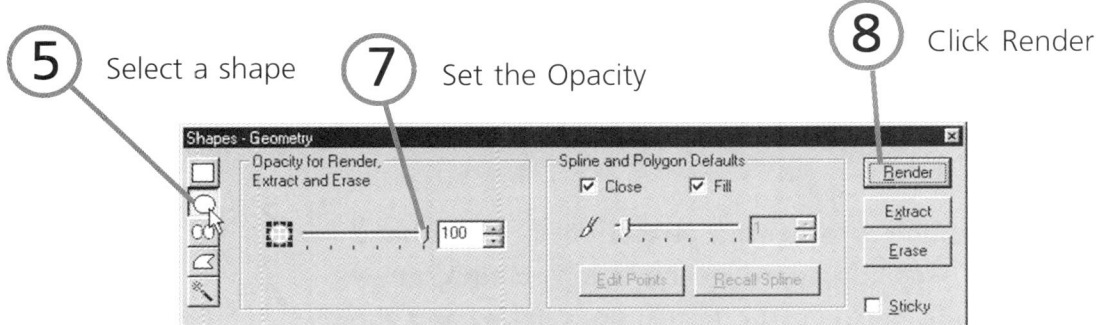

5 Select a shape **7** Set the Opacity **8** Click Render

Working with sprites

A sprite can be a scanned image which you have imported, lettering created using the Text tool palette, or a design created from scratch.

To move or edit a sprite, you must select it first. The best way to do this is to press the Tab key, which jumps to each sprite in turn. Once a sprite is selected, it will have a Bounding Box around it with handles at the corners and sides; click and drag on these to resize or rotate it.

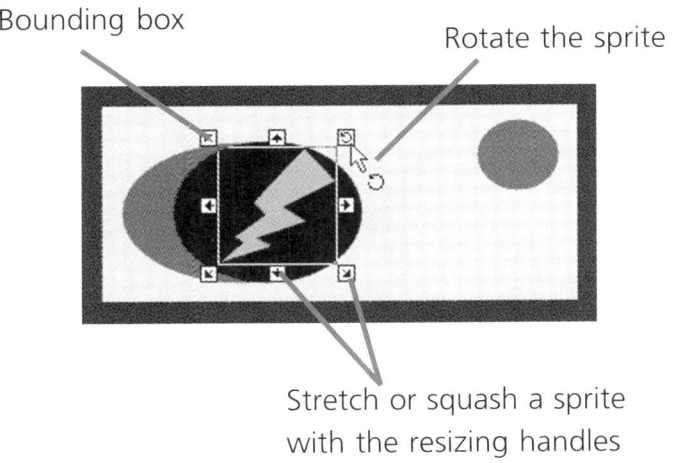

Bounding box

Rotate the sprite

Stretch or squash a sprite with the resizing handles

Shaped sprites

As an alternative to creating regular shaped backgrounds and painting on them, simple shapes can be created with the **Polygon** ⬠ or **Spline** ∞ buttons. The advantage of these will become clear when you start them layering them.

Creating a spline is rather like stretching a rubber band around the pegs in a board – each time you click a new point, the line between the first point clicked and the most recent is stretched around it.

Checking the **Fill** field creates a solid shape – if it is unchecked, just the outline is created.

1 Open the **Shapes** tool palette.

2 Click the **Polygon** or **Spline** button.

3 For a polygon, click to set each vertex.

4 For a spline, click to add a point which the line is stretched around.

5 Choose whether to **Fill** the shape or just use an outline.

6 Click **Render** to complete the shape.

1 Open the Shapes palette   **6** Click Render

2 Choose Spline or Polygon   **5** Fill?

Take note

When you select a sprite which is behind another, you will only see the bounding box, and you may have to move it out to see which one it is!

Polygons

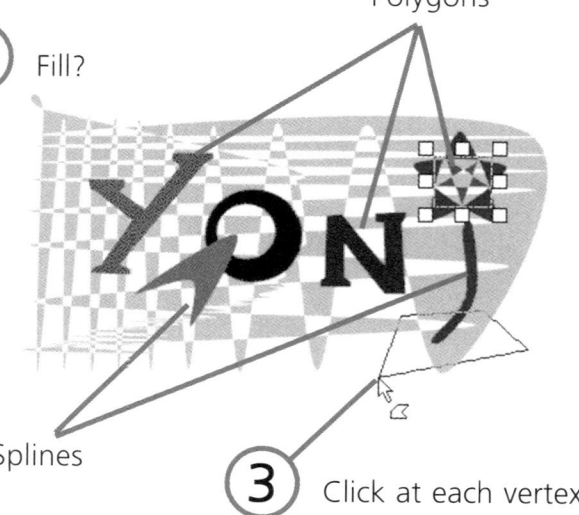

Splines   **3** Click at each vertex

Basic steps

1 Arrange the sprites roughly on top of each other.

2 Click the **Arrange** icon in the **Toolbox**.

3 Use the **Tab** key to select a sprite.

4 Click the **To Front** icon.

5 Switch to the next sprite with the **Tab** key.

6 Click the **Bring Forward** or **Send Backward** icon to shuffle it through the stack.

7 If necessary, repeat this with the other circle until the sprites are in the right order.

8 Arrange the sprites as you want them.

The finished arrangement

Sprites can be layered one on top of another and the order shuffled about to achieve the desired effect. By default, the sprites are layered in the order they were created – most recent on the top.

In the following example, I have created four sprites; a green circle, a larger black circle and a yellow lightning flash and orange explosion (using the **Polygon** button on the **Shapes** tool palette).

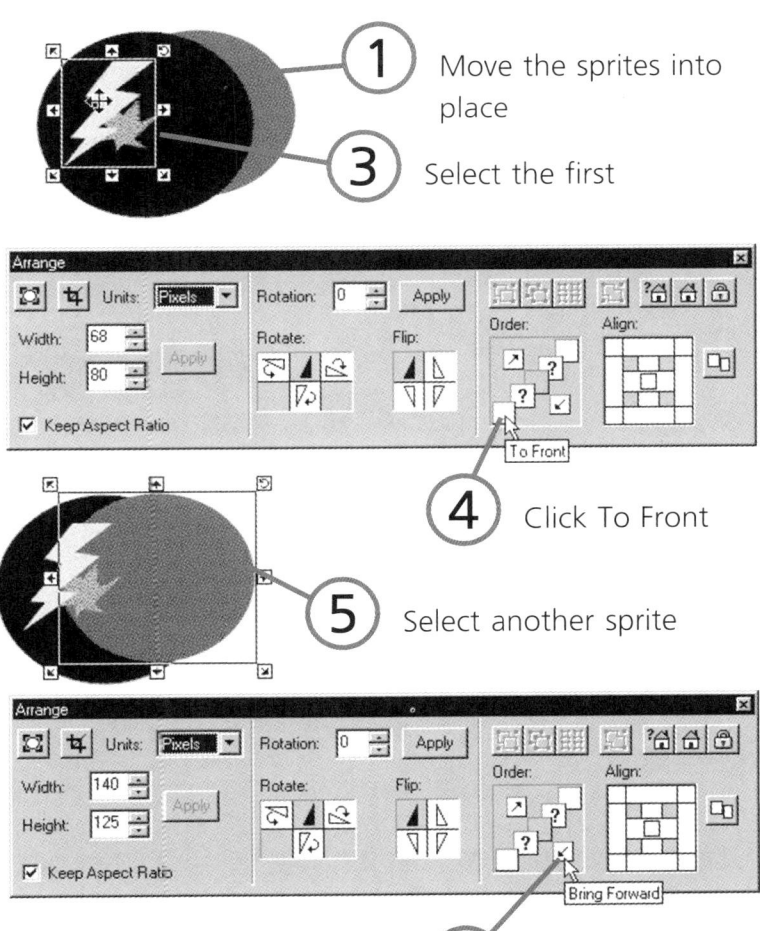

① Move the sprites into place

③ Select the first

④ Click To Front

⑤ Select another sprite

⑥ Shuffle into order

Art effects, warps and filters

There is no limit to what you can achieve with a combination of effects – the settings for each one radically affect the outcome, as does the order in which you perform a series of transformations on a sprite.

When you are experimenting with effects, it is a good idea to make a few copies of the sprite you are working on because the **Undo** button will only undo the last change you made.

Basic steps

1 Select a sprite.

2 Click the **Duplicate** button 🔲 a few times.

3 Select an effect.

4 Adjust the settings.

5 Click **Apply**

6 Try other effects on the duplicates.

7 Delete ✖ the ones you don't want.

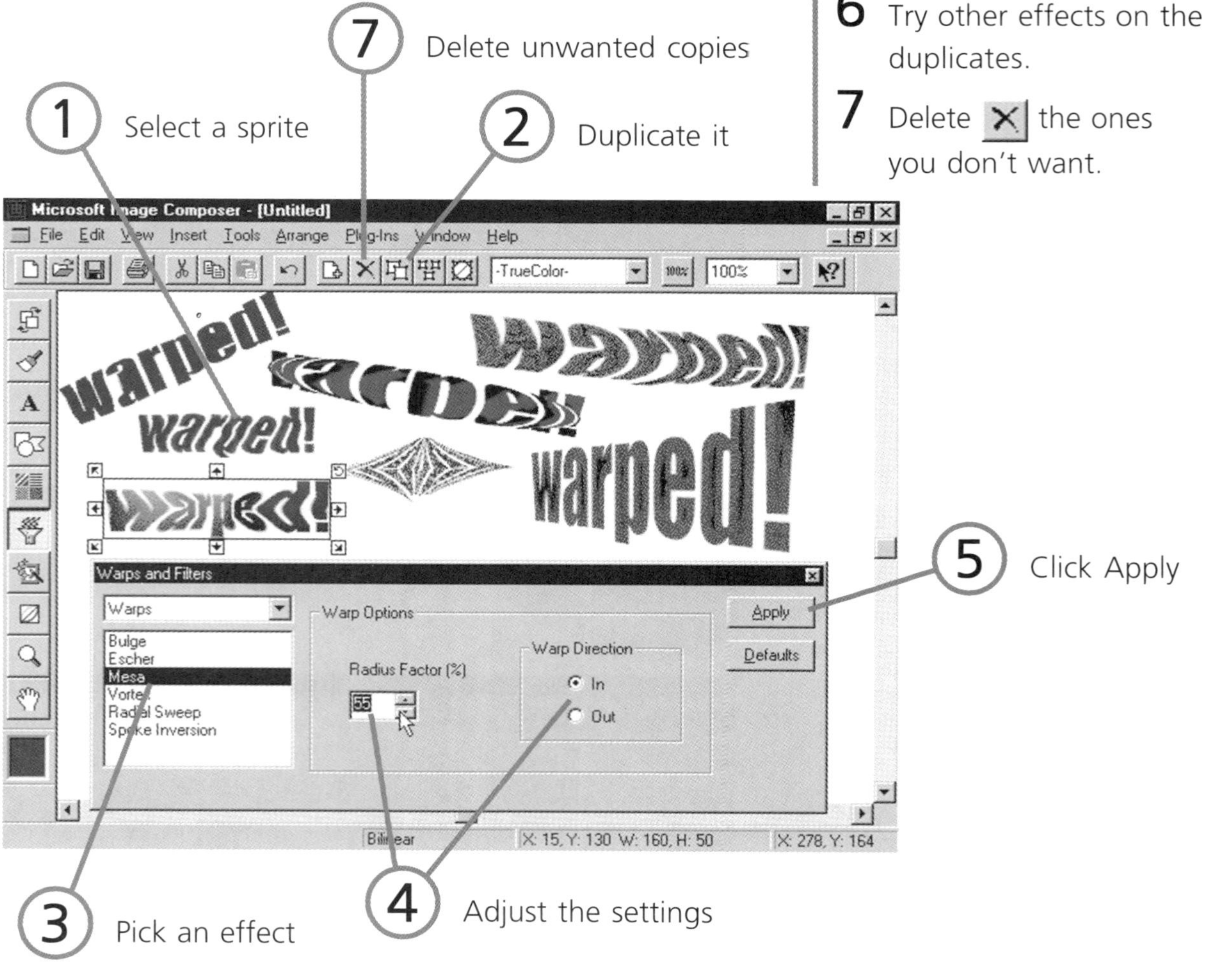

⑦ Delete unwanted copies

① Select a sprite

② Duplicate it

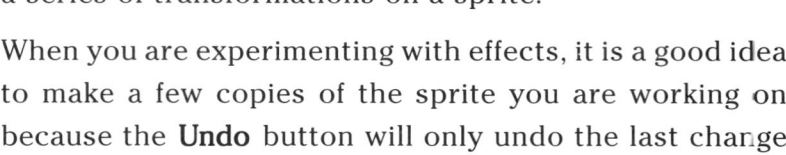

⑤ Click Apply

③ Pick an effect

④ Adjust the settings

Basic steps

1 Select a sprite.
2 Click the **Duplicate** button a few times.
3 Choose **Warp Transforms** from the drop-down menu.
4 Choose **Interactive Warps.**
5 Select a type of warp.
6 Click and drag the frame to set the warp's size and direction.
7 Click **Apply**.

Settings

Each effect has different settings according to what it is supposed to do, but there are a couple of common controls:

- **Opacity** ▦ sets how 'thickly' the effect is laid on.
- **Smoothness** controls how smooth the resulting surface appears. Move the slider to the left for more contour and detail; to the right for less definition.
- **Stroke length/pressure** lets you choose a brushstroke to imitate a painting or drawing technique.

Interactive warps

Whereas some warps like *Bulge* just have a direction – In or Out – the interactive warps are much more controllable.

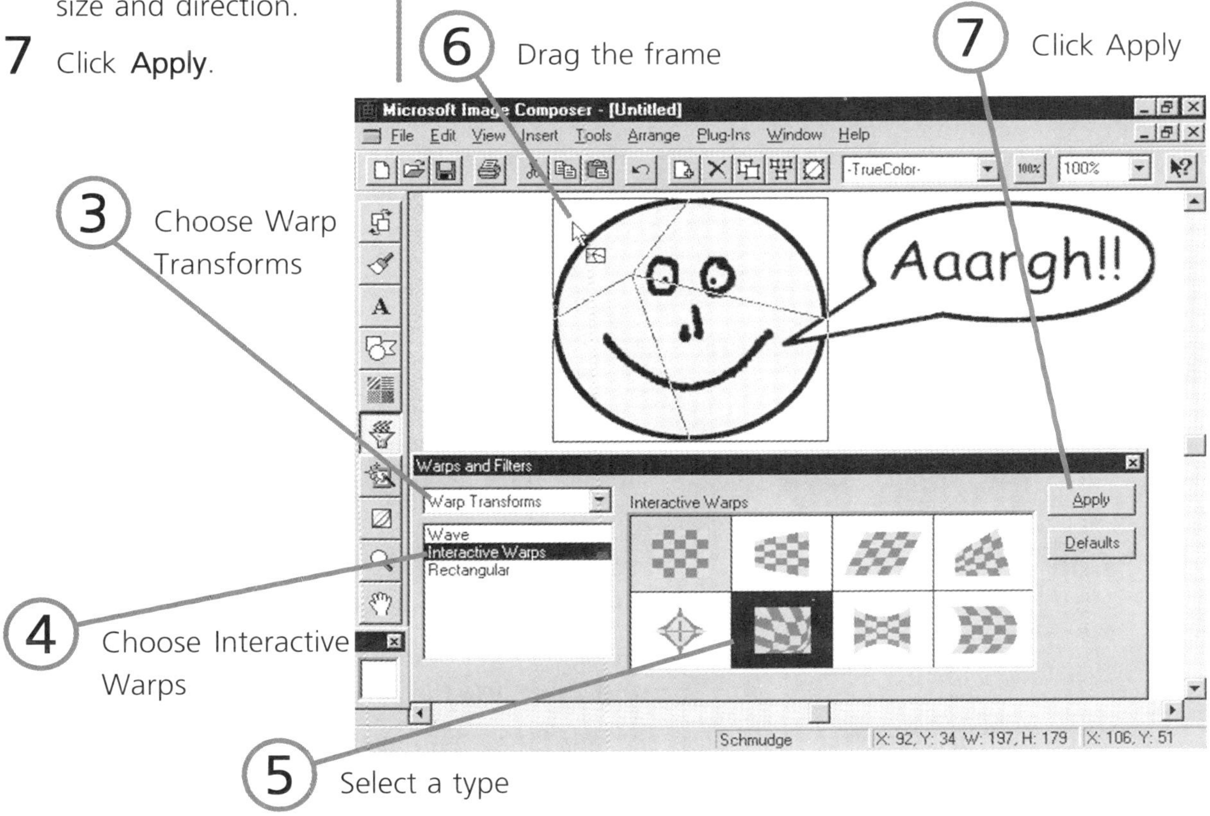

⑥ Drag the frame   ⑦ Click Apply

③ Choose Warp Transforms

④ Choose Interactive Warps

⑤ Select a type

43

Grouping and flattening

Once you have an arrangement of sprites which you want to keep together, you can **Group** them together and move them around as a single entity.

Flattening sprites works in much the same way, but once flattened, sprites cannot be separated again. The advantage to flattening sprites is that you can edit the whole arrangement as a single sprite – grouped sprites cannot be resized or rotated, nor can you apply any special effects to them.

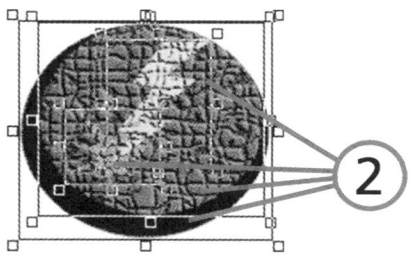

Click the sprites you want to group

1 Click the **Arrange** icon to bring up the palette.

2 Hold the **Shift** key and click on each sprite you want to add to the group.

3 Click the **Group** button.

❑ *To edit an individual sprite*

4 Select the grouped sprites.

5 Click the **Ungroup** button.

Flattened sprites can be edited freely

Tip

If you are likely to want to change any part of the image at a later date, save the whole page, extra bits and all, as a **.mic** file before you flatten the sprites. The **.mic** format preserves the individual sprites.

Basic steps

1 Create a sprite to use as a source for the pattern or fill.

2 Move the source sprite over the sprite to apply the effect to.

3 Select the sprite beneath using **[Tab]**.

4 Choose a **Sprite to Sprite** effect.

5 Click **Apply**.

6 When prompted, choose another sprite to copy from.

7 Select the source sprite and Delete it.

Patterns and Fills

As with other effects, make several copies of a sprite so that you can experiment freely. Using the **Sprite to Sprite** effects, you will need two sprites; one to alter and one to take the colour or shape from. The second will often have to cover or overlap the first to have any effect because it is used almost like a transfer or brass rubbing.

2 Move the source over the top

6 Choose another

5 Click Apply

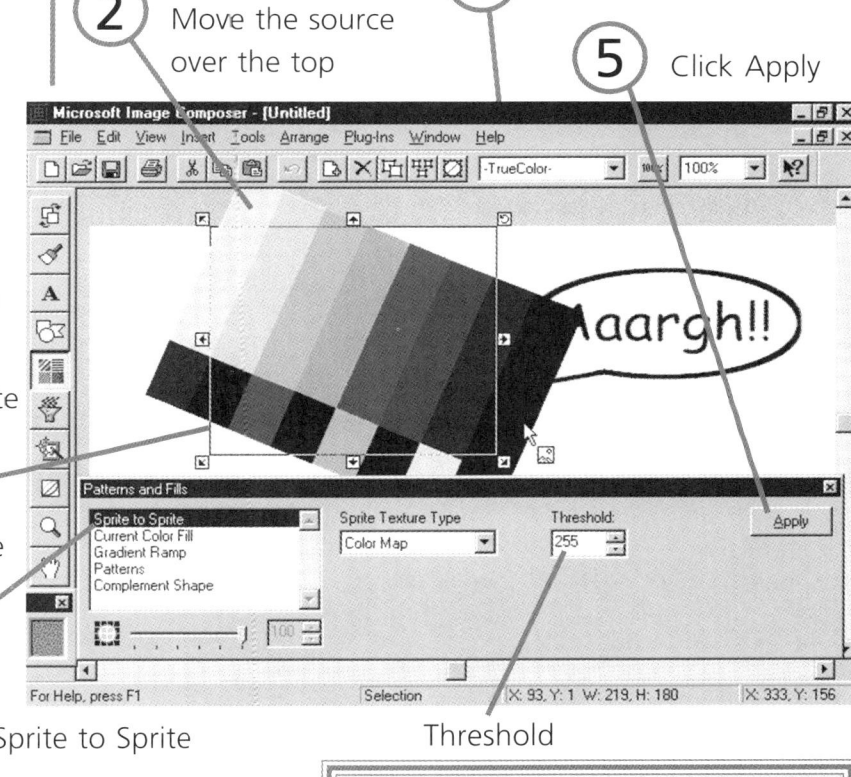

3 Select the Sprite beneath

4 Choose Sprite to Sprite

Threshold

> ## Tip
>
> **The settings are important. To transfer the Color Bars faithfully, the Threshold must be set at maximum (255).**

45

Erasing

When you Erase part of a sprite or flattened group of sprites it is made transparent, allowing sprites beneath it to show through. The Opacity control determines to what extent sprites beneath are visible – 100 cuts erased areas completely, 1 allows virtually nothing to show through.

● You can use Erase from the Paint palette, or cut out areas with the Shapes tools.

Basic steps

1 Select a sprite.

2 Click the **Erase** button on the **Paint** palette.

3 Choose a shape for the eraser.

4 Adjust its size.

5 Adjust the **Opacity**.

6 Erase from the sprite.

or

7 Select a shape from the **Shapes** palette.

8 Use the shape to select an area.

9 Click **Erase**.

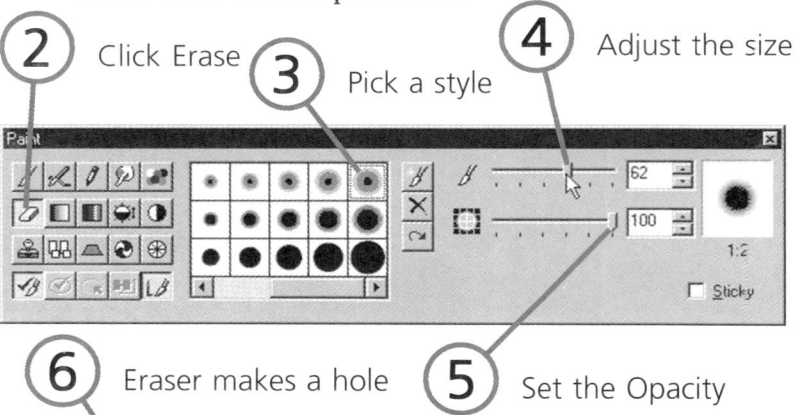

② Click Erase ③ Pick a style ④ Adjust the size

⑥ Eraser makes a hole ⑤ Set the Opacity

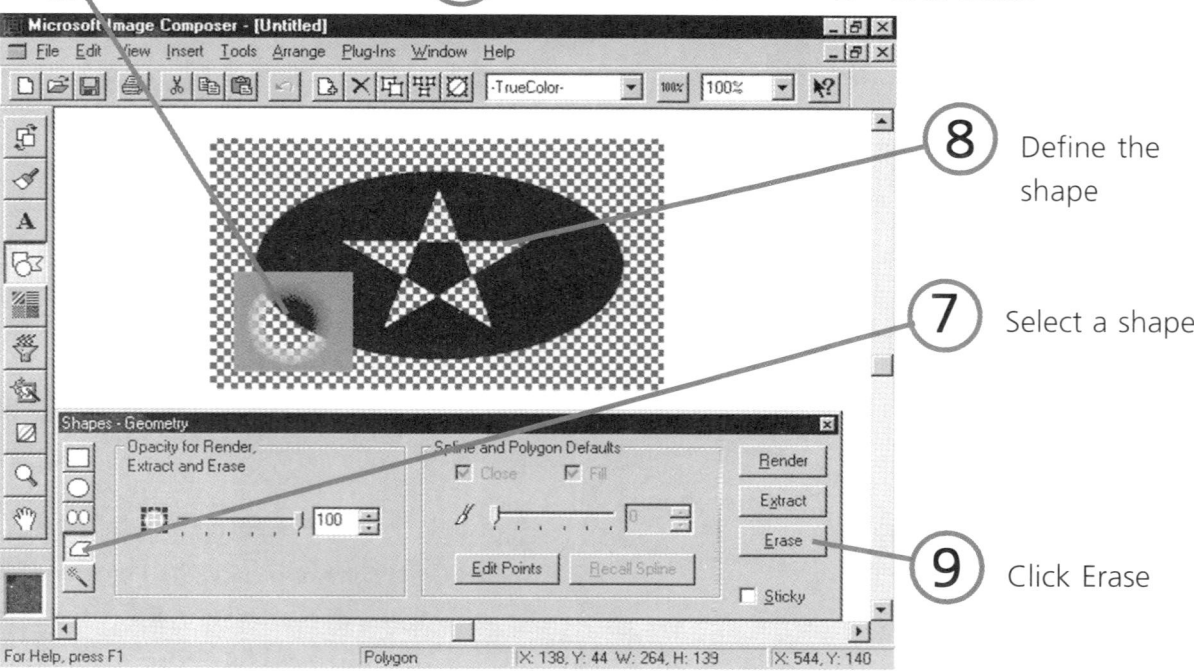

⑧ Define the shape

⑦ Select a shape

⑨ Click Erase

Basic steps

1 Click the **Select All** button 🔡.

2 Click **Flatten** 🔲 on the **Arrange** palette.

3 Select a shape from the **Shapes** palette.

4 Use the shape to select the part you want.

5 Click **Extract**.

6 Choose **Save Selection As** from the **File** menu.

7 If you are going to use this image in a web page, you should save it as a .gif or .jpg file.

8 Click **Save**.

Extracting

By the time you are satisfied with an image, you may have some extraneous bits and pieces around it – even if you cut these, the space is preserved when you save the image. To save only the part you want, flatten the sprites into one group and then use the Shapes palette to define an area. A new sprite is then created which includes only the selected part of the image. The old one can now be discarded.

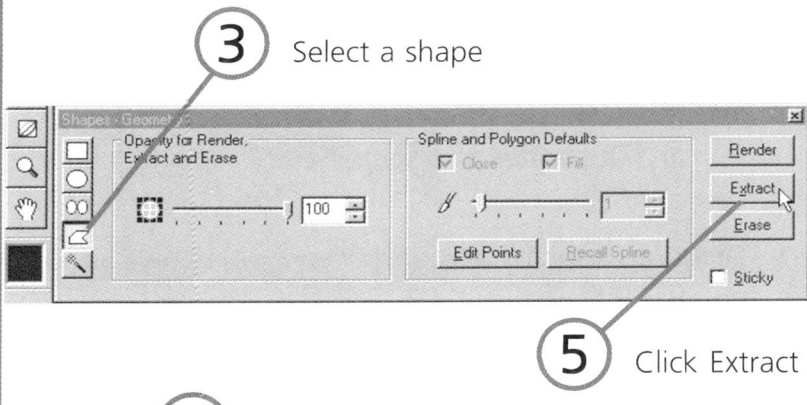

③ Select a shape

⑤ Click Extract

⑥ Choose File – Save Selection As...

⑦ Save as a .gif or .jpg

⑧ Click Save

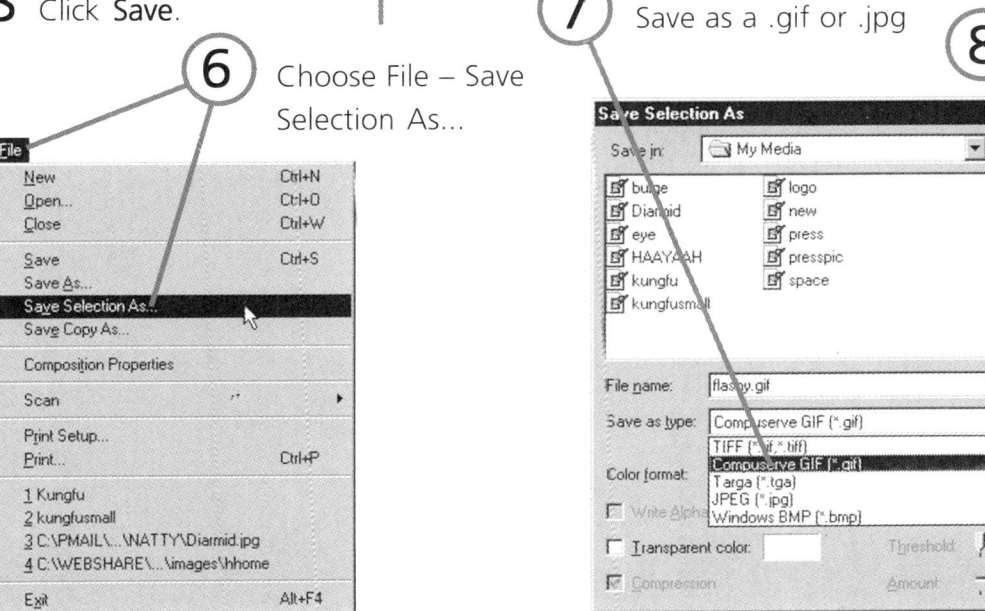

Summary

- You can **Configure** FrontPage to use your favourite **image Editor** instead of MS Image Composer.

- **Sprites** are individual images which are used to make up the 'collage' of an Image Composer design.

- Create **new sprites** using the **Shapes** or **Text** tool palettes.

- Use the **Arrange** palette to shuffle the order in which sprites are layered.

- Edit sprites using the various tool palettes – **Patterns and Fills**, **Warps and Filters**, and **Art Effects** (remember to make **Duplicates** of a sprite before zapping it with special effects!).

- **Group** an arrangement of sprites so that they can all be moved together.

- **Flatten** sprites so that you can use the **Extract** command from the **Shapes** palette to select an area of your design.

- Save a design in the **.mic** format to preserve the individuality of its sprites, or as a **.gif** or **.jpeg** file to use it in a web.

- You can **erase** part of a sprite so that an underlying sprite shows through.

4 Active content

Active sorcery 50

AVI video clips 51

Other video formats 53

Marquees 54

Animated GIFs 56

Java, ActiveX and JavaScript 59

Summary 60

Active sorcery

This is where building a web really gets to be fun!

It's all very well having pretty pictures and snappy text in bright colours, but you can do that on ordinary paper – what makes web sites so different is their potential for movement and action.

The following pages explain how to add digital video clips and create your own animated text and graphics so that you can bring your pages to life with a little active sorcery...

At the time of writing, there was an excellent GIF animation source page at:

http://www.acute.com/promote/graphics/1gifani.htm

Check it out – it should still be there.

Tip

When constructing your web pages, try to strike a balance between impressive looking graphics, movie clips and other attention-grabbers, and the boredom involved in waiting for large files to download.

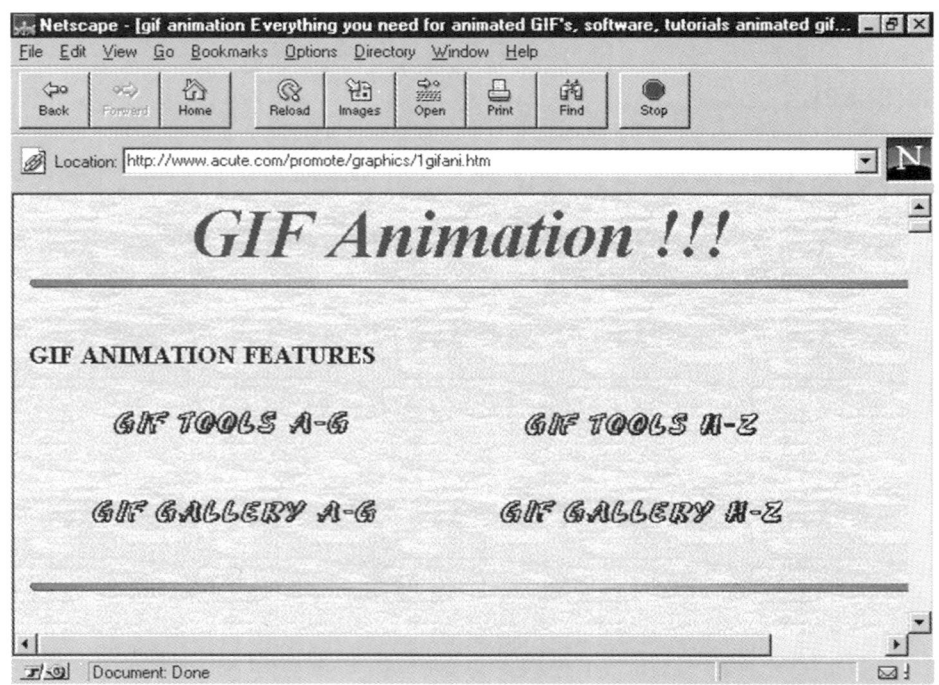

Basic steps

1 From the **Insert** menu, choose **Video**...

2 Choose from a video already in the **Current Front Page Web**

or

3 Click on the **Other Location** tab.

4 **Browse**... for a video file on your computer.

or

5 Enter the World Wide Web **Location** of a file.

6 Click **OK**.

Take note

AVI stands for Audio-Visual Interleaved and is the format used by Windows' Media Player.

AVI video clips

The way video clips are displayed varies from browser to browser. FrontPage is designed for use with **AVI** files, and will not display files of other formats in the **Current FrontPage Web**.

If you use **AVI** files and your visitors use MS Explorer, video clips will be played wherever you put them on the page, and you can also customise the way they are displayed.

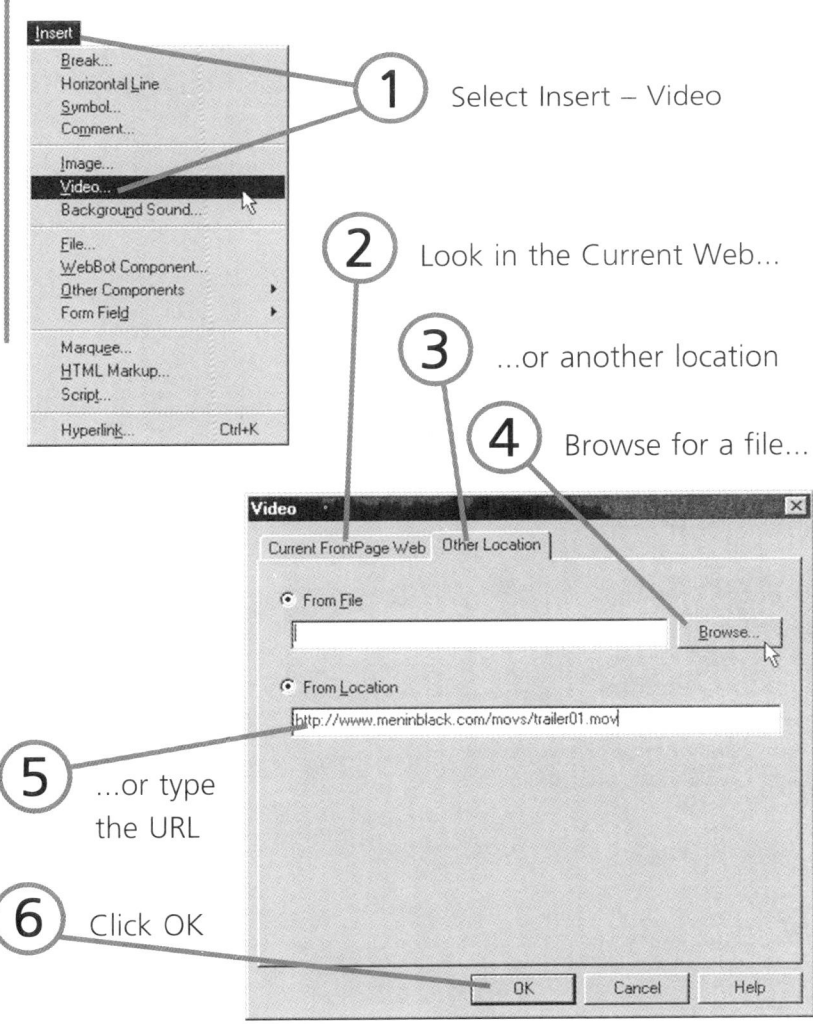

① Select Insert – Video

② Look in the Current Web...

③ ...or another location

④ Browse for a file...

⑤ ...or type the URL

⑥ Click OK

AVI display options

There are a few options that you can set to control how the .avi clip is displayed.

- **Show controls in browser** – if this is checked, it allows visitors to stop and start the clip.

- **Loop** – specifies the number of times to repeat the clip.

- **Forever** – sets the clip into a continuous loop.

- **Loop Delay** – the delay between repeat showings.

- **Start On File Open** – starts the animation as soon as the clip is loaded.

- **Start On MouseOver** – loads the clip and waits for the cursor to move over the first frame before starting to play.

Basic steps

1 Right-click on the video image.

2 Choose **Image Properties...**

3 Click on the **Video** tab.

4 Set the options as required.

5 Click **OK**.

| Cut |
| Copy |
| Paste |
| Page Properties... |
| Image Properties... Alt+Enter |

(2) Select Image Properties

(3) Go to the Video panel

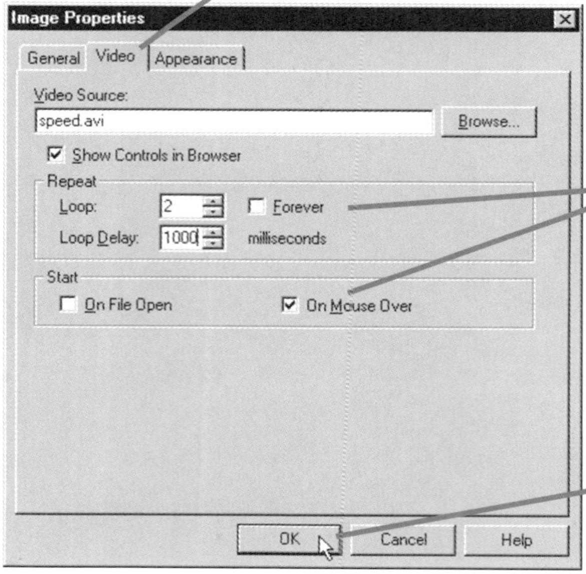

Take note

These options only apply to AVI files.

Image Properties

General | Video | Appearance

Video Source:
speed.avi   Browse...

☑ Show Controls in Browser

Repeat
Loop: 2   ☐ Forever
Loop Delay: 1000 milliseconds

Start
☐ On File Open   ☑ On Mouse Over

(4) Set options

OK   Cancel   Help

(5) Click OK

52

Basic steps

1 In the Explorer window, choose **Import...** from the **File** menu.

2 Click **Add File...**

3 Browse for a file.

4 Click **OK**.

5 In the Editor window, select text or an image to serve as a link.

6 Click the **Create Hyperlink** button.

7 Enter the name of the file in the **Page** field.

8 Click **OK**.

Unfortunately for FrontPage users, many clips available are in **.mov** or **.mpeg** formats, and many people prefer to use a Netscape browser! Perhaps the simplest way to get around the problem is to create a link to the video file instead of embedding it into a page, though this does mean that you lose the extra display options.

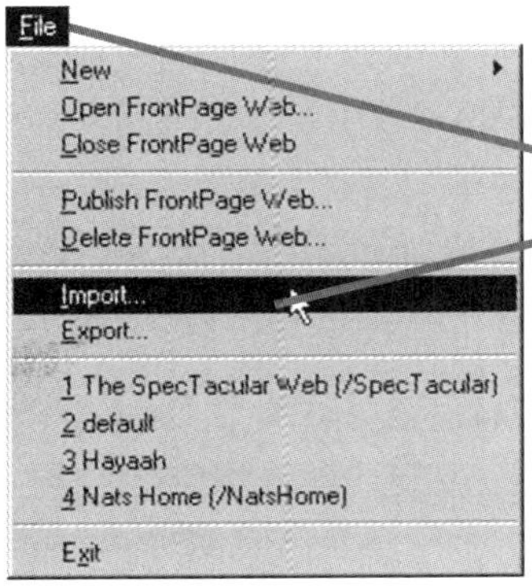

File menu:

File
New ▶
Open FrontPage Web...
Close FrontPage Web

Publish FrontPage Web...
Delete FrontPage Web...

Import...
Export...

1 The SpecTacular Web (/SpecTacular)
2 default
3 Hayaah
4 Nats Home (/NatsHome)

Exit

(1) Use File – Import

(2) Click Add File

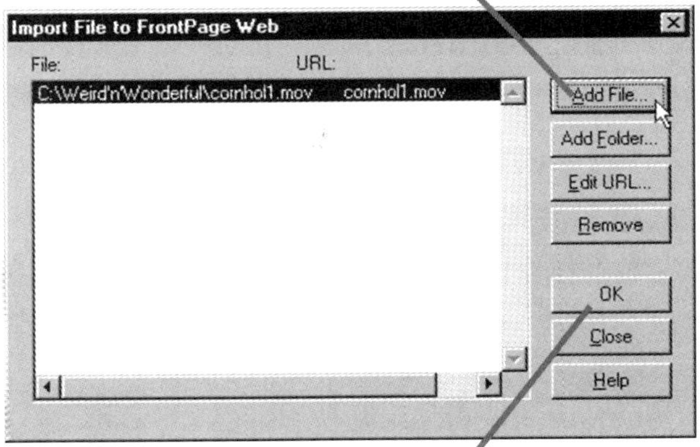

Import File to FrontPage Web

File: URL:
C:\Weird'n'Wonderful\cornhol1.mov   cornhol1.mov

Add File...
Add Folder...
Edit URL...
Remove

OK
Close
Help

(4) Click OK

(7) Enter the filename

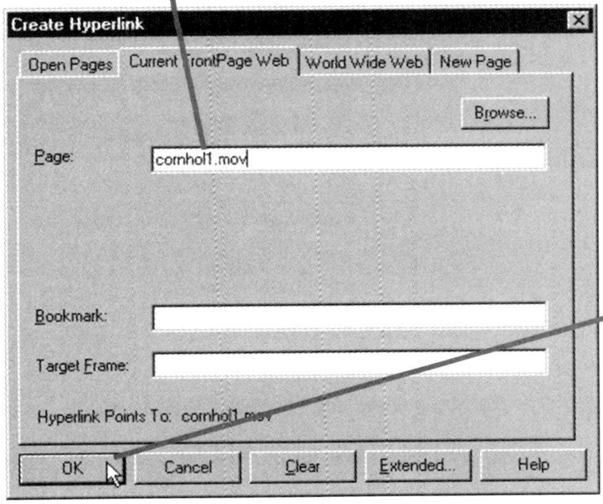

Create Hyperlink

Open Pages | Current FrontPage Web | World Wide Web | New Page

Browse...

Page: cornhol1.mov

Bookmark:

Target Frame:

Hyperlink Points To: cornhol1.mov

OK   Cancel   Clear   Extended...   Help

(8) Click OK

Marquees

A Marquee is a FrontPage component which will make text scroll or bounce from left to right across the screen. There are several properties which you can edit:

- **Direction** determines whether the text scrolls to the Left or Right.

- **Movement Speed** sets the Delay in milliseconds before repeating the motion – *Amount* is an odd term to describe speed, but that's what it does: more means faster.

- **Behavior** – *Scroll* runs text onto the marquee box at one side and off the other;

  Slide makes text slide onto the marquee and stay still when it reaches the other side

  Alternate makes text slide back and forth.

- **Align with text** sets the vertical alignment of any text surrounding the marquee.

- **Specify Width** and **Height** – by default, these are determined by the size of the text in the marquee, but you can set values if you wish.

- **Repeat** makes the action repeat *Continuously* or for a specified number of *Times*.

- **Background color** – change the background colour.

1 From the **Insert** menu, choose **Marquee...**

2 Type a message.

3 Set the **Direction** and **Speed** of motion.

4 Select a **Behavior** style.

5 Set text alignment.

6 Specify the **Width** and/or **Height**.

7 Decide how many times the action is repeated.

8 Set a **Background color**.

9 Click **OK**.

Tip

A marquee's text can be formatted as normal - just highlight it and use the toolbar to set the font, size and colour.

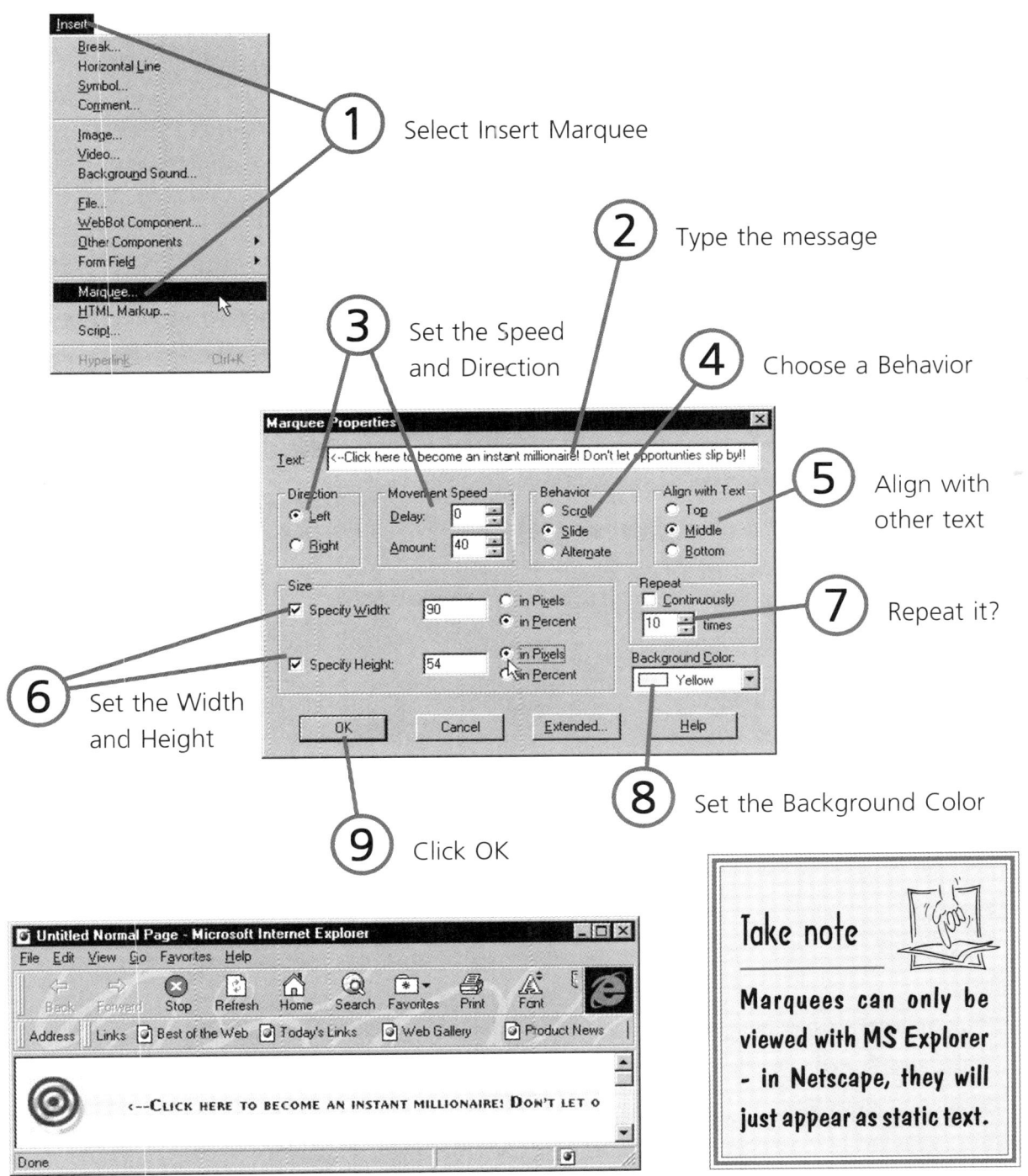

1 Select Insert Marquee

2 Type the message

3 Set the Speed and Direction

4 Choose a Behavior

5 Align with other text

6 Set the Width and Height

7 Repeat it?

8 Set the Background Color

9 Click OK

Take note

Marquees can only be viewed with MS Explorer - in Netscape, they will just appear as static text.

Animated GIFs

GIF files are the graphics format most commonly used on the Internet, but as well as being used for static images, several GIF images can be stored as a single file and displayed in turn as an animation.

There are a number of shareware (try before you buy) and freeware (free!) packages designed for animating GIFs, including Gif Animator from Microsoft.

Animation frames

You will first need to create a series of images to insert as animation frames. The more you have, the smoother the animation, but the fewer you can get away with, the faster your pages will download, so be minimal.

Besides copying images and changing certain parts of them, you can also use warps and effects to produce successive images, as with the 'warped' hearts below.

Frame1

Frame2

Frame3

Tip

The easiest way to create your set of images is to save the first, then adapt that to create the second — saving it with a new name. Adapt the second to produce the third, and so on. This helps to get a smooth transition from one to the next, and also ensures that all the images are the same size.

Take note

GIF animator is now being supplied as part of Microsoft's Image Composer software. You can download a copy free from:

http://www.microsoft.com/imagecomposer/gifanimator/gifanin.htm

Basic steps

Gif Animator

1 Click the **Open** button on the toolbar and choose an image.

2 Click the **Insert** button to add further images.

continued...

This is a nice user-friendly package; you can easily insert images, set the speed of animation, the order of the sequence and the number of times it is run. The Preview button ▶ gives you a fairly accurate idea of how it will look in action.

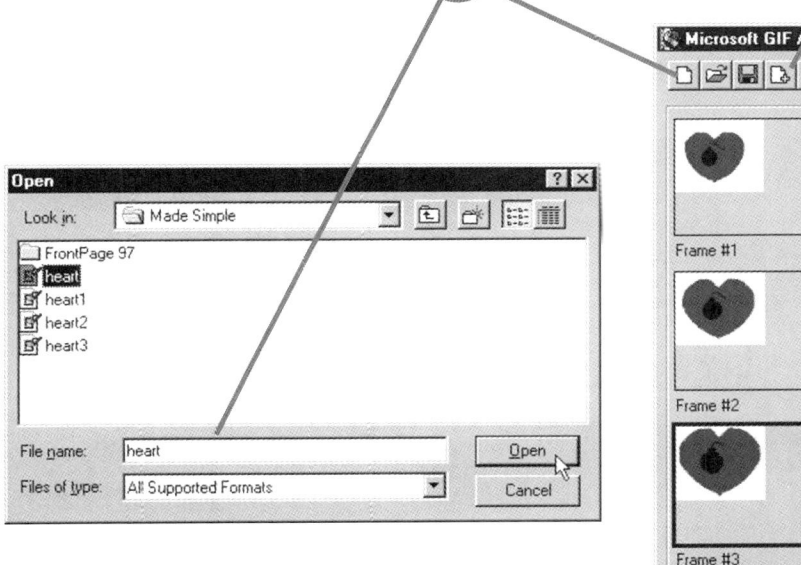

① Open an image

② Insert more images

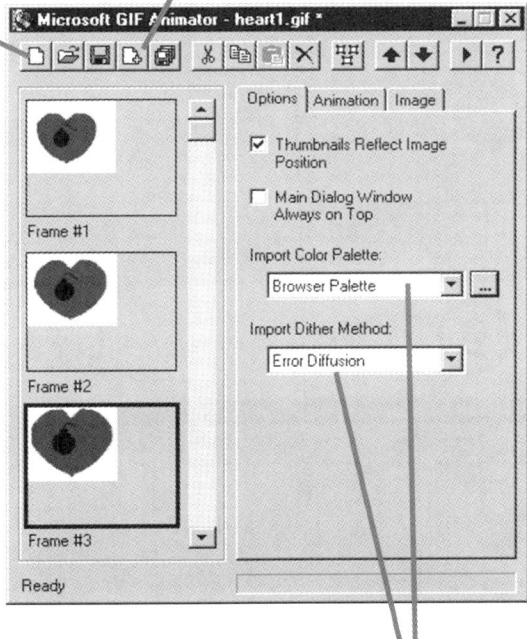

Leave the Options at their default settings unless you have used a special colour palette for your GIFs

Take note

You don't have to worry about getting the order right as you insert the images: click on a frame and you can shuffle it through the stack with the Move Up ⬆ and Move Down ⬇ icons.

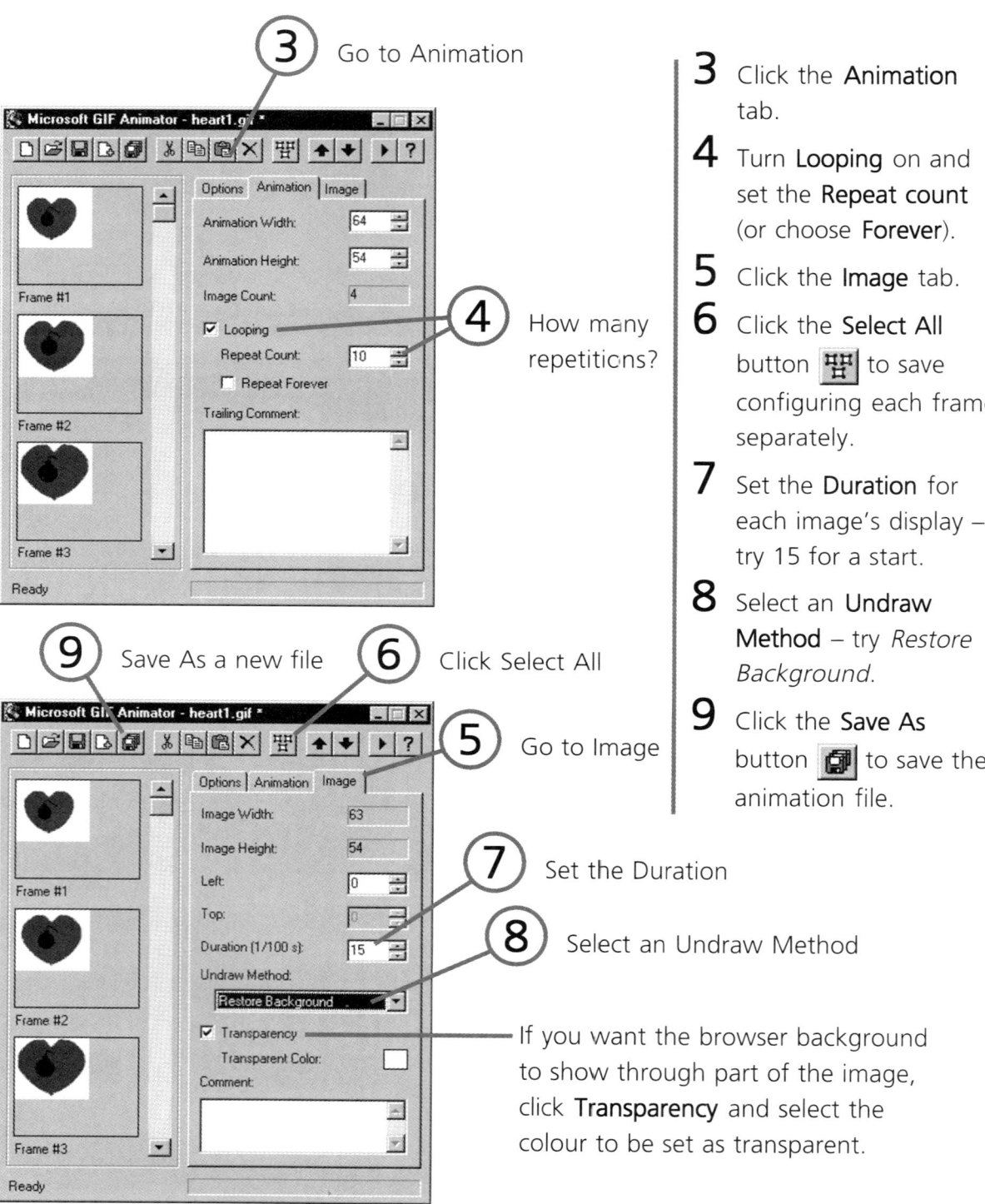

3 Go to Animation

4 How many repetitions?

9 Save As a new file

6 Click Select All

5 Go to Image

7 Set the Duration

8 Select an Undraw Method

If you want the browser background to show through part of the image, click **Transparency** and select the colour to be set as transparent.

3 Click the **Animation** tab.

4 Turn **Looping** on and set the **Repeat count** (or choose **Forever**).

5 Click the **Image** tab.

6 Click the **Select All** button 🏓 to save configuring each frame separately.

7 Set the **Duration** for each image's display – try 15 for a start.

8 Select an **Undraw Method** – try *Restore Background*.

9 Click the **Save As** button 🗗 to save the animation file.

58

Java, ActiveX and JavaScript

These are complex computer language systems which you would need time and training to master. Fortunately for those of us who don't have a spare couple of years to become expert programmers, small chunks of program written by experts can be used by amateurs.

Java

Java applets are mini-programs which are loaded onto your hard drive and then run from your machine – they might run animations, or allow users to interact with the on-screen display, for example.

ActiveX

ActiveX controls are simple modules of code which can be linked together to perform more complex tasks – even if they are stored in different sites around the Internet.

JavaScript

This is considerably easier to learn than either of the others, but is more limited in what it can do. Small blocks of JavaScript code can be attached to the elements in your pages and forms, to make them more interactive. Unfortunately, only those visitors who use Netscape or Internet Explorer 4.0 will be able to get the real benefit, as earlier version of Internet Explorer cannot handle JavaScript (a Netscape development)!

To make the best of the ready-made applets or controls available, it is useful to have some understanding of how they work and how they can be used, and there isn't really space here to get into it properly.

Tip

Don't reject the idea of using these langauges – the Links and Resources page (page 143) has the addresses of a couple of good sites where you can get simple advice and instruction on how to use them, as well as links to other sites showing what them at work.

If you want to learn these languages, why not try *Java Made Simple* and *JavaScript Made Simple*.

Summary

❏ Embed **AVI video clips** wherever you want in a page and set control options.

❏ **Video clips in other file formats** will need to have a hyperlink to the file set up.

❏ Make text scroll or slide to and fro like a banner with the **Marquee** feature.

❏ Build animated images with a program such as **GIF Animator**.

❏ Check out the Java, ActiveX and JavaScript sites listed on the **Links and Resources** page to see how to make your site truly interactive.

5 Tables

Creating a table 62

Table properties 64

Merging cells 66

Editing Cells 69

Importing table data 70

Tables in page design 71

Complex designs 72

Filling in the table 74

Troubleshooting 75

Summary 76

Creating a table

The first thing you need to decide when creating a table is the number of rows and columns it will have. You can add and delete them later on, but before you set any of the table's properties, you should give it a basic framework.

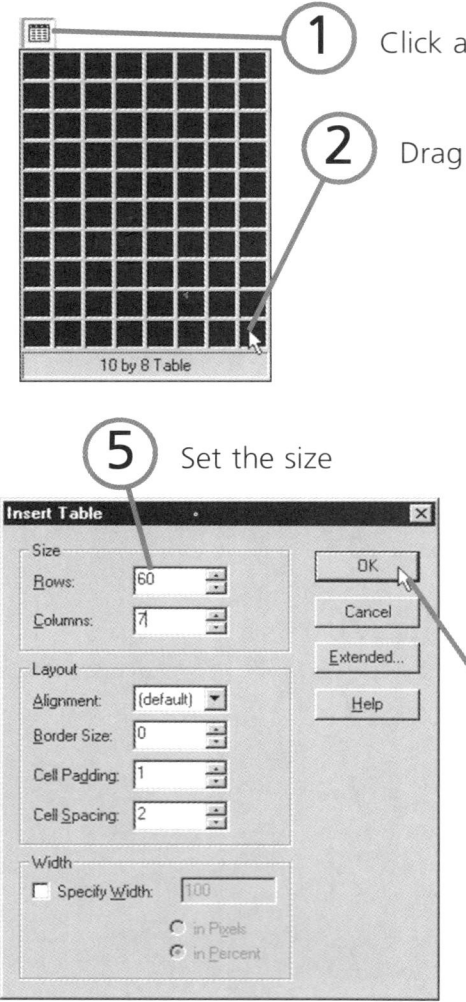

① Click and hold Insert Table

② Drag to the required size

④ Select Table – Insert Table

⑤ Set the size

⑥ Click OK

Layout options can be set now, or later through the Table Properties dialog box

1 On the Toolbar, click and hold the **Insert Table** button 🎞

2 Drag the cursor down and to the right until you have the size you want.

3 Release the mouse button.

or

4 Choose **Insert Table** from the **Table** menu.

5 Set the number of rows and columns.

6 Click **OK**.

Take note

In theory, you can set tables to have 100 rows by 100 columns, but in practice, they are very memory-intensive, and even a 50 by 50 table can slow your system to a snail's pace. Where possible, divide large tables into manageable chunks.

Basic steps

To insert lines

1 Place the cursor in the table where you want to insert a new row or column.

2 Choose **Insert Rows or Columns…** from the **Table** menu.

3 Select **Rows** or **Columns**.

4 Set the number to insert.

5 Choose where to put them in relation to where the cursor is.

To delete lines

6 Move the cursor to the left or top edge of the table until it turns into a solid black arrow, then click to select the entire row or column.

7 Hold the mouse button and drag it to select more than one at a time.

8 Press **[Backspace]** or **[Delete]**.

Adjusting the size

If you want to change the size of a table, rows and columns can be easily inserted or deleted.

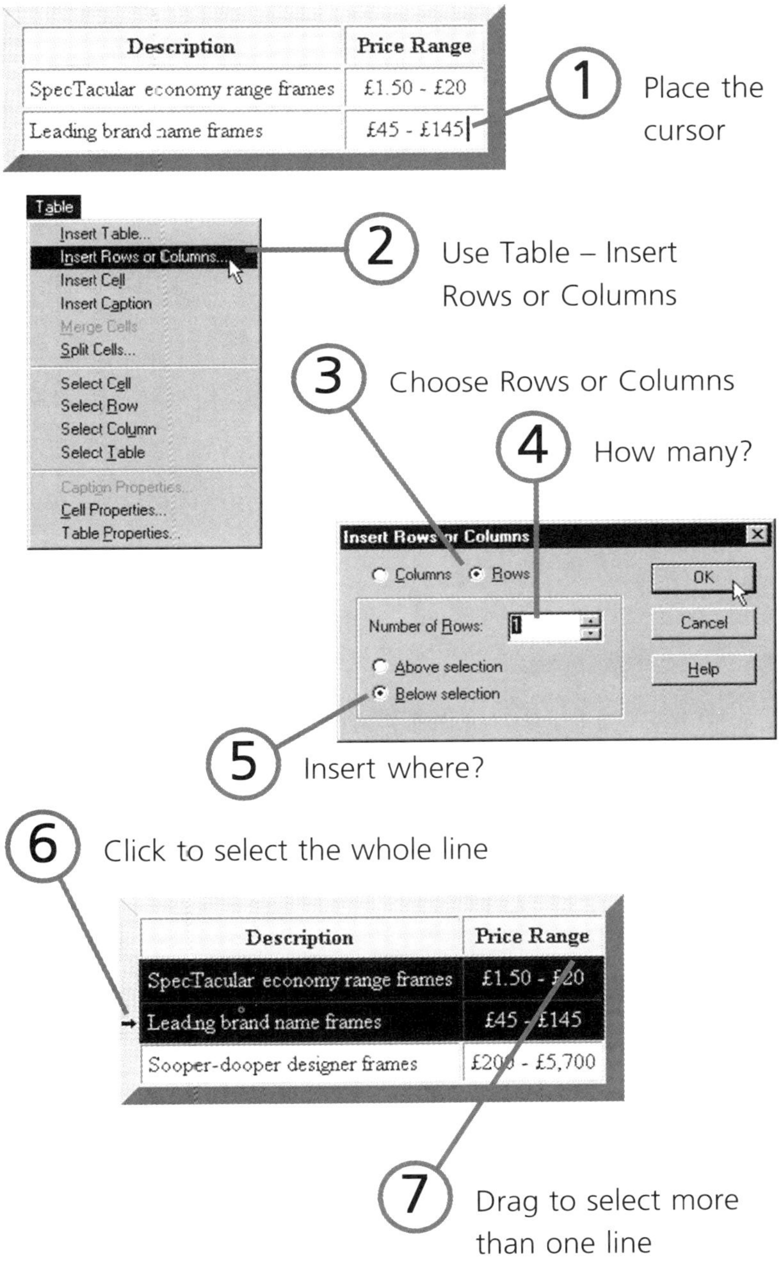

Description	Price Range
SpecTacular economy range frames	£1.50 - £20
Leading brand name frames	£45 - £145

1 Place the cursor

Table
- Insert Table…
- **Insert Rows or Columns…**
- Insert Cell
- Insert Caption
- Merge Cells
- Split Cells…
- Select Cell
- Select Row
- Select Column
- Select Table
- Caption Properties…
- Cell Properties…
- Table Properties…

2 Use Table – Insert Rows or Columns

3 Choose Rows or Columns

4 How many?

Insert Rows or Columns

○ Columns ⊙ Rows

Number of Rows: 1

○ Above selection
⊙ Below selection

OK   Cancel   Help

5 Insert where?

6 Click to select the whole line

Description	Price Range
SpecTacular economy range frames	£1.50 - £20
Leading brand name frames	£45 - £145
Sooper-dooper designer frames	£200 - £5,700

7 Drag to select more than one line

63

Table properties

A table consists of cells, which can be coloured individually – but there are certain properties in the **Table Properties** dialog box which apply to all cells, or to the whole table:

● **Alignment** sets the position across the page.

● **Width** can be set in pixels or as a percentage of the browser window. If a width is not specified, the table size is determined by its contents.

● **Border** – the thickness in pixels of the table's outer border. A value of 0 will arrange data in a table format, but without a border or gridlines.

● **Cell padding** – the margin between a cell's contents and its inner edge, set in pixels.

● **Cell spacing** – the gap between cells, also in pixels.

Basic steps

1 Right-click on the table and choose **Table Properties…**

2 Select an **Alignment** from the drop-down menu.

3 Set the **Border**, **Cell Padding** and **Cell Spacing** values.

4 Click **Specify Width**.

5 Enter a value, in **Pixels** or **Percent**.

6 Click **OK**.

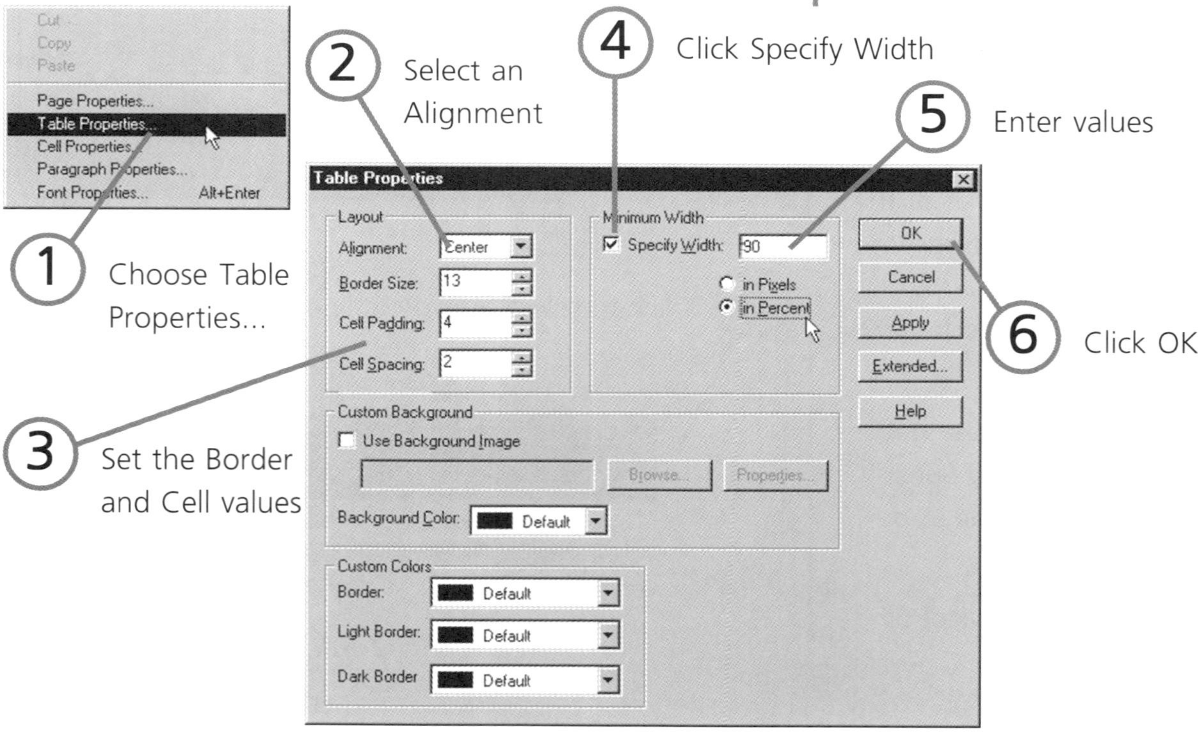

② Select an Alignment

④ Click Specify Width

⑤ Enter values

① Choose Table Properties…

③ Set the Border and Cell values

⑥ Click OK

Cut
Copy
Paste

Page Properties…
Table Properties…
Cell Properties…
Paragraph Properties…
Font Properties…   Alt+Enter

Table Properties

Layout
Alignment: Center
Border Size: 13
Cell Padding: 4
Cell Spacing: 2

Minimum Width
☑ Specify Width: 90
○ in Pixels
◉ in Percent

OK
Cancel
Apply
Extended…
Help

Custom Background
☐ Use Background Image
Browse…   Properties…
Background Color: Default

Custom Colors
Border: Default
Light Border: Default
Dark Border: Default

Basic steps

1 Open the **Table Properties...** dialog box.

2 Choose a **Background Color**.

or

3 Click **Use Background Image** and browse for the one you want.

4 Choose a colour for a flat border.

or

5 Choose **Light** and **Dark** for a 3-D border.

6 Click **OK**.

Colours and images

You can choose the background colour of the cells, or set a background image to be tiled across the whole table.

For the table border, set a colour for a plain flat **Border**, or give it a 3-D effect with a **Light Colour** and a **Dark Colour** (you need a border width of a few pixels to notice this).

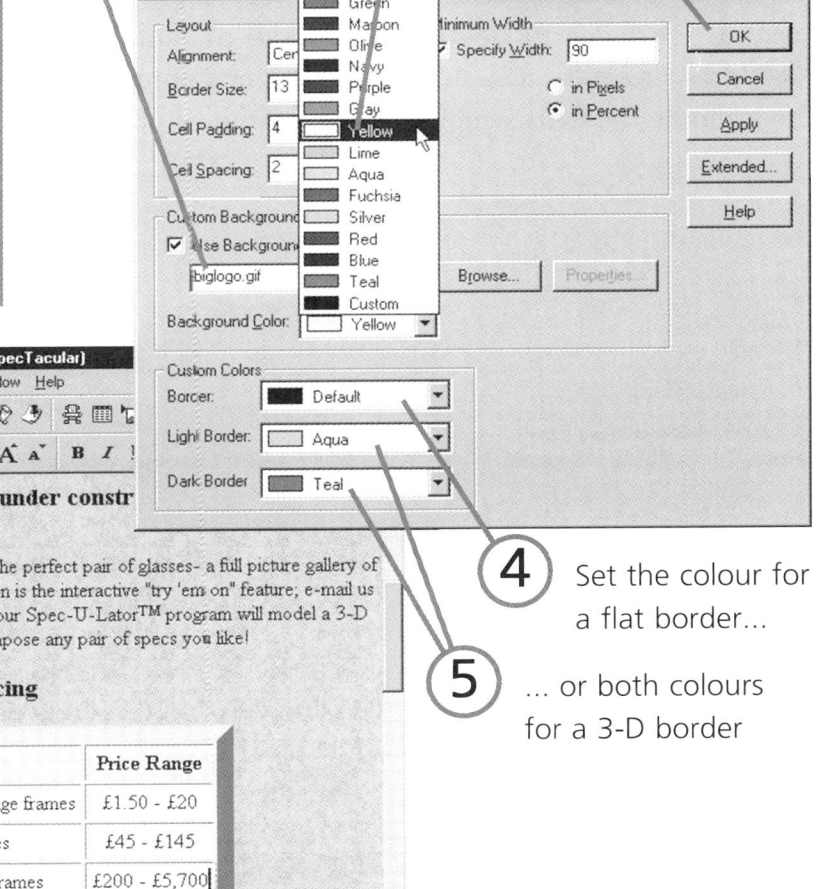

② Set a Background Color...

③ ...or use an image

⑥ Click OK

④ Set the colour for a flat border...

⑤ ... or both colours for a 3-D border

Merging cells

Often, you may want to have a header cell which spans two or three sub-columns, so you will need to merge a range of cells into one large one. Merging cells also becomes important when using <u>tables in page design</u> (page 71).

Merging small blocks

Because of the way HTML code is read by browsers, you can only use this method for merging entire rows or columns, or consecutive cells – if you have a 5x5 table, for instance, you will find that you can't select just the bottom 2x2. If you want to do this, you have to edit a cell's properties to make it span several rows and columns and then delete the cells which are pushed out of place.

1 Place the cursor anywhere in the first of the cells you want to merge.

2 Click and drag the cursor to anywhere in the last cell.

3 Choose **Merge Cells** from the **Table** menu.

4 Place the cursor in the upper left cell of the block you want to merge.

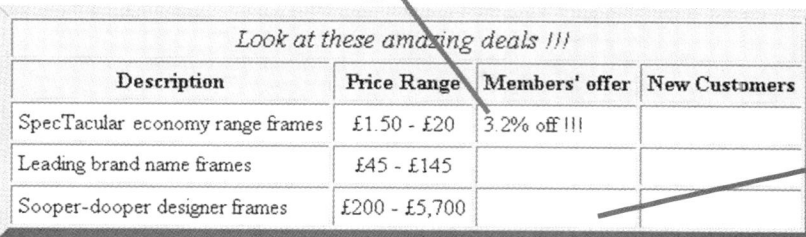

Start in the first cell

Drag to the last

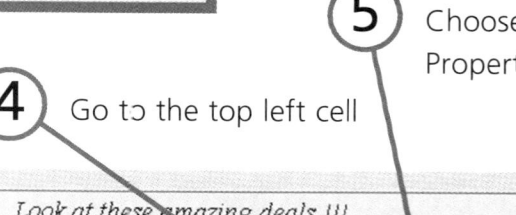

Select Table – Merge Cells

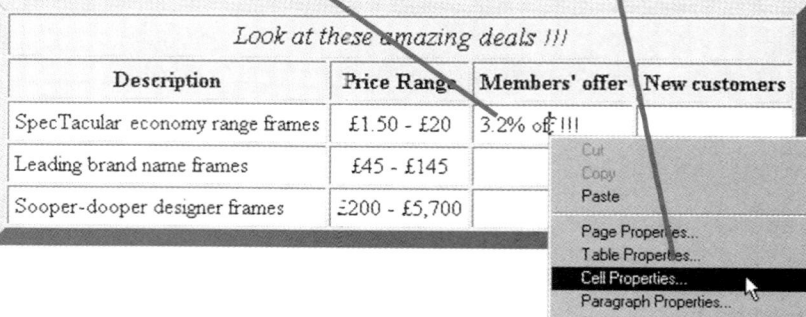

Go to the top left cell

Choose Cell Properties

5 Right-click and choose **Cell Properties…**

6 Increase the values in the appropriate **Cell Span** fields.

7 Click **OK**.

8 Select the columns which are sticking off the edge of the table.

9 Press **[Delete]**.

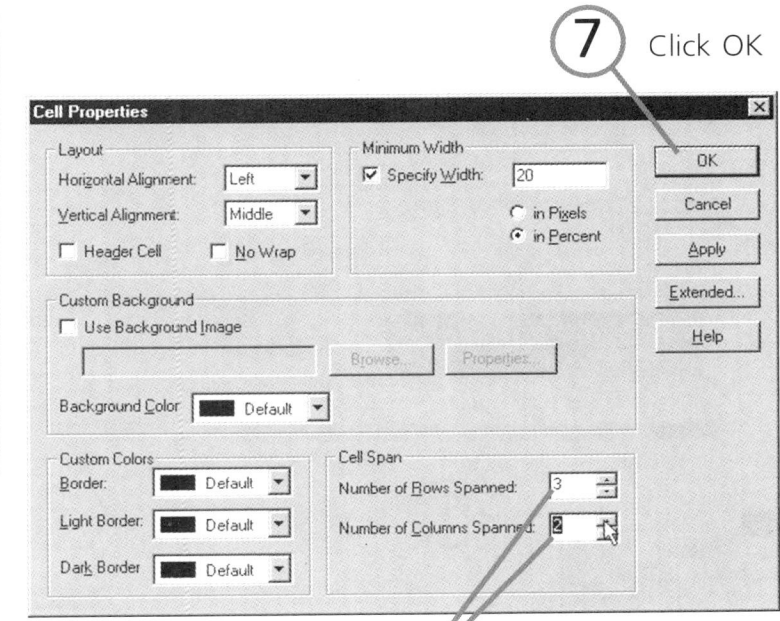

⑦ Click OK

⑥ Set the numbers of cells to be spanned

Look at these amazing deals !!!			
Description	**Price Range**	**Members' offer**	**New customers**
SpecTacular economy range frames	£1 50 - £20		
Leading brand name frames	£45 - £145	3.2% off !!!	
Sooper-dooper designer frames	£200 - £5,700		

⑧ Select the surplus cells

The enlarged cell can be coloured or its text formatted to make it stand out

Look at these amazing deals !!!			
Description	**Price Range**	**Members' offer**	**New customers**
SpecTacular economy range frames	£1.50 - £20		
Leading brand name frames	£45 - £145	An unbelievable 3.2% off !!!	
Sooper-dooper designer frames	£200 - £5,700		

Splitting cells

Dividing a cell into smaller cells is often easier than expanding one, as it doesn't upset the table structure by forcing other cells out of the way.

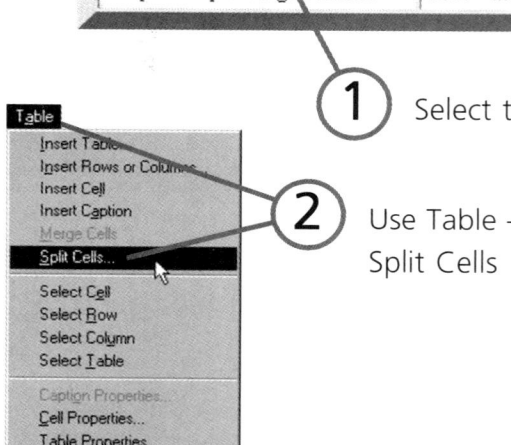

(1) Select the cell(s)

(2) Use Table – Split Cells

Basic steps

1 Select the cell(s) to be divided.

2 Choose **Split Cells...** from the **Table** menu.

3 Choose **Split into Columns** or **Rows**.

4 Enter the number of rows or columns.

5 Click **OK**.

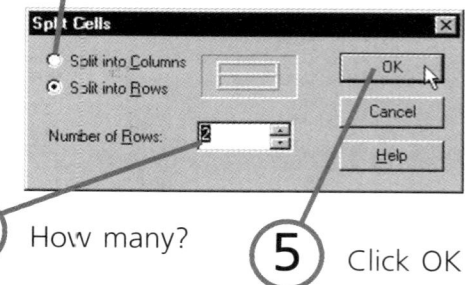

(3) Split into Rows or Columns?

(4) How many?

(5) Click OK

Look at these amazing deals !!!

Description	Price Range
SpecTacular economy range frames	£1.50 - £20
Leading brand name frames	£45 - £145
Fake designer frames	
Sooper-dooper designer frames	£200 - £5,700

If you want to split the existing text in the cell, you will have to cut and paste it

Tip

Try to think of where you could split cells before you add rows and merge cells. In this example, an extra row could have been added to take 'Fake designer frames', then the two cells in the Price column merged — but it was simpler to split one cell instead.

Basic steps

1 Click and drag the cursor to select a cell or range of cells.

2 Right click and choose **Cell Properties...**

3 Edit the properties.

4 Click **Apply**.

5 Click **OK**.

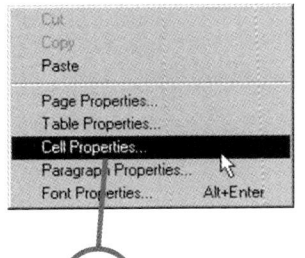

② Select Cell Properties

Editing cells

To enter or edit text, just place the cursor in a cell and type as usual, using the arrow keys or **Tab** to move between cells. You can select a cell or range of cells and change their properties from the **Cell properties** dialog box:

- **Horizontal** and **Vertical Alignment** – determines how the contents of a cell are aligned within it.

- **Width** – specify a minimum cell width in pixels or as a percentage of the table width.

- **Header Cell** – sets text in the cell in bold type.

- **No Wrap** – tells browsers to make the page wider rather than wrap text onto a new line within the cell.

- **Colours** – highlight an area of a table by changing colour settings from the default values for the table.

- **Cell Span** – increase the size of a cell to span several rows or columns (see <u>Merging cells</u>, page 66).

④ Click Apply

⑤ Click OK

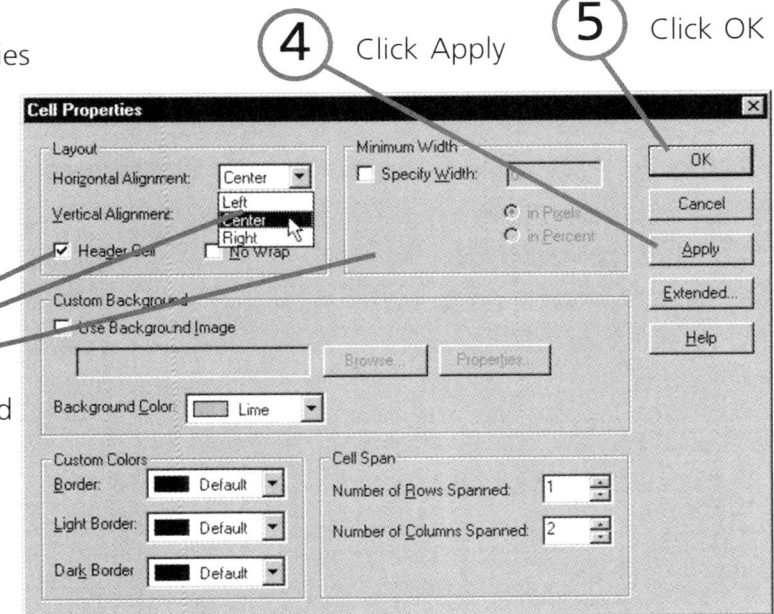

③ Edit as required

Importing table data

FrontPage can convert Microsoft Excel spreadsheet data directly into tables – each worksheet is created as a separate table. Some of the formatting is lost, but that can be retouched from the Table Properties dialog box.

Basic steps

1 Place the cursor where you want the table.

2 Choose **File…** from the **Insert** menu.

3 Select the **File of type** from the list.

4 Select a file.

5 Click **Open**.

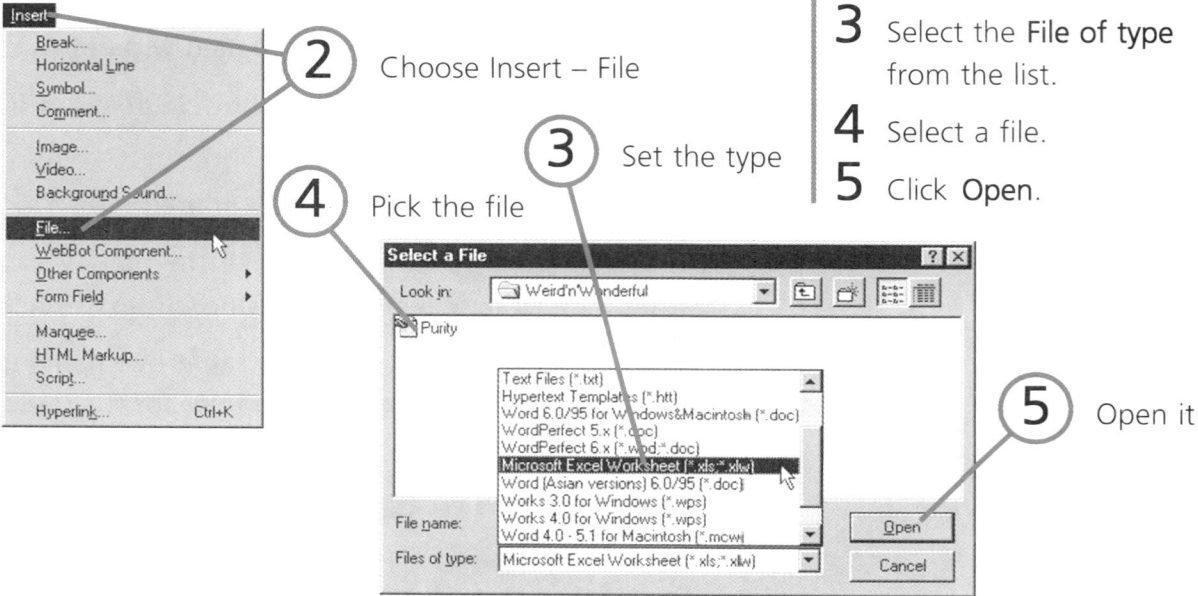

Choose Insert – File

Set the type

Pick the file

Open it

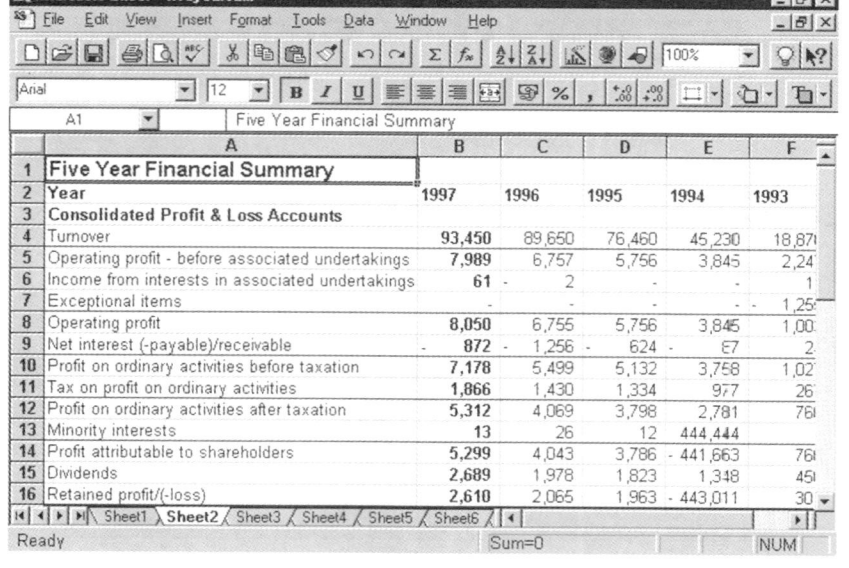

Tip

You can also copy cells from Excel and paste them into a web page. This seems to copy the data more faithfully, but you can only import one worksheet at a time.

Basic steps

1 Create a table.

2 Insert images and text into the cells.

❑ **Highlighting**

3 Click ⊞ and insert a 1x1 table into a cell.

4 Edit the **Table Properties** to give it a border.

5 Insert into this inner table the images or text you want to draw attention to.

Besides arranging data, tables have another important function in FrontPage. Since there is no way of setting tabs, and only one space can be typed between words or words and images, text and graphics are often arranged on a page using tables.

With their border thickness set to zero, the dashed lines which you can see in the Editor window do not show up in browser windows.

If you want to highlight a particular element in the table, you can insert a table inside a cell and give this inner table a border.

② Arrange text and images in the table

③ Insert a table into a cell

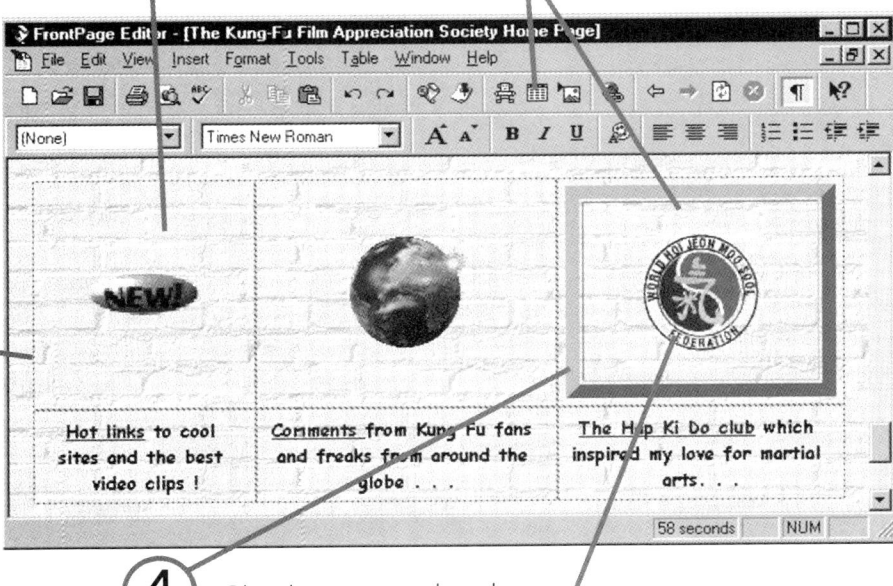

FrontPage shows guide lines, even with the border width set to 0

④ Give it a strong border

⑤ Add the material you want to highlight

Complex designs

If your page layout is going to be fairly complicated, it is a good idea to sketch it out on paper and box the elements into a labelled grid so that you can plan how to set up the table.

In the example below, the basic format is three newspaper-style columns, so we'll start with a 2 by 3 table, so that the pairs of cells 3-4 and 7-8 are initially in one column, the pairs 5-9 and 6-10 are in one row, and cells 7-8-11-12 are all in one block.

The top right-hand cell can then be split into two (cells 3 and 4), cells 1, 2 and 3 merged into one, and cells 7-8-11-12 split into two: 7-8 and 11-12.

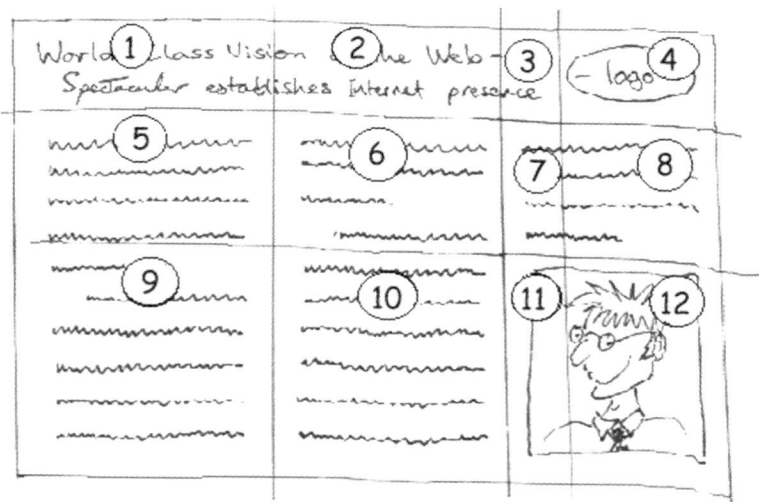

1 Click and drag the Insert Table button to create a 2 by 3 table.

2 Select the top right-hand cell.

3 Choose Split cells... from the Table menu.

4 Split the cell into two columns.

5 Select cells 1, 2 and 3.

6 Choose Merge cells from the Table menu.

7 Select the bottom right-hand cell.

8 Split the cell into 2 rows.

Take note

If you had decided to start with a 3 by 4 table and merge and delete cells, you would have found that the whole process was much more convoluted — it really is worth taking time to assess the best approach to the design.

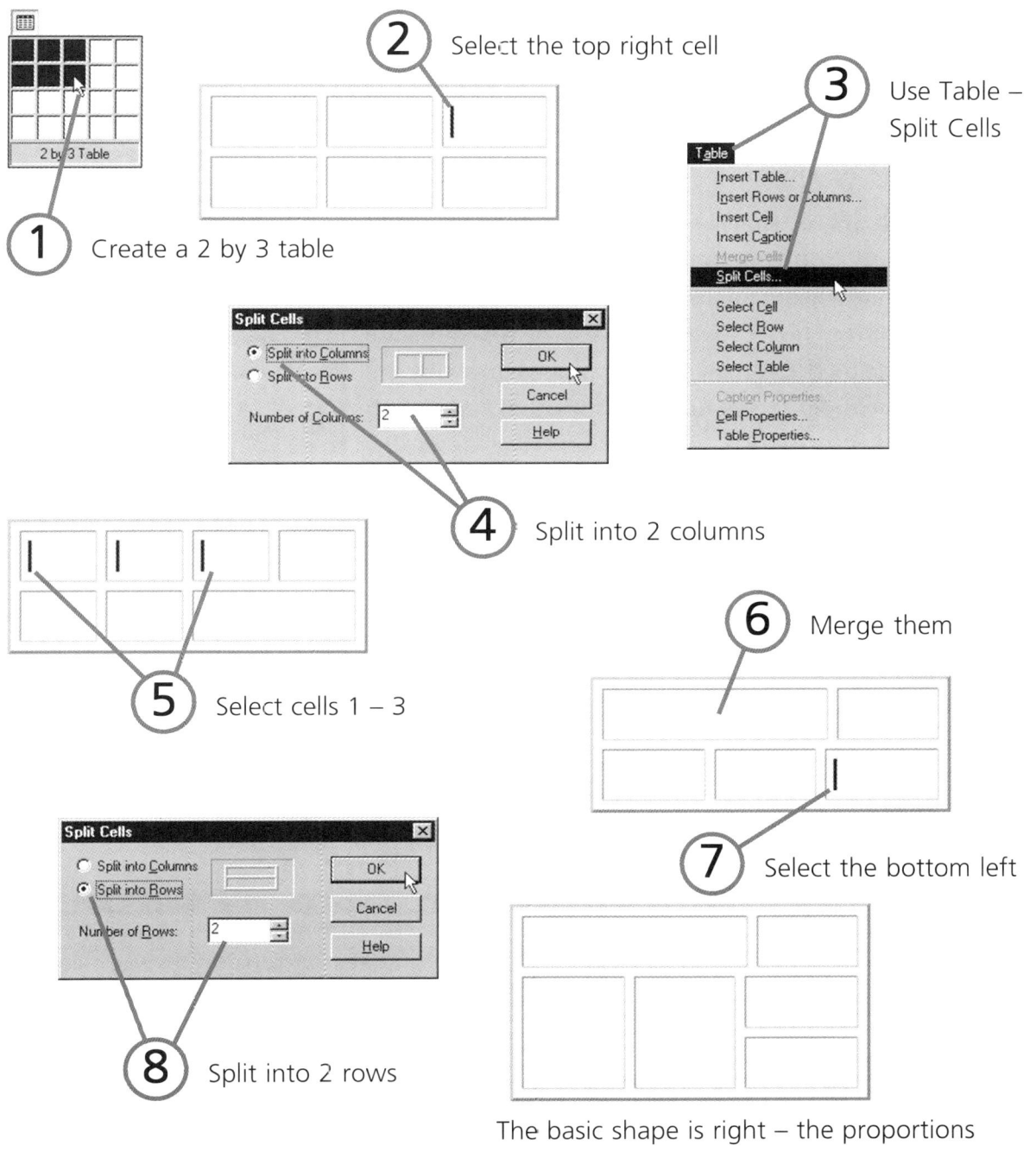

① Create a 2 by 3 table

② Select the top right cell

③ Use Table – Split Cells

④ Split into 2 columns

⑤ Select cells 1 – 3

⑥ Merge them

⑦ Select the bottom left

⑧ Split into 2 rows

The basic shape is right – the proportions will be corrected later

Filling in the table

We now find that we have an empty table in roughly the right shape for our purposes which just needs to have some text and images dropped in. However, it's never quite that simple, and there will always be some adjustments to be made.

For instance, it may be that the title we had planned for the article won't fit into the space as planned, so the cell needs to be made wider. When you do this, you may find that the width you specify seems to bear little resemblance to what you see on the screen. If this happens, preview the page in your browser to see how it has worked and switch back to adjust it further.

1 Position the cursor in a cell.

2 Right-click and choose **Cell Properties...**

3 Choose **Pixels** or **Percent**.

4 Enter a new **Width**.

5 Preview the page in your browser.

6 Adjust the cell width if necessary.

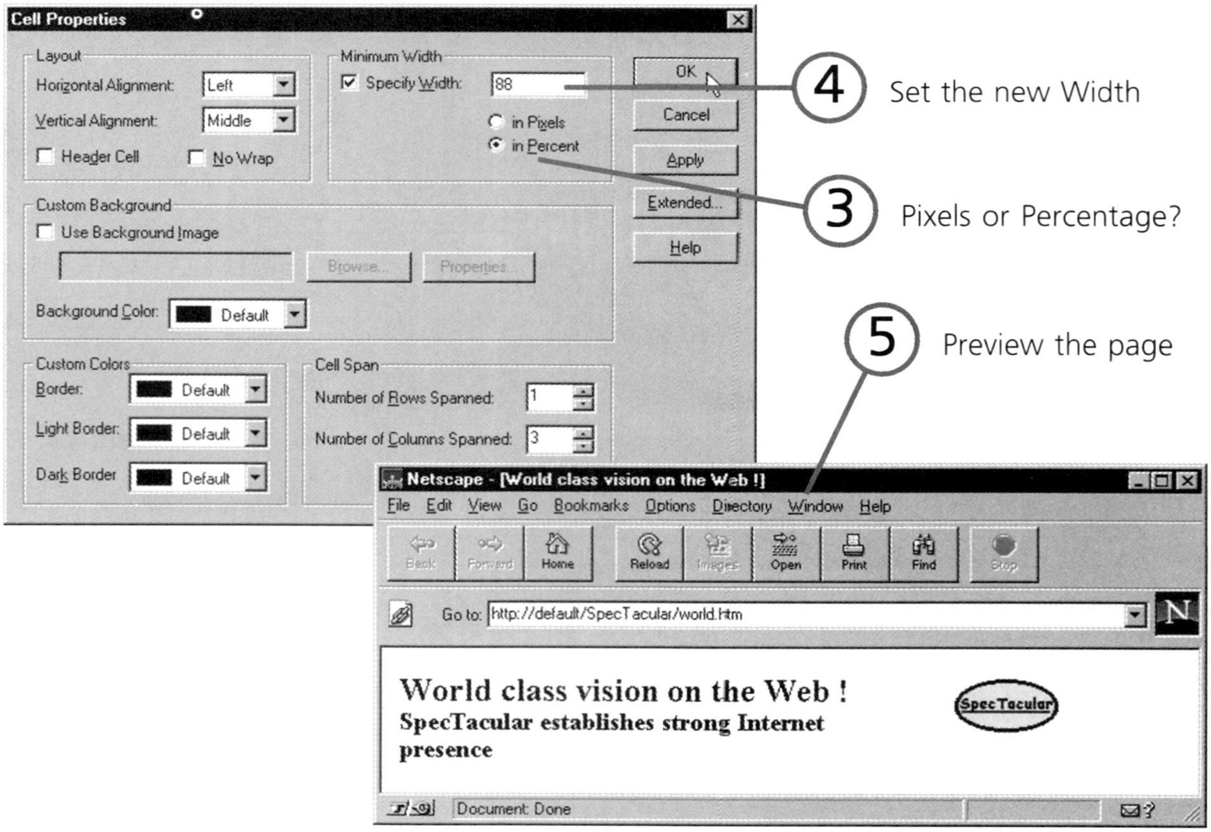

Cell Properties

Layout
Horizontal Alignment: Left
Vertical Alignment: Middle
☐ Header Cell   ☐ No Wrap

Minimum Width
☑ Specify Width: 88
   ○ in Pixels
   ● in Percent

OK
Cancel
Apply
Extended...
Help

Custom Background
☐ Use Background Image
Browse...   Properties...
Background Color: Default

Custom Colors
Border: Default
Light Border: Default
Dark Border: Default

Cell Span
Number of Rows Spanned: 1
Number of Columns Spanned: 3

④ Set the new Width

③ Pixels or Percentage?

⑤ Preview the page

Netscape - [World class vision on the Web !]

File Edit View Go Bookmarks Options Directory Window Help

Back Forward Home Reload Images Open Print Find Stop

Go to: http://default/SpecTacular/world.Htm

World class vision on the Web !
SpecTacular establishes strong Internet presence

SpecTacular

Document: Done

74

Troubleshooting

Sometimes you will come across inexplicable problems – my press release had a large white space left between the end of the text and the picture below, and no amount of fiddling seemed to fix it. In this case, there was no actual need to have the picture in a separate cell to the one above – the two cells could be merged and the image inserted straight after the last line of text.

This is the sort of unexpected difficulty which you will inevitably run into when laying out pages using tables, and unfortunately there are no universal solutions. With a little lateral thinking and some splitting and merging of cells, there is almost always a way around the problem.

Tip

Remember that you can insert tables within tables if you want to fine-tune the positioning of elements in a cell.

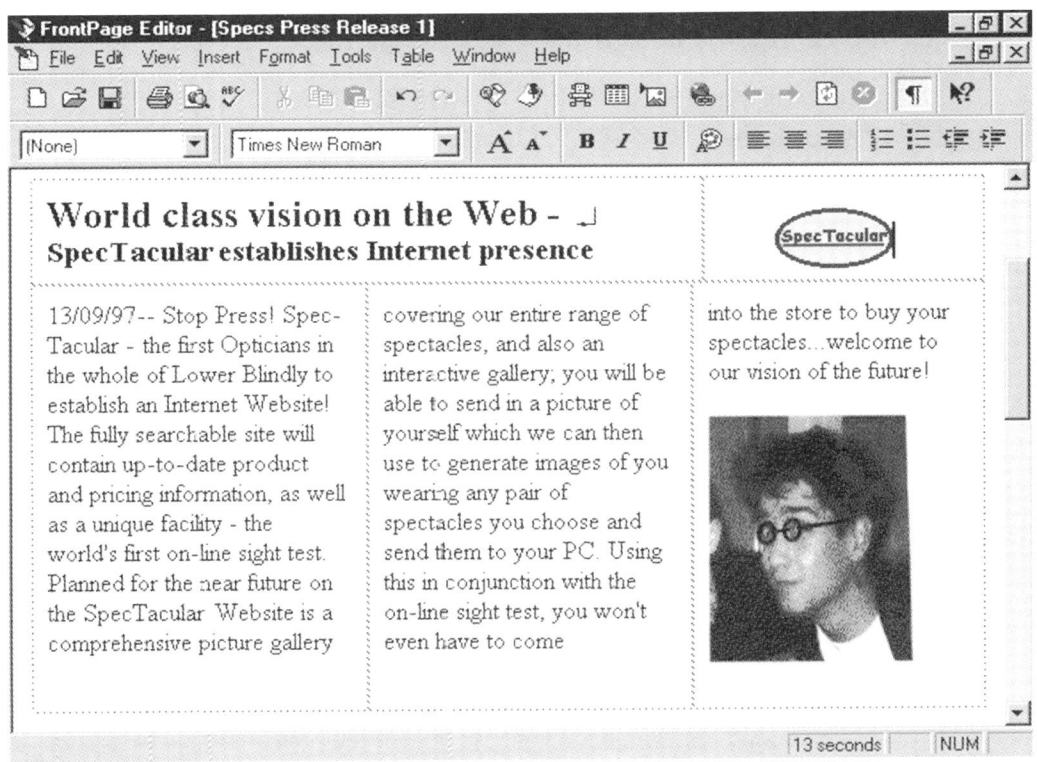

Summary

❑ Use tables to present data or to arrange text and graphics on the page.

❑ Configure the table's properties from the **Table properties...** dialog box.

❑ Change individual **Cell properties** to highlight areas of the table.

❑ **Merge** and **Split** cells to position the contents of the table where you want them.

❑ **Add** rows and columns as needed, or select and **Delete** unwanted ones.

❑ You can import **spreadsheet data** directly onto a page. FrontPage will automatically create a table for it, which you can then edit as usual.

❑ Be patient and think creatively when perfecting the **layout** of your tables!

6 Bookmarks and links

Using Bookmarks 78

Links to other pages 80

Links to Web pages 83

Using images as links 84

Recalculating hyperlinks 87

Checking your hyperlinks 88

Summary .90

Using Bookmarks

Bookmarks are reference points which tell a browser which part of a page to display on screen when it follows a hypertext **link**.

In the Editor window, a Bookmark is denoted by dashed underlining or a flag icon: ![flag] (not shown by browsers). When a browser reads a link to a Bookmark, it displays the line with the flag icon in it at the top of the window.

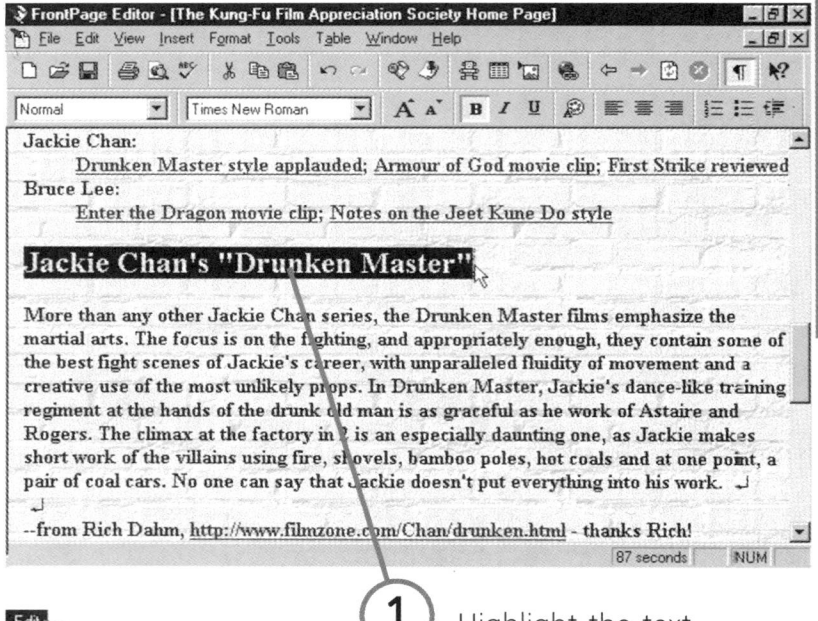

Basic steps

1 Place the cursor in a suitable place, or highlight some text.

2 Choose **Bookmark...** from the **Edit** menu.

3 Type a name for the Bookmark.

4 Click **OK**.

❑ **To remove a Bookmark**

5 Highlight the Bookmark.

6 Choose **Bookmark...** from the **Edit** menu.

7 Click **Clear**.

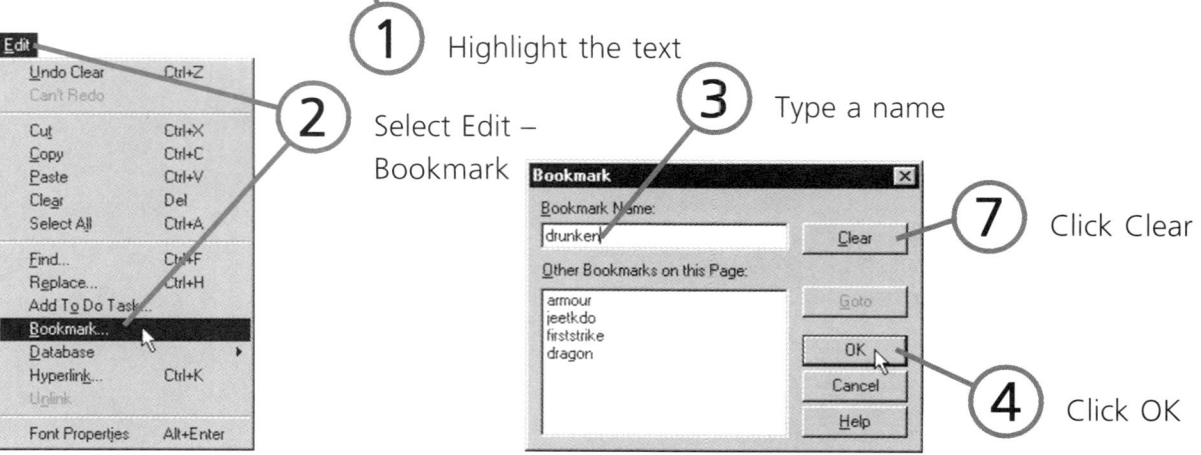

① Highlight the text

② Select Edit – Bookmark

③ Type a name

⑦ Click Clear

④ Click OK

Links to Bookmarks

1 Highlight the text
which you want to use
as a link.

2 Click the **Create or Edit
Link** button .

3 Leave the **Page** field
blank – the default is
the current page.

4 Type the name of the
Bookmark.

5 Click **OK**.

Having links to different parts of a page is useful if it is
much longer than a screen's height. Being able to jump
from a directory at the top to something which interests
you and back again saves a lot of tedious scrolling up and
down.

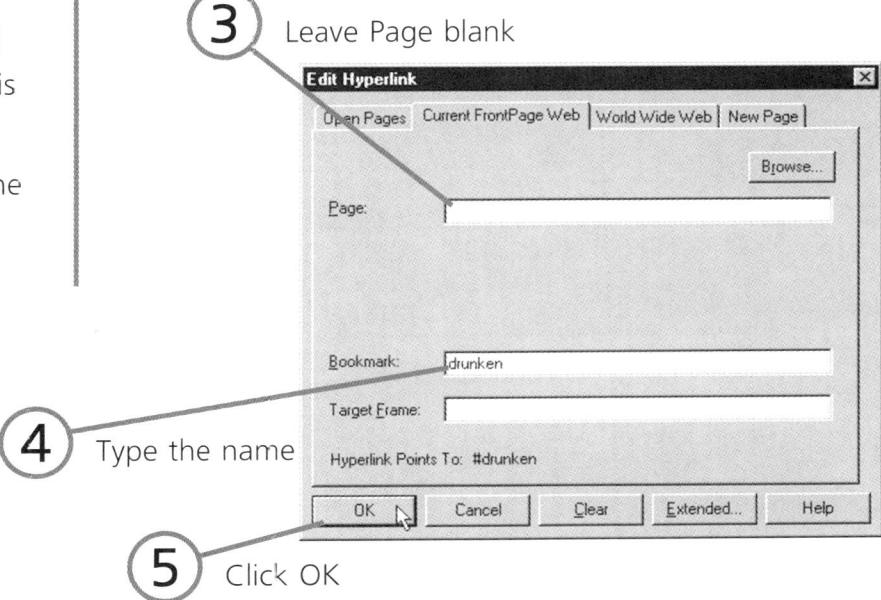

③ Leave Page blank

④ Type the name

⑤ Click OK

Navigating with Bookmarks

You can use Bookmarks to move around a page as you are
editing it. In the Bookmark dialog box, select a Bookmark
from the list and click Goto.

Tip

**To follow hyperlinks
between pages, position
the cursor over the linked
text or image, hold [Ctrl]
and click the left mouse
button.**

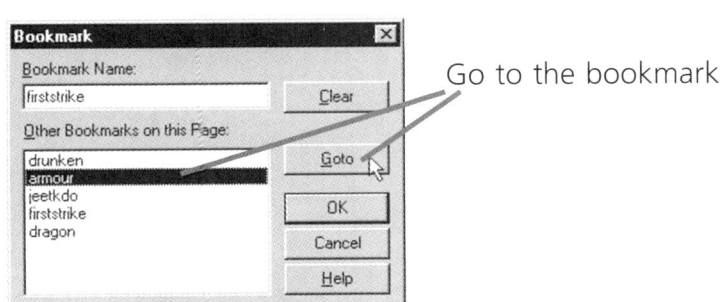

Go to the bookmark

Links to other pages

Links turn a collection of files into a web. Think about your material, and decide which pages should be linked, and where those links should fit.

It's often a good idea to link your pages as you construct them. The Open Pages panel makes this simple.

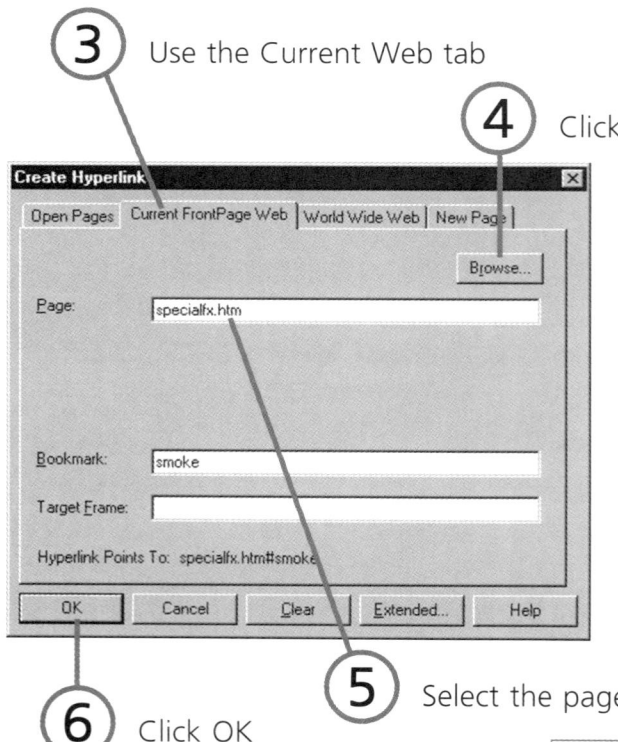

③ Use the Current Web tab

④ Click Browse

⑥ Click OK

⑤ Select the page

1 Highlight the text you want to use as a link.

2 Click the **Create or Edit Link** button .

3 Click the **Current FrontPage Web** tab if it is not already showing.

4 Next to the Page field, click **Browse…**

5 Select the page.

6 Click **OK**.

or

7 Click the **Open Pages** tab.

8 Select a page.

9 Click **OK**.

Take note

You can create a link to a specific part of another page by typing a name into the **Bookmark** field as well as a page reference (it doesn't matter whether you create the link or the Bookmark first).

Tip

To ensure that all your pages are linked, include a navigation bar or give each page a link back to a home page or table of contents page.

(7) Go to Open Pages

(8) Pick a page

(9) Click OK

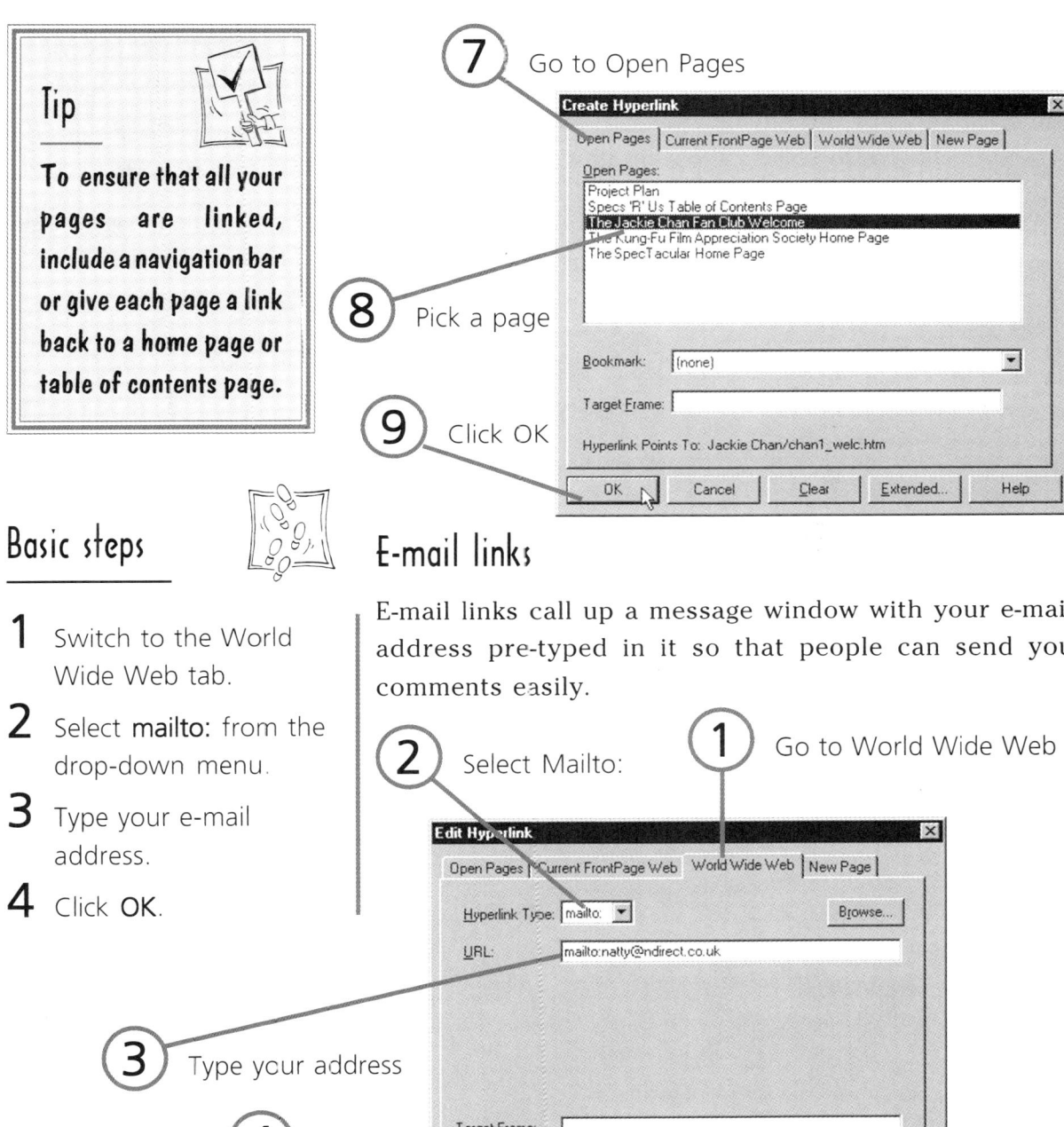

Basic steps

1 Switch to the World Wide Web tab.

2 Select **mailto:** from the drop-down menu.

3 Type your e-mail address.

4 Click **OK**.

E-mail links

E-mail links call up a message window with your e-mail address pre-typed in it so that people can send you comments easily.

(2) Select Mailto:

(1) Go to World Wide Web

(3) Type your address

(4) Click OK

Links to a new page

If you want something to have a page of its own, you can set up a link to a page which does not exist yet. FrontPage will create a blank page, which you can edit immediately, or add to the **To Do List** as a job for another day.

② Click the Link button

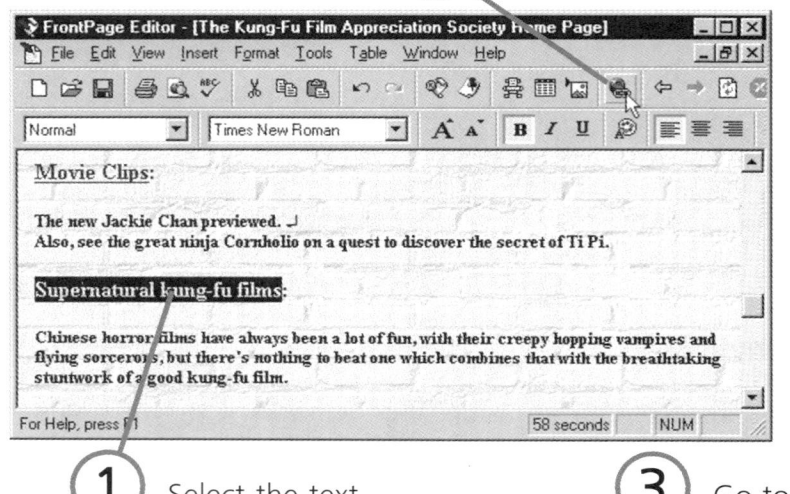

① Select the text

③ Go to New Page

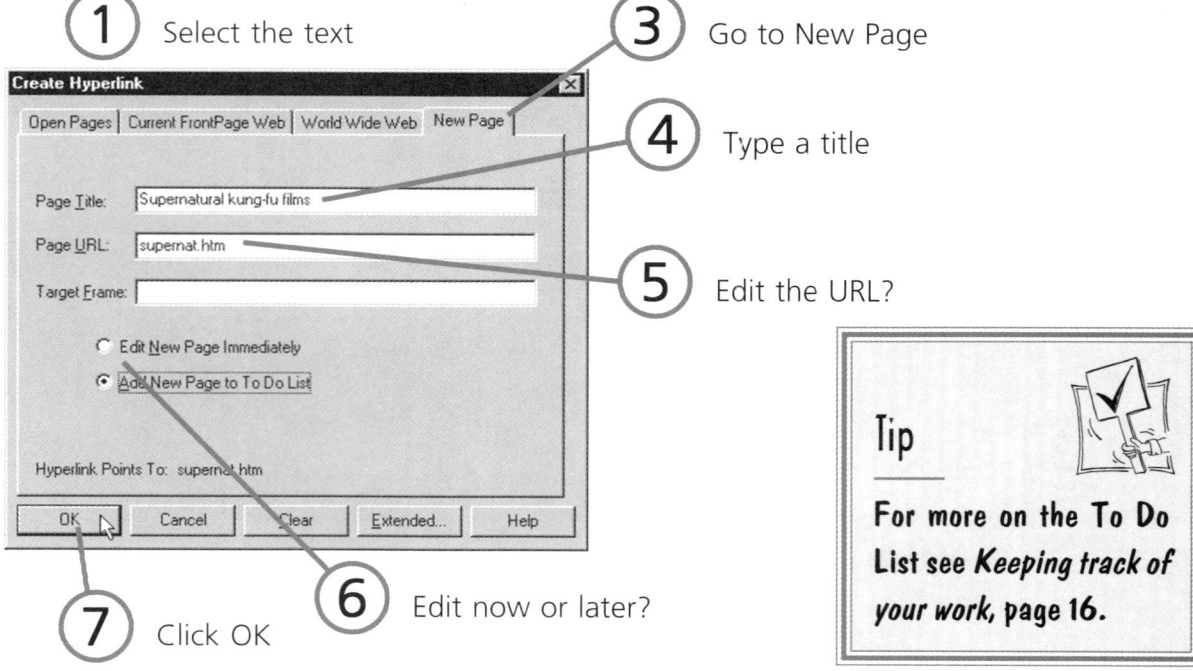

④ Type a title

⑤ Edit the URL?

⑥ Edit now or later?

⑦ Click OK

Basic steps

1 Highlight the text you want to use as a link.

2 Click the **Create or Edit Link** button 🔗.

3 Click on the **New Page** tab.

4 Type a **title**.

5 If you want, edit the suggested **URL**.

6 Choose whether to **Edit** the **New Page Immediately** or **Add** it **to** the **To Do List**.

7 Click **OK**.

Tip

For more on the To Do List see *Keeping track of your work*, page 16.

82

Links to Web pages

Basic steps

1 Highlight the text you want to use as a link.

2 Click the **Create or Edit Link** button .

3 Click on the **World Wide Web** tab.

4 Click **Browse...** and surf to the page.

5 Switch back to the Editor window – the URL is there.

or

6 Select the kind of location from the **Hyperlink Type** menu.

7 Type the URL into the field.

Take note

The Browse button only works if Internet Explorer is your default browser. However, you can visit a page in Netscape and the URL will still appear when you switch to FrontPage.

External hyperlinks are very important – many organisations increase the number of visitors to their sites by establishing reciprocal links with other sites.

Browse the Internet to find a site you want to link to, then switch back to FrontPage and the URL of the site will be entered for you.

Other World Wide Web locations

Links can be created to other types of World Wide Web locations – to an FTP site so that visitors can download software, for example, or to a newsgroup.

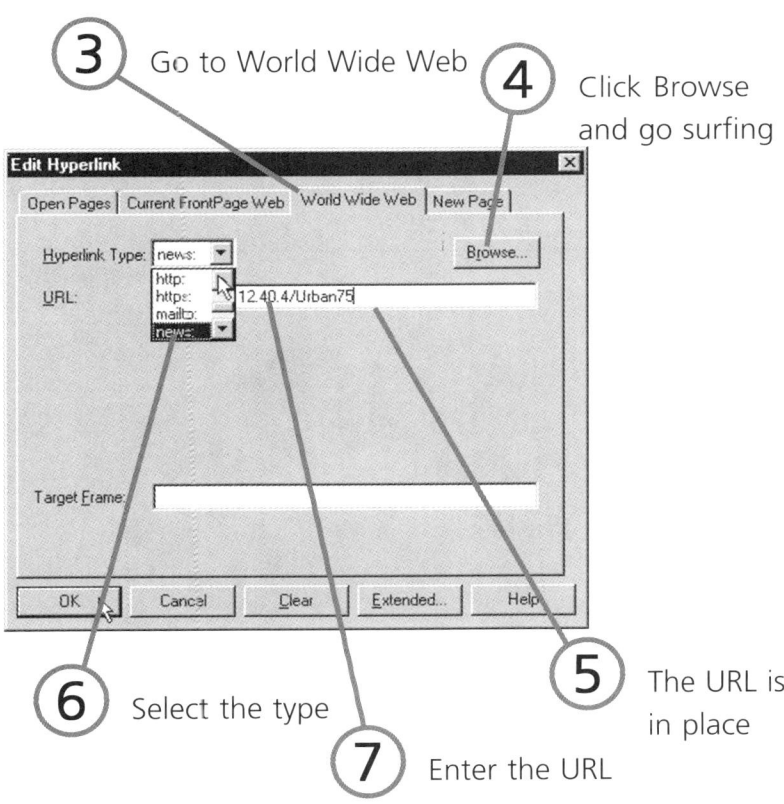

3 Go to World Wide Web

4 Click Browse and go surfing

6 Select the type

7 Enter the URL

5 The URL is in place

Using images as links

There are two ways of using images as links. In the first case, the whole picture acts as a link, so you just highlight the image and create a link as you would for text.

Image maps

The second way of using images is to designate different areas of a picture (**hotspots**) as links to different locations. FrontPage makes light work of these **image maps**, and allows you to adjust the hotspots after you have created them.

1 Select the image

2 Pick the Rectangle

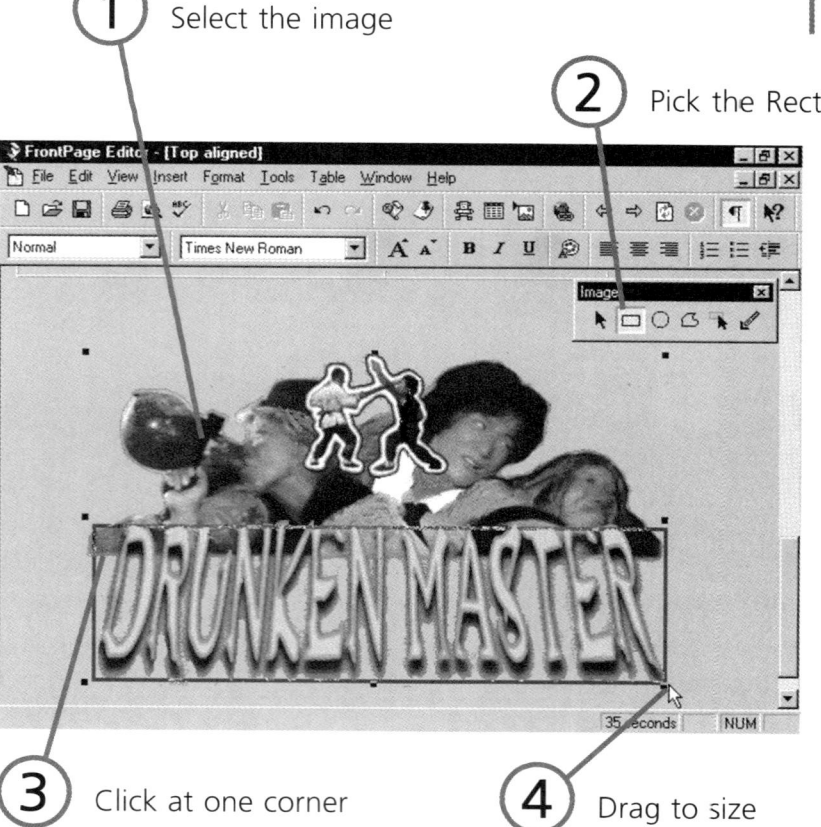

3 Click at one corner

4 Drag to size

Basic steps

1 Click on the image to select it and bring up the **Image** toolbar.

2 Click the **Rectangle** button.

3 Position the cursor at one corner of the area you want to be a hotspot.

4 Drag to the opposite corner of the area.

Take note

If your hotspots overlap, FrontPage gives priority to the most recently created one.

84

❑ **Circle hotspots**

1 Click the **Circle** button.

2 Point at the *centre* of the hotspot.

3 Drag the cursor to expand the circle.

❑ **Polygon hotspots**

4 Click the **Polygon** button.

5 Move the cursor around the hotspot, clicking once to create each vertex.

6 Double-click to end.

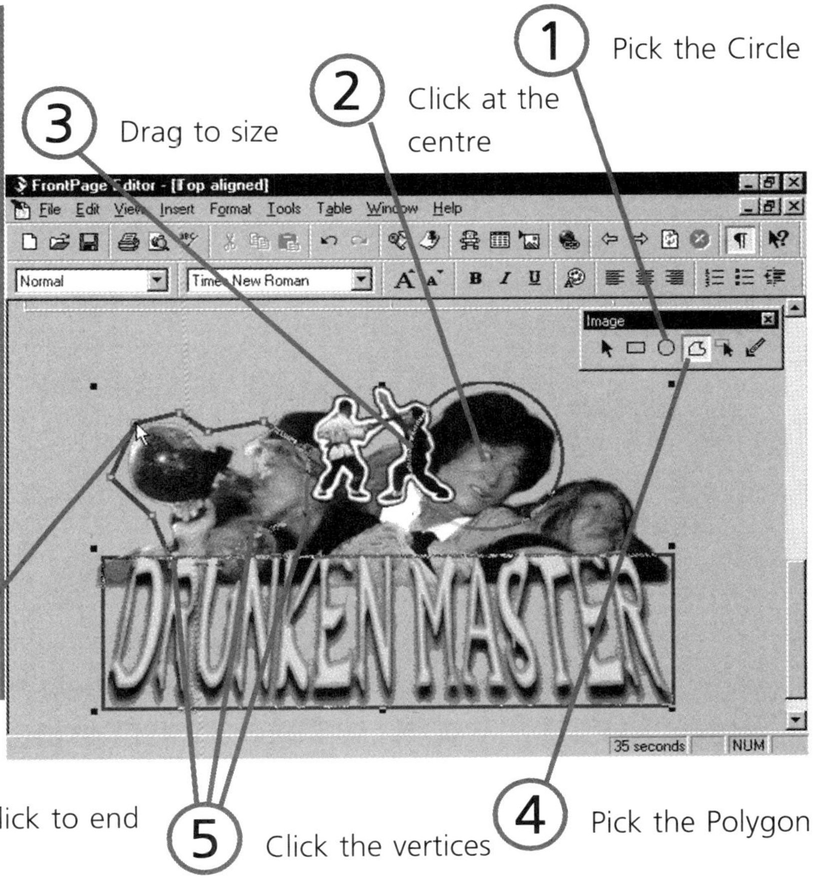

Pick the Circle

(2) Click at the centre

(3) Drag to size

(6) Double-click to end

(5) Click the vertices

(4) Pick the Polygon

Take note

When the **Create Hyperlink** dialog box opens, type or Browse for the page as usual.

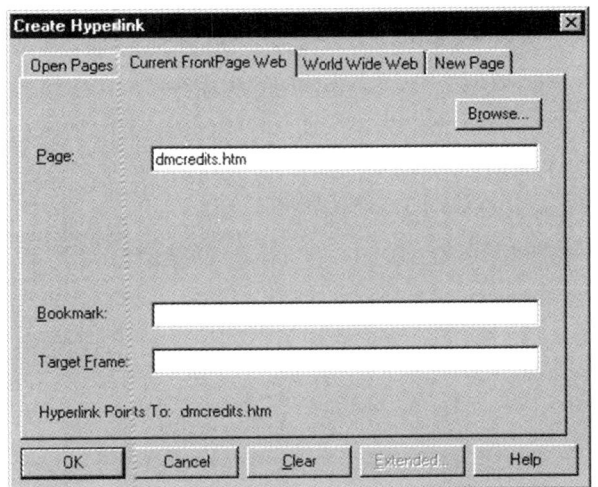

Editing hotspots

Once you have created a hotspot, you can change the destination of its link, move it, or adjust its shape.

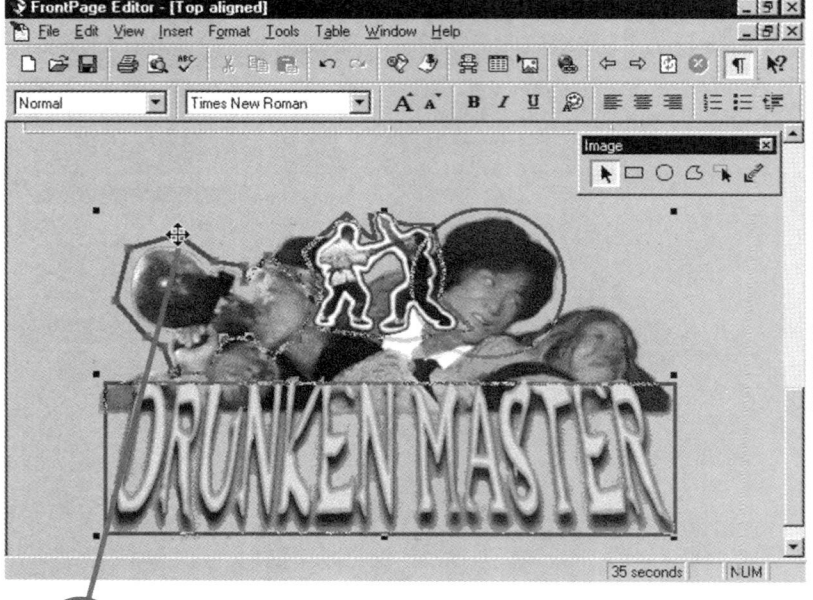

(2) Drag the handles to resize

Basic steps

❏ **To edit the link**

1 Double click on the hotspot to reopen the **Create Hyperlink** dialog box.

❏ **To edit the hotspot**

2 Click once and drag the handles.

❏ **To delete a hotspot**

3 Select it and press [Delete].

Background links

As well as creating hotspots on an image, you can set the rest of it (the 'cold background', as it were) to be a link. Browse for a destination or type the URL into the **Default Hyperlink** field in the **Image Properties** dialog box (see page 27).

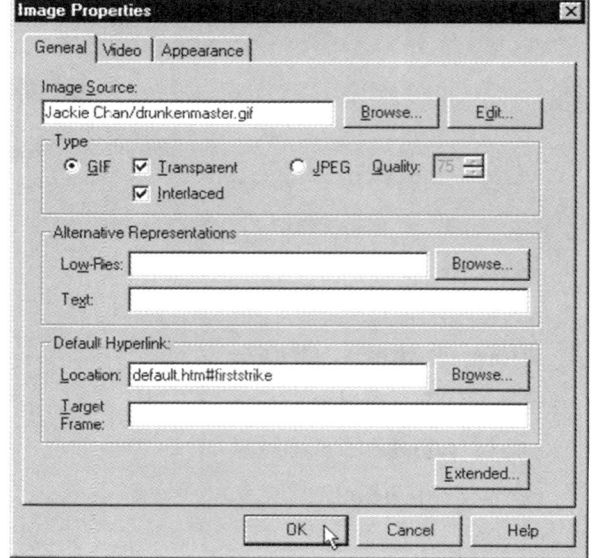

Recalculating Hyperlinks

1 Switch to the Explorer window.

2 Choose **Recalculate Hyperlinks...** from the **Tools** menu.

3 Click **Yes** – unless your web is really huge, it doesn't take that long!

When FrontPage recalculates your hyperlinks it performs two functions. It goes through the contents of every file in your web to:

● make sure that the automatically-generated parts of the web structure are up-to-date – if a **WebBot Include** (see page 120) component is moved, for instance, any page containing it may need updating.

● update the text index which a **WebBot Search** (see page 127) component uses.

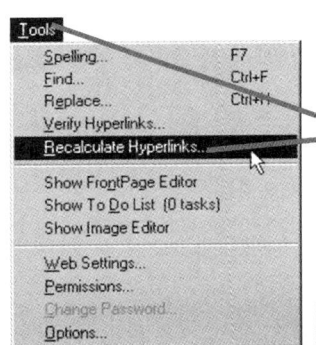

Choose Tools – Recalculate Hyperlinks

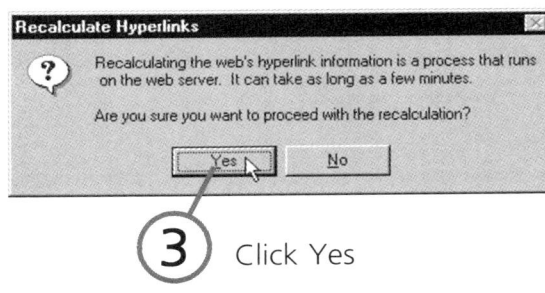

Click Yes

With this many pages and links, it is quite a relief to get them checked automatically

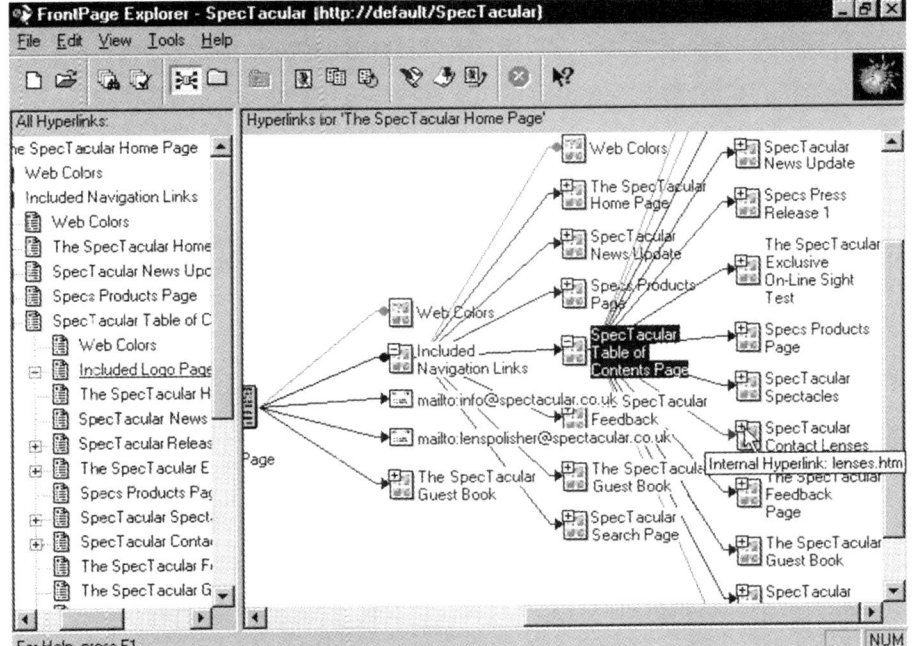

Checking your hyperlinks

The **Verify Hyperlinks** command checks your web's links to make sure that they lead somewhere. The dialog box initially shows any internal links which are broken and all external links – to check these, you must connect to the Internet.

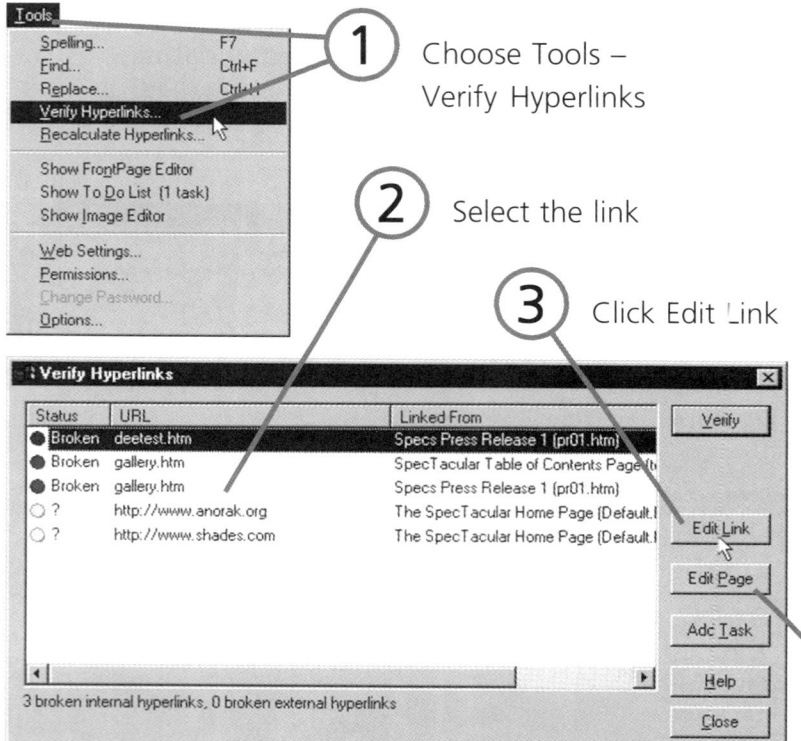

Choose Tools –
Verify Hyperlinks

Select the link

Click Edit Link

Click Edit Page

1 In the Explorer window, choose **Verify Hyperlinks…** from the **Tools** menu.

2 Select a broken link.

3 Choose **Edit Link** to change the target URL.

4 Type the correct URL.

5 The default option is to update all pages containing the broken link. Leave this as it is.

6 Click **OK**.

or

7 Choose **Edit Page** to change or remove the link on that page only.

Tip

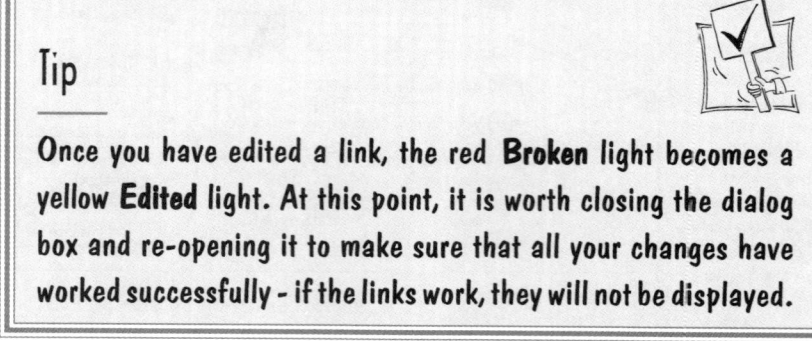

Once you have edited a link, the red **Broken** light becomes a yellow **Edited** light. At this point, it is worth closing the dialog box and re-opening it to make sure that all your changes have worked successfully - if the links work, they will not be displayed.

(5) Change all pages   (4) Type the URL

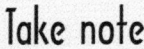

Take note

Remember to save any recent work you have done on your pages, otherwise FrontPage won't be able to check it. Similarly, click the **Refresh** button in the Editor window to update any changes.

Edit Link

Replace: deetest.htm

With: seetest.htm   Browse...

⊙ Change all pages with this hyperlink
○ Select pages to change

pr01.htm

    OK   Cancel   Help

(6) Click OK

Basic steps

1 Connect to the Internet.

2 Choose **Verify Hyperlinks** from the **Tools** menu.

3 Click **Verify**.

4 **Edit** Broken **Links** or the **Page** containing them as before.

5 Click **Close**.

External links

When you check your external links, FrontPage connects briefly to each linked World Wide Web site in turn to make sure that it exists. Those which do exist are marked with a green **OK** light; sites which are not found are given a red **Broken** one.

(3) Click Verify

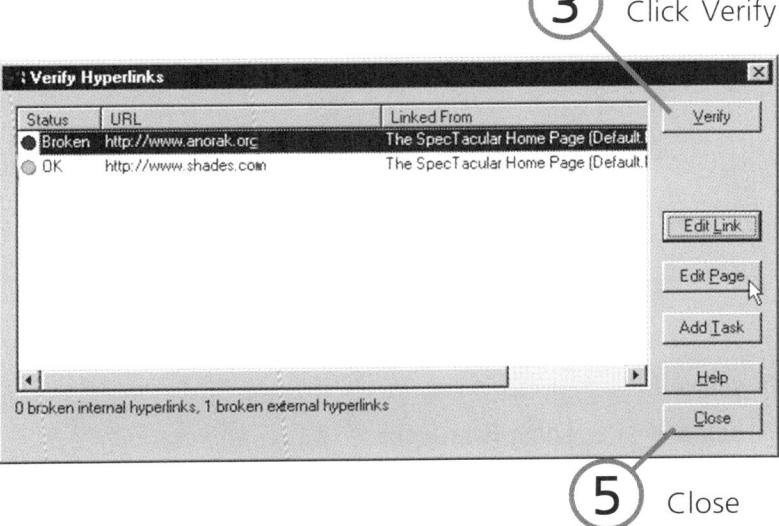

Verify Hyperlinks

Status	URL	Linked From		Verify
● Broken	http://www.anorak.org	The SpecTacular Home Page (Default...		
○ OK	http://www.shades.com	The SpecTacular Home Page (Default...		

Edit Link

Edit Page

Add Task

Help

Close

0 broken internal hyperlinks, 1 broken external hyperlinks

(5) Close

Summary

❑ Use **Bookmar**ks to define specific sections of a page as destinations for hyperlinks.

❑ Create **links within a page** to make it easier to find your way around it.

❑ Set up **links between the pages** in your web to make it an interconnected site.

❑ Create **links to other World Wide Web locations**, including newsgroups and FTP sites.

❑ Set the **Type** of hyperlink to **mailto:** to launch a message window addressed to you.

❑ Use **text**, **images** or **image hotspots** as links.

❑ **Recalculate Hyperlinks** to update the parts of your web which relate to WebBot components.

❑ Make sure your hyperlinks are working with the **Verify Hyperlinks...** command.

7 Frames

What are frames? 92

Working with frames 93

Creating a Frame Set 94

Editing frames 96

Custom grids 98

Target frames 100

Summary 102

What are frames?

Frames are a way of breaking up the browser window into sections, each of which has a separate page displayed in it. When a new page is displayed in a frame, other frames in the set– the whole browser window – are not changed.

Typically, a frame set might consist of a main frame in which new pages are displayed, and a contents page which remains unchanged so that visitors can always use it to navigate around your web.

Take note

Some old browsers do not support frames, so you may want to construct a frameless alternative page with the same information and links.

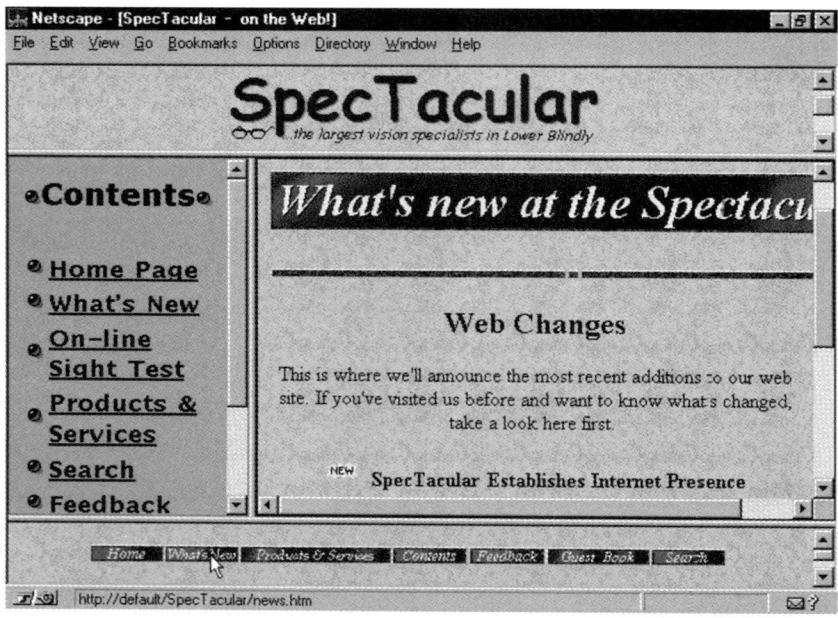

Tip

When a page is loaded into a frame, the frame is treated as a screen in its own right, so text is wrapped around to fit within the margins. Images which fit comfortably on a full screen may fall off the edge of a frame, as with the What's New banner above. To avoid this, specify the width of large images as a percentage.

Working with frames

Tip

If you have a frame for your logo, make sure that it is a small one. A large frame may well fix your name in visitors' minds — but it will be associated with an irritating waste of space!

Frames can make navigating a web more user-friendly, but don't overcomplicate things by having too many of them. Besides being potentially confusing, they actually take up quite a lot of space — imagine trying to read anything in the four narrow frames in the example screen below.

That nice thin line in FrontPage doesn't take into account the blank margins around a page's contents, nor the scrollbars which will probably be needed in a browser window.

Also, when using frames, hyperlinks have to specify which frame to put the new page in. With more than a handful of frames, you will find it difficult to keep track of which page is to be displayed in which frame at which time!

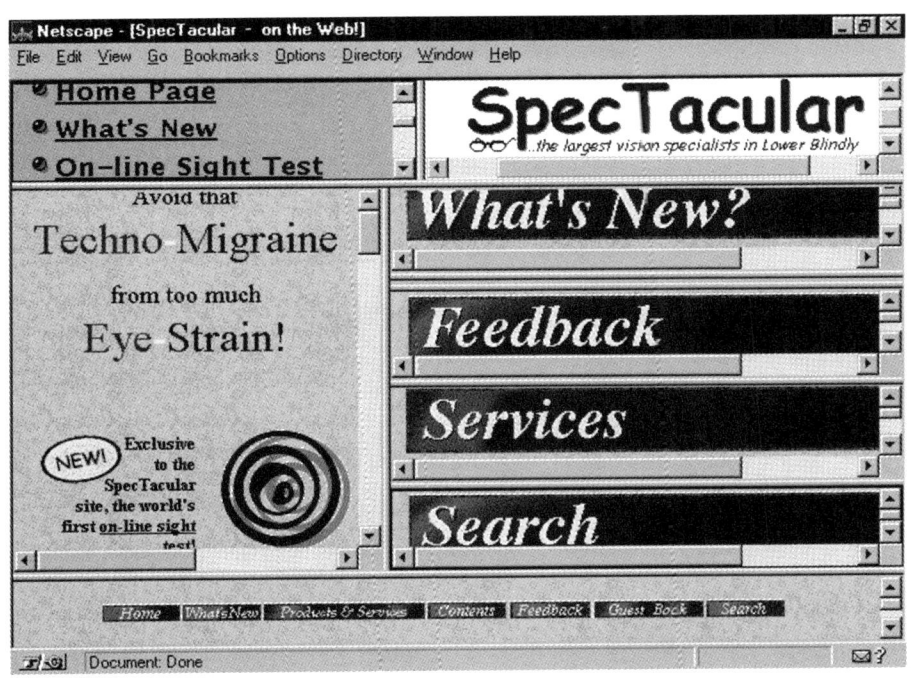

Don't overdo the sub-division into frames!

Creating a Frame Set

Oddly, FrontPage cannot create or edit frame sets in the same WYSIWYG format as any other feature. You have to use the Frames Wizard to create one, then view it in your web browser and return to the wizard to make any adjustments.

In practice, you may have to spend quite some time switching to your browser window and reloading the page, then switching back to the Explorer window and re-opening the Frames Wizard.

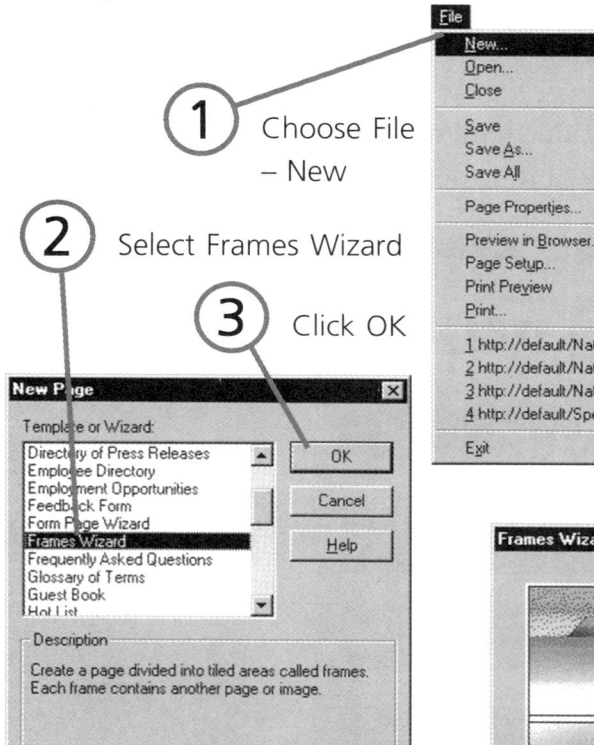

① Choose File – New

② Select Frames Wizard

③ Click OK

④ Use a template

Basic steps

1 Choose **New...** from the **File** menu.

2 Select **Frames Wizard** from the list.

3 Click **OK**.

4 Select **Pick a template** (see page 98 for **custom grids**).

5 Choose a template.

6 If you wish, **Browse...** for an alternate page for browsers that do not support frames.

7 Select one and click **OK**.

8 Type a **Title** and **URL** for the frame set.

9 Click Finish.

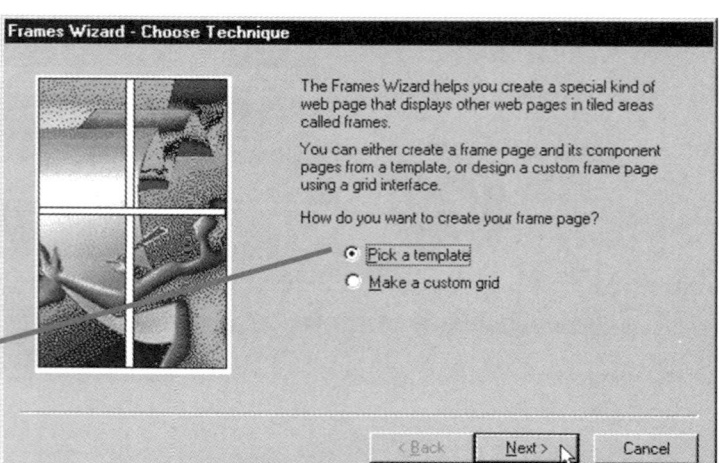

94

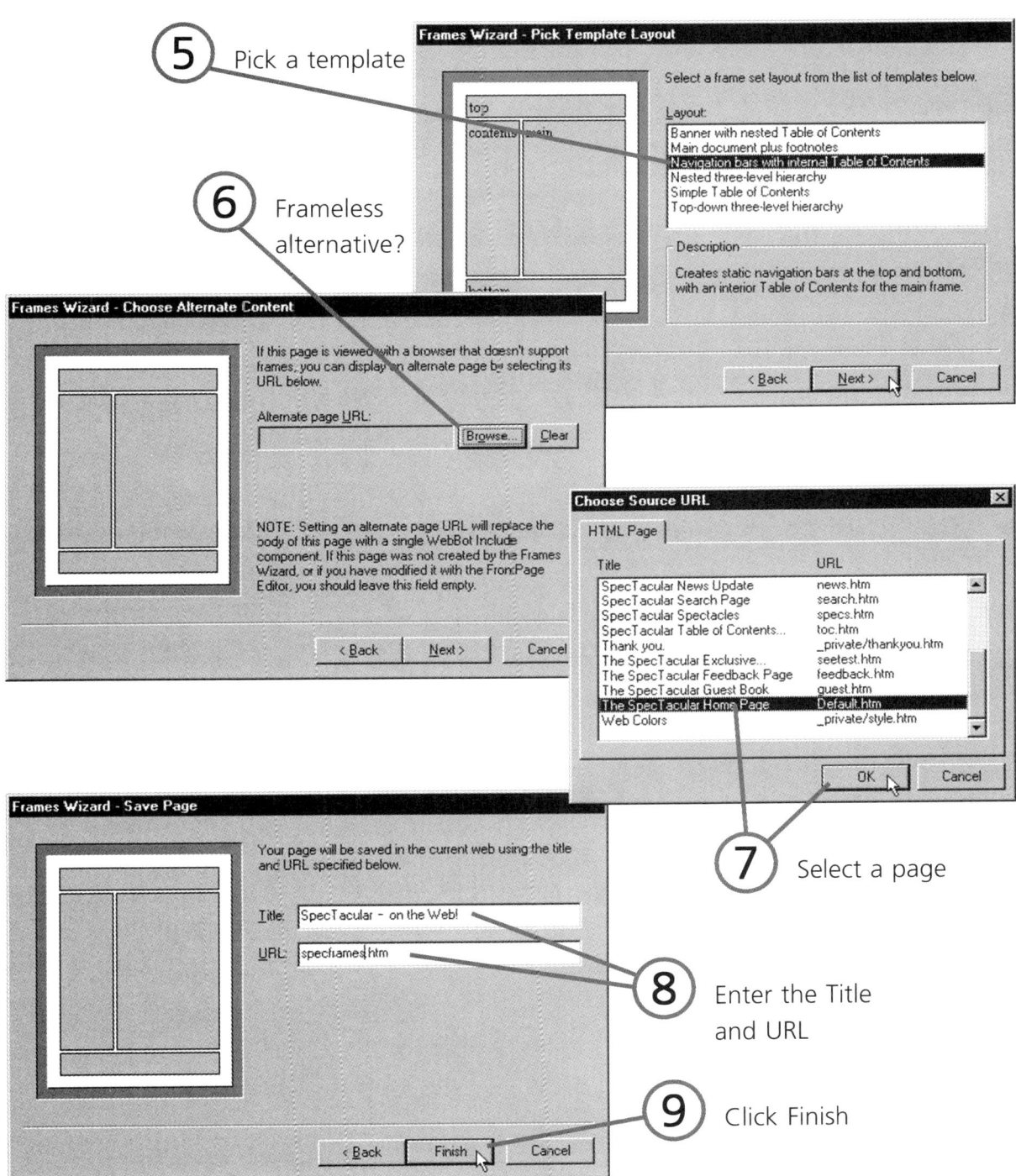

5 Pick a template

6 Frameless alternative?

Frames Wizard - Pick Template Layout

Select a frame set layout from the list of templates below.

Layout:
Banner with nested Table of Contents
Main document plus footnotes
Navigation bars with internal Table of Contents
Nested three-level hierarchy
Simple Table of Contents
Top-down three-level hierarchy

Description
Creates static navigation bars at the top and bottom, with an interior Table of Contents for the main frame.

< Back   Next >   Cancel

Frames Wizard - Choose Alternate Content

If this page is viewed with a browser that doesn't support frames, you can display an alternate page by selecting its URL below.

Alternate page URL:

Browse...   Clear

NOTE: Setting an alternate page URL will replace the body of this page with a single WebBot Include component. If this page was not created by the Frames Wizard, or if you have modified it with the FrontPage Editor, you should leave this field empty.

< Back   Next >   Cancel

Choose Source URL

HTML Page

Title	URL
SpecTacular News Update	news.htm
SpecTacular Search Page	search.htm
SpecTacular Spectacles	specs.htm
SpecTacular Table of Contents...	toc.htm
Thank you.	_private/thankyou.htm
The SpecTacular Exclusive...	seetest.htm
The SpecTacular Feedback Page	feedback.htm
The SpecTacular Guest Book	guest.htm
The SpecTacular Home Page	Default.htm
Web Colors	_private/style.htm

OK   Cancel

7 Select a page

Frames Wizard - Save Page

Your page will be saved in the current web using the title and URL specified below.

Title: SpecTacular - on the Web!

URL: specframes.htm

8 Enter the Title and URL

9 Click Finish

< Back   Finish   Cancel

95

Editing frames

In the Explorer window, double-click on the frame set you have just created. The Frames Wizard is re-activated at the Edit Frameset Grid dialog box. From here you can adjust the size of your frames (you can also split and merge them – see page 98).

Click **Next** and the Edit Frame Attributes dialog box appears, where you can do the following:

● Change the name. FrontPage sets a default which is used when you specify target frames for hyperlinks.

● Change the Source URL. See opposite.

● Set the width in pixels of the **Margins** between a frame's edges and its contents.

● Set a frame to be **resizable** – allowing visitors to change its size in their browser windows – or **Not**.

● Set **Scrolling** options. **Auto** puts scroll bars in if necessary; **Yes** or **No** turn them on or off absolutely.

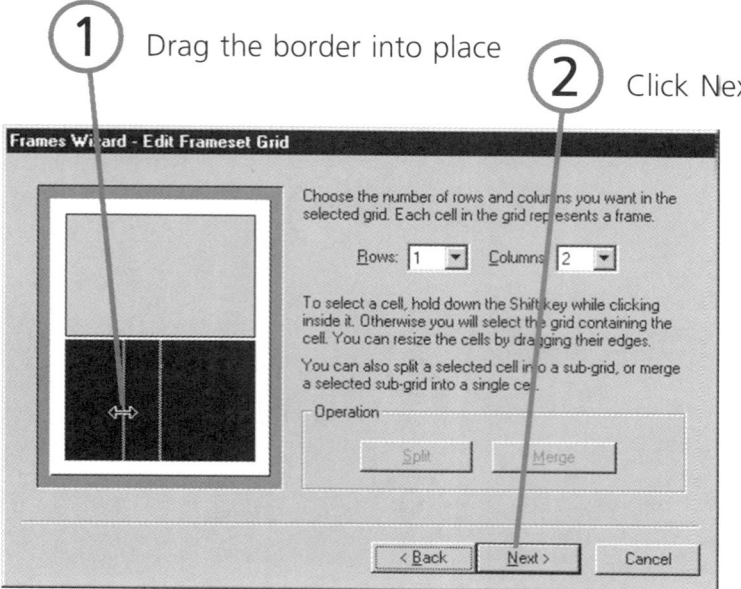

① Drag the border into place

② Click Next

Basic steps

1 Position the cursor over the border between two frames, then click and drag the border into place.

❑ **Setting attributes**

2 Click **Next** to move on to the **Edit Frame Attributes** dialog box.

3 Select a frame.

4 Set the **Margin** widths.

5 Click **Not resizable** to prevent visitors altering your layout in their browser windows.

6 Select a **Scrolling** option from the list.

❑ **Setting the source URL**

7 Click **Browse...**

8 Choose an **HTML page** from your web.

or

9 Click on the **Image** tab to choose from a list of images.

10 Click **OK**.

Setting the contents

The **Source URL** is the location of the page to be displayed in each frame when the frameset is first opened. FrontPage will already have created default URLs for you, but you may want to replace these with existing pages, or with images.

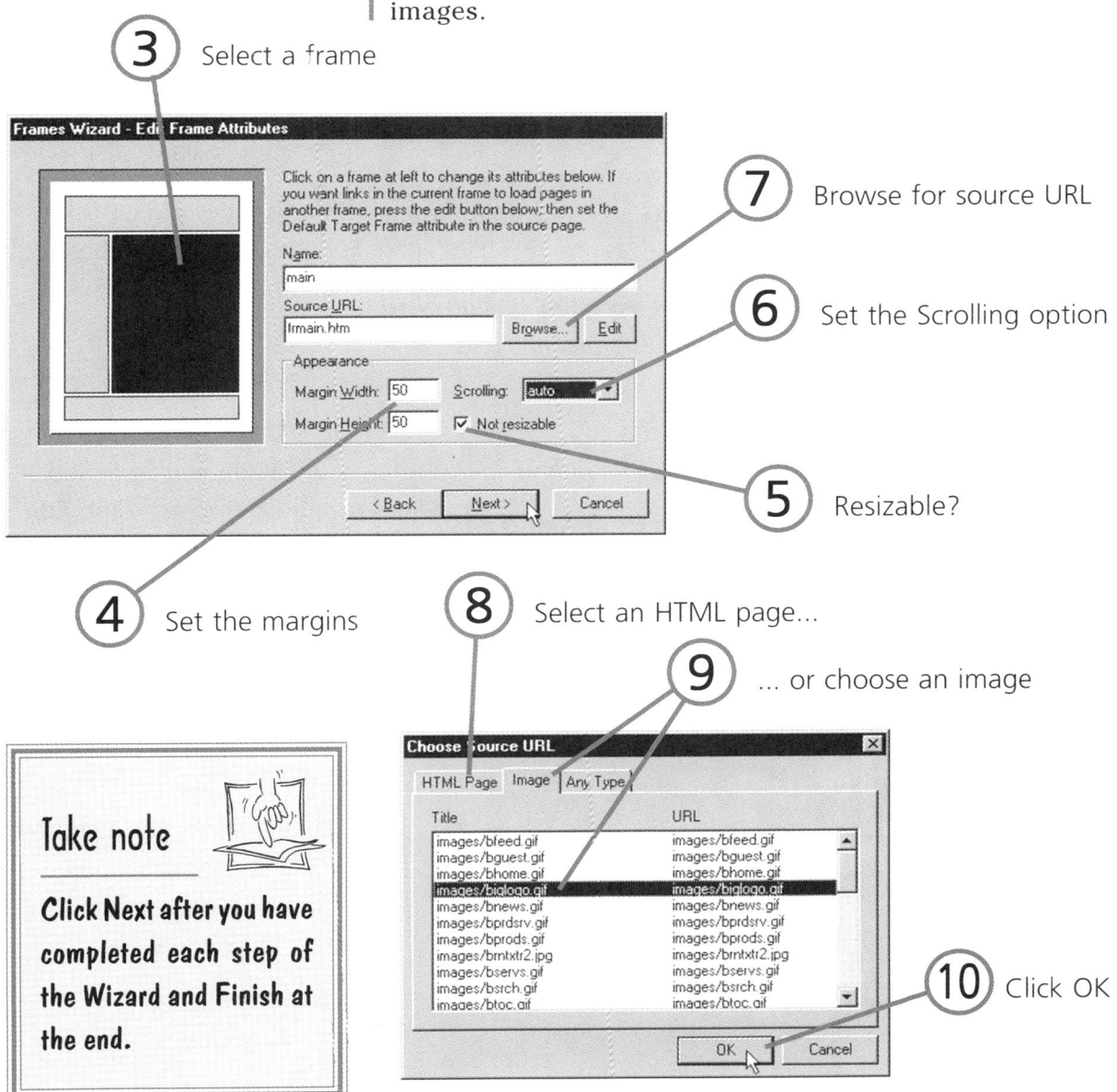

③ Select a frame

⑦ Browse for source URL

⑥ Set the Scrolling option

⑤ Resizable?

④ Set the margins

⑧ Select an HTML page...

⑨ ... or choose an image

⑩ Click OK

Take note

Click Next after you have completed each step of the Wizard and Finish at the end.

Custom grids

When you choose **Make a custom grid** instead of **Pick a template**, you work with grids and frames. The window is divided into a grid; each frame in the grid can be split into smaller grids to create the layout you want.

Note that you can only merge *all* the frames in a grid together; you can't merge some and leave others alone. If for instance you wanted to have one frame on the top half of the screen and the bottom half divided into three, you should set the initial grid to have two rows and only one column. You can then select the bottom row and divide it into three columns.

If you start with two rows and three columns. then try to merge just the top three frames, you'll find that you can't!

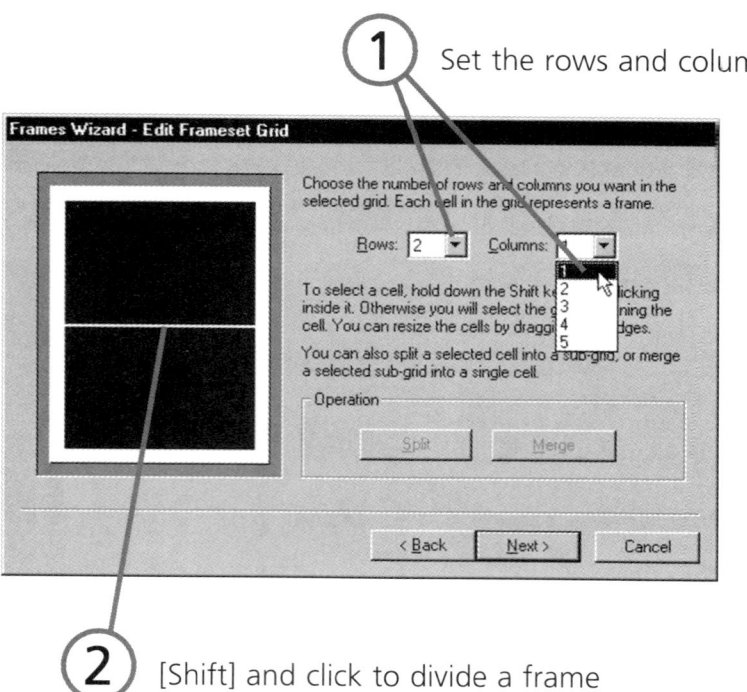

Set the rows and columns

[Shift] and click to divide a frame

Basic steps

1 Choose the number of rows and columns you want to start with.

2 Select a frame to subdivide by holding the **[Shift]** key and clicking in the frame.

3 Click **Split**.

4 Set the number of rows and columns for the sub-division.

5 Adjust the size of each frame by dragging the borders.

6 When you have laid out frames in the **Edit Frameset Grid** dialog box, click **Next** to edit the attributes.

7 Select a frame.

8 Type a **Name** for the frame.

9 **Browse...** for a source URL, or type a new filename (and create that page later!)

❑ Edit the **Frame attributes** as before.

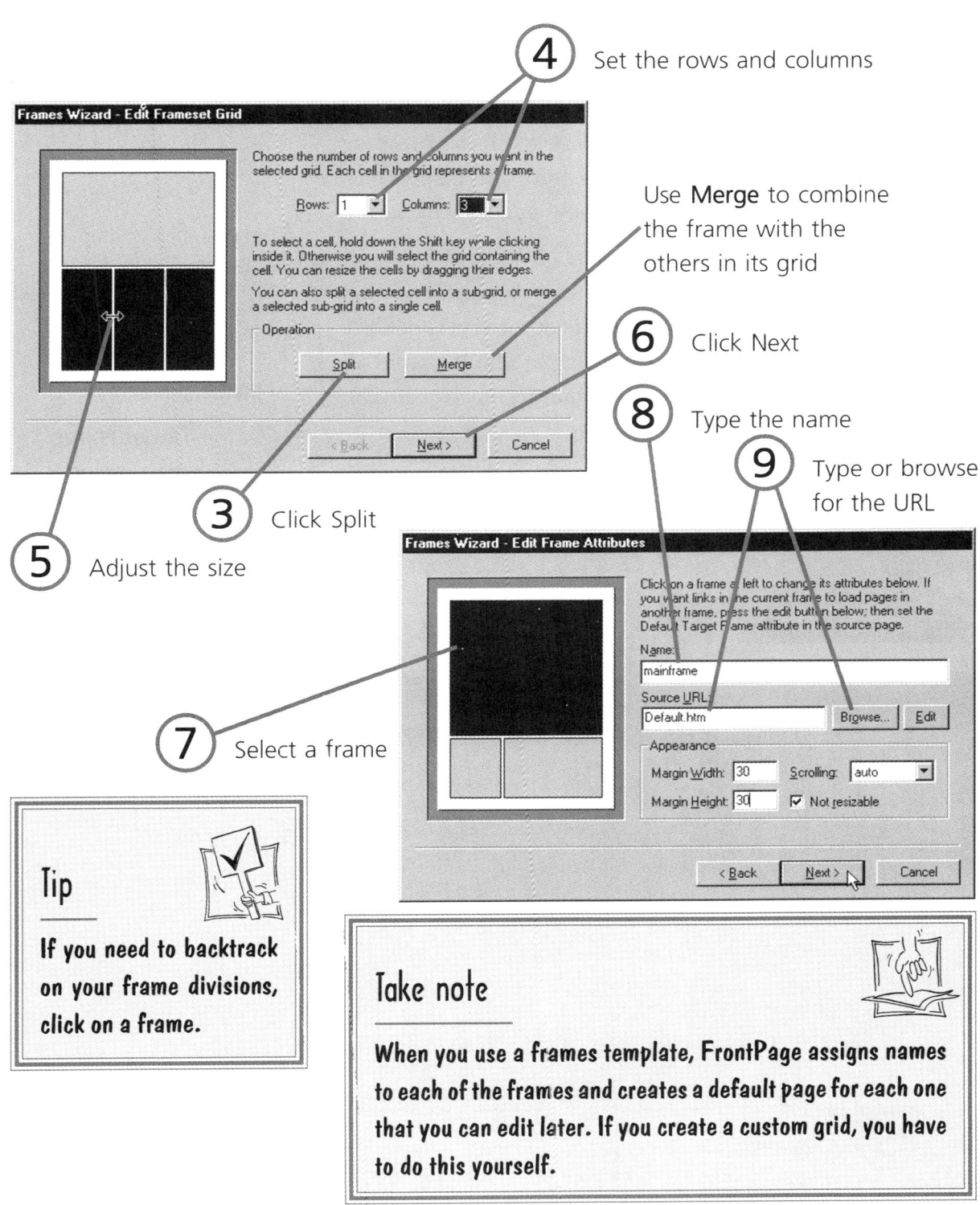

4 Set the rows and columns

Use **Merge** to combine the frame with the others in its grid

6 Click Next

8 Type the name

9 Type or browse for the URL

3 Click Split

5 Adjust the size

7 Select a frame

Tip

If you need to backtrack on your frame divisions, click on a frame.

Take note

When you use a frames template, FrontPage assigns names to each of the frames and creates a default page for each one that you can edit later. If you create a custom grid, you have to do this yourself.

Target frames

When you are working with frames, you need to specify **target frames** for your hyperlinks. These tell the browser where to display the new page. If you don't specify a target, the browser will open the new page in the frame which contained the link, replacing itscontents.

A default target frame can be set for each page, and this will apply to all links on the page unless otherwise specified. Contents pages, for instance, often use a default so that all linked pages are displayed in the main frame.

Basic steps

1 Create a new hyperlink.

or

2 Right-click on an existing hyperlink for the context menu.

3 Choose **Hyperlink properties...**

4 In the **Target Frame** field, type a name.

5 Click **OK**.

❑ **To set a default target**

6 Open the **Page Properties...** dialog box.

7 Type the name of a frame in the **Default Target Frame** field.

8 Click **OK**.

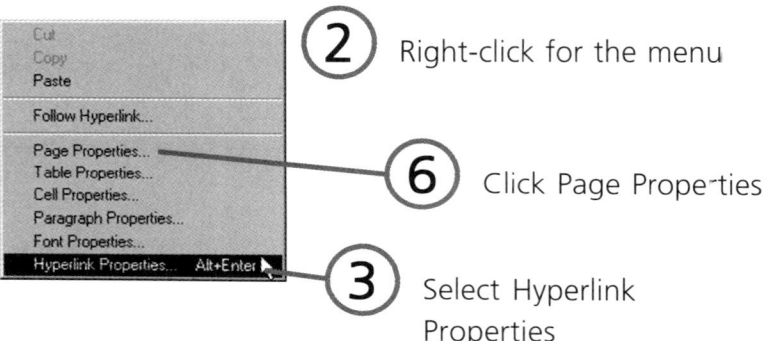

(2) Right-click for the menu

(6) Click Page Properties

(3) Select Hyperlink Properties

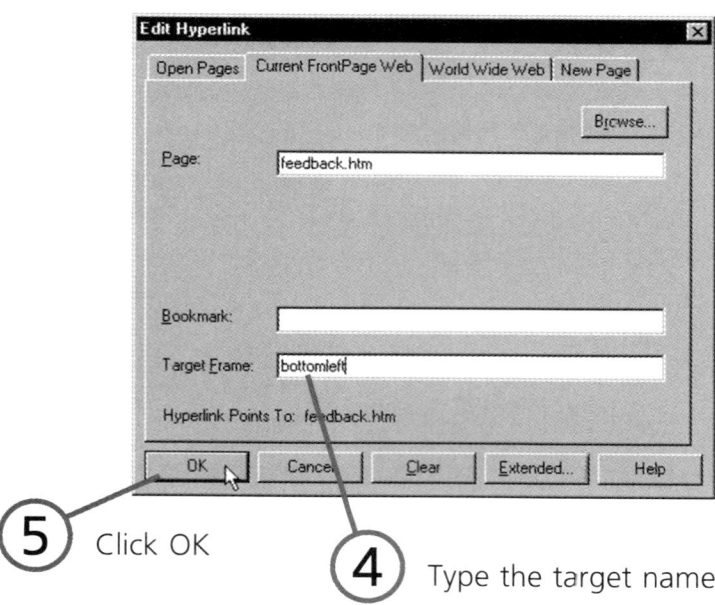

(5) Click OK

(4) Type the target name

7 Type the default target name

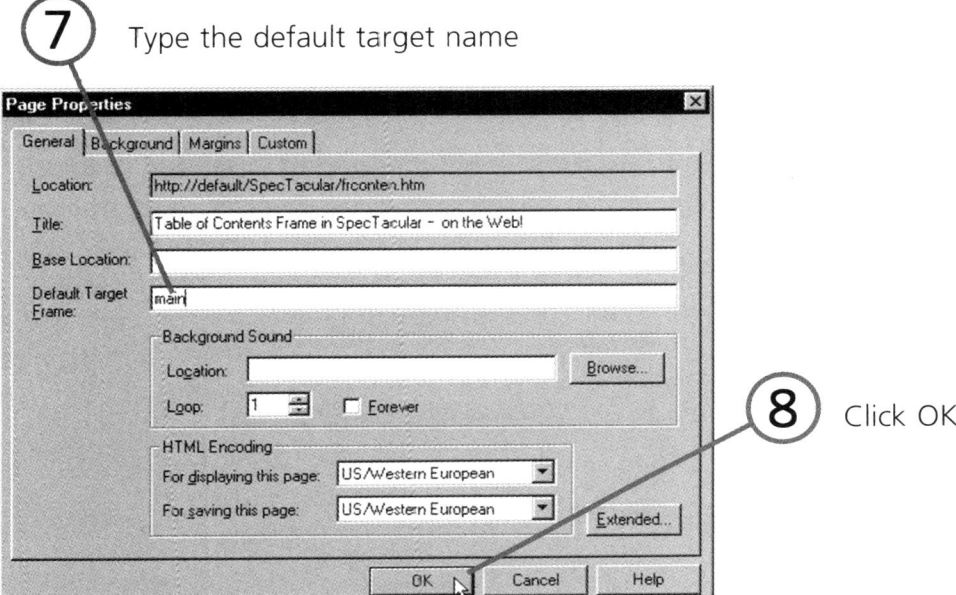

8 Click OK

Special frames

There are four pre-defined frame names which have special functions and cannot be used as name for any of your own frames.

These names can be entered into the **Target Frame** field, not at the stage where you assign names to frames.

- **_blank** tells the browser to open a new window to display the page in.

- **_self** sets the target frame as the frame containing the hyperlink.

- **_parent** is used when you have a frame set within a frame; it tells the browser to put the new page into the frame which contains the sub- frame set.

- **_top** removes all frames from the browser window and replaces them with the new page.

Summary

- ❑ Use **frames** to divide the browser window into independent sections.

- ❑ You can create a **frame set** from one of the FrontPage **templates**.

- ❑ You can create a **customised** frame set by splitting the grid into as many frames as you want.

- ❑ Check the appearance of a frame set page in your browser.

- ❑ **Edit** the number and size of frames in the **Edit Frames** dialog box.

- ❑ **Edit** a frame's **margins**, turn the **Scrolling** on or off or make it **Not resizable** in the **Edit Frame Attributes** dialog box.

- ❑ Choose the **Source URL** as the page or image which is called up into a frame when the frame set is first loaded.

- ❑ Specify **Target Frames** for hyperlinks so that browsers know where to display a new page.

8 Forms and feedback

What are forms? 104

Names and values 105

Handling form data 106

Creating a form 108

Setting out your form 109

Text boxes 110

Text box validation 111

Push buttons 113

Radio buttons 114

Check boxes 115

Drop-down menus 116

Summary 118

What are forms?

Forms are sections of a page which request information from visitors to your web. Visitors type answers to your prompts or questions into the blank spaces on the page, and the form is then sent back to your web server where you can access the results.

Radio buttons

One-line text box

Check boxes

Drop-down menu

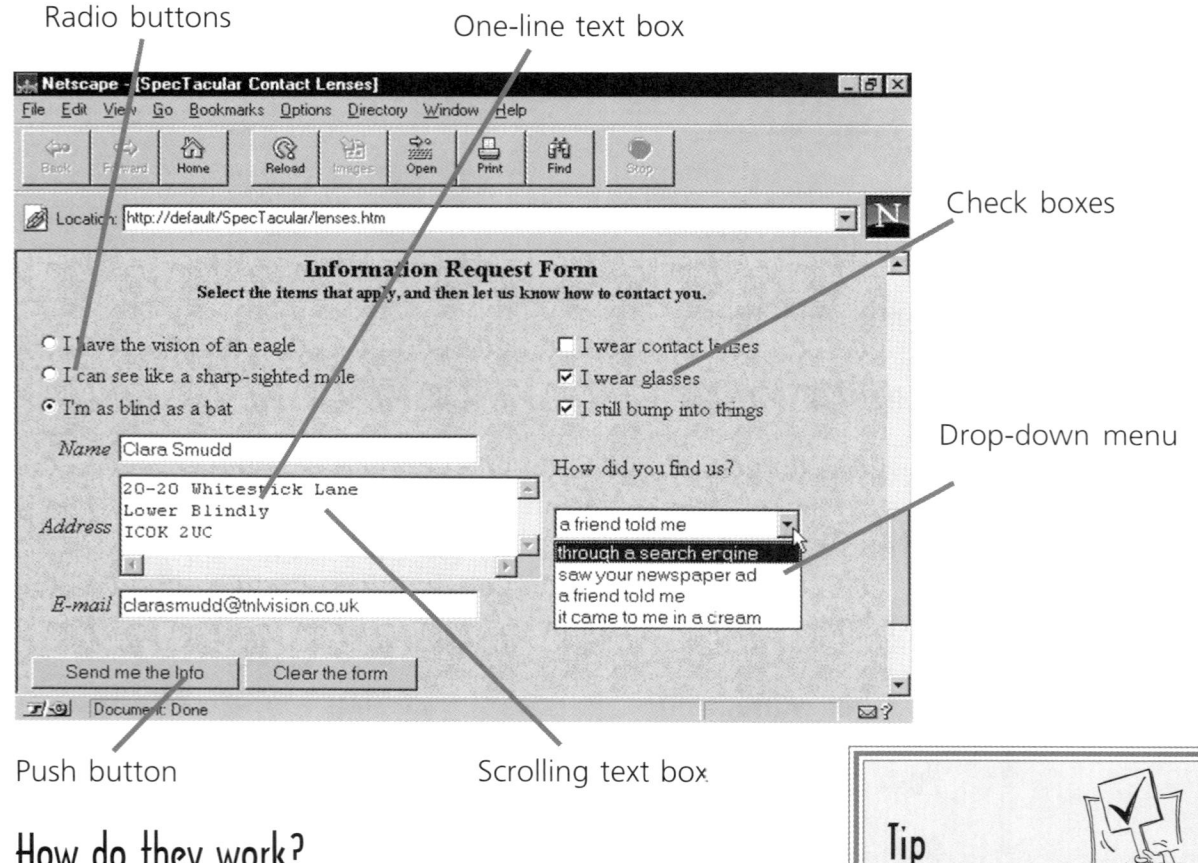

Push button

Scrolling text box

How do they work?

If your Internet Service Provider (ISP) supports <u>FrontPage Extensions</u> (page 124), the data sent by visitors is collated by the Extensions on your ISP's server into a database or HTML file. If your ISP does not support the Extensions, you will need a CGI script, to handle incoming data. These also run on your ISP's server. Talk to your ISP about this.

> ## Tip
>
> **Use forms to gather data and build a visitor database, or to invite visitors to submit feedback and questions to you.**

Names and values

Items of information submitted from a form have two main attributes:

- a **name**, which identifies the items when you access the results file where returned form data is stored.

- a **value**, which is the information itself. Sometimes, this will be whatever the user types in; in other cases, you will set the values for *either/or* responses. Some values can be returned automatically, such as the time and date that the form was submitted.

Names

Values

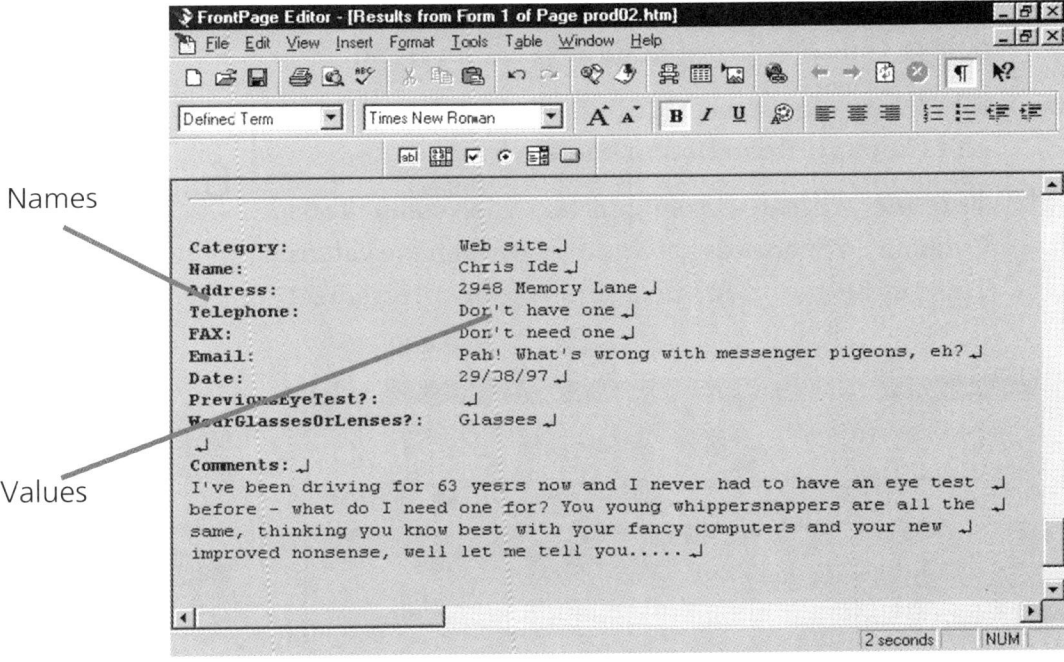

Tip

Matt's Script Archive has handy scripts for a wide range of uses — find it at http://worldwidemart.com/scripts (see page 141).

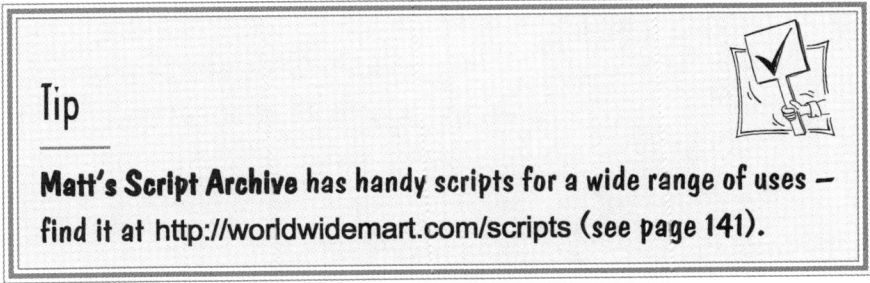

Handling form data

The simplest way to handle the data you receive from a form is to leave it to the **WebBot Save Results Component**. Using this, you can save data in various file formats when it is submitted. The results can be accessed later from the Explorer window:

- **HTML** – the default style, which collates information and displays it as ordinary text in an HTML page.

- **Formatted text** – preserves tabs and spaces as they were entered by the user (HTML does not recognise tabs or multiple spaces). This creates a text file unless you select **Formatted text within HTML**.

- **HTML List** – creates an HTML page with Name-Value pairs set as a **Definition** or **Bulleted** list.

- **Text file** – creates a simple text file, using **Tabs**, **Commas** or **Spaces** as separators between the values. This can be imported into a database or spreadsheet.

Basic steps

1 Right-click on the form and choose **Form Properties…**

2 Click **Settings…**

3 Edit the suggested **File name**, if desired.

4 Select a **Format** for submitted data from the drop-down menu.

5 Check the boxes for the **Additional information** you want.

6 Click **OK**.

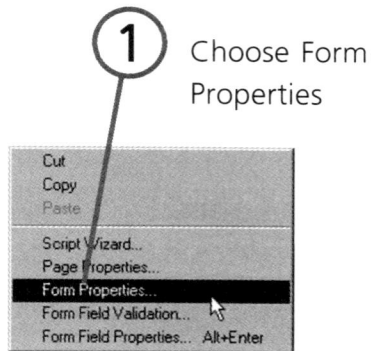

① Choose Form Properties

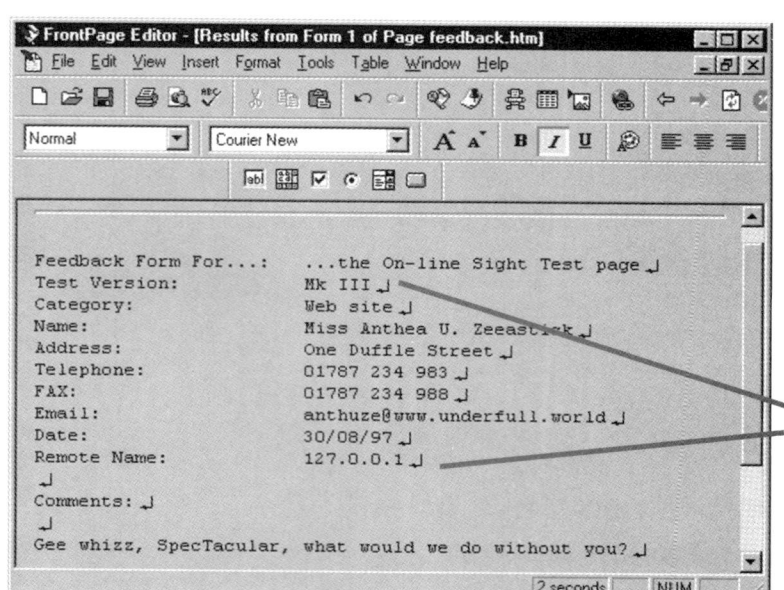

Hidden fields can be a useful source of information

106

Hidden fields

❑ **Hidden fields**

7 Click **Add...**

8 Enter a **Name**.

9 Enter a **Value**.

10 Click **OK**.

To help you identify the information when you access your results page, you can set Hidden fields which cannot be seen by the user, but which are returned to you along with each submitted form.

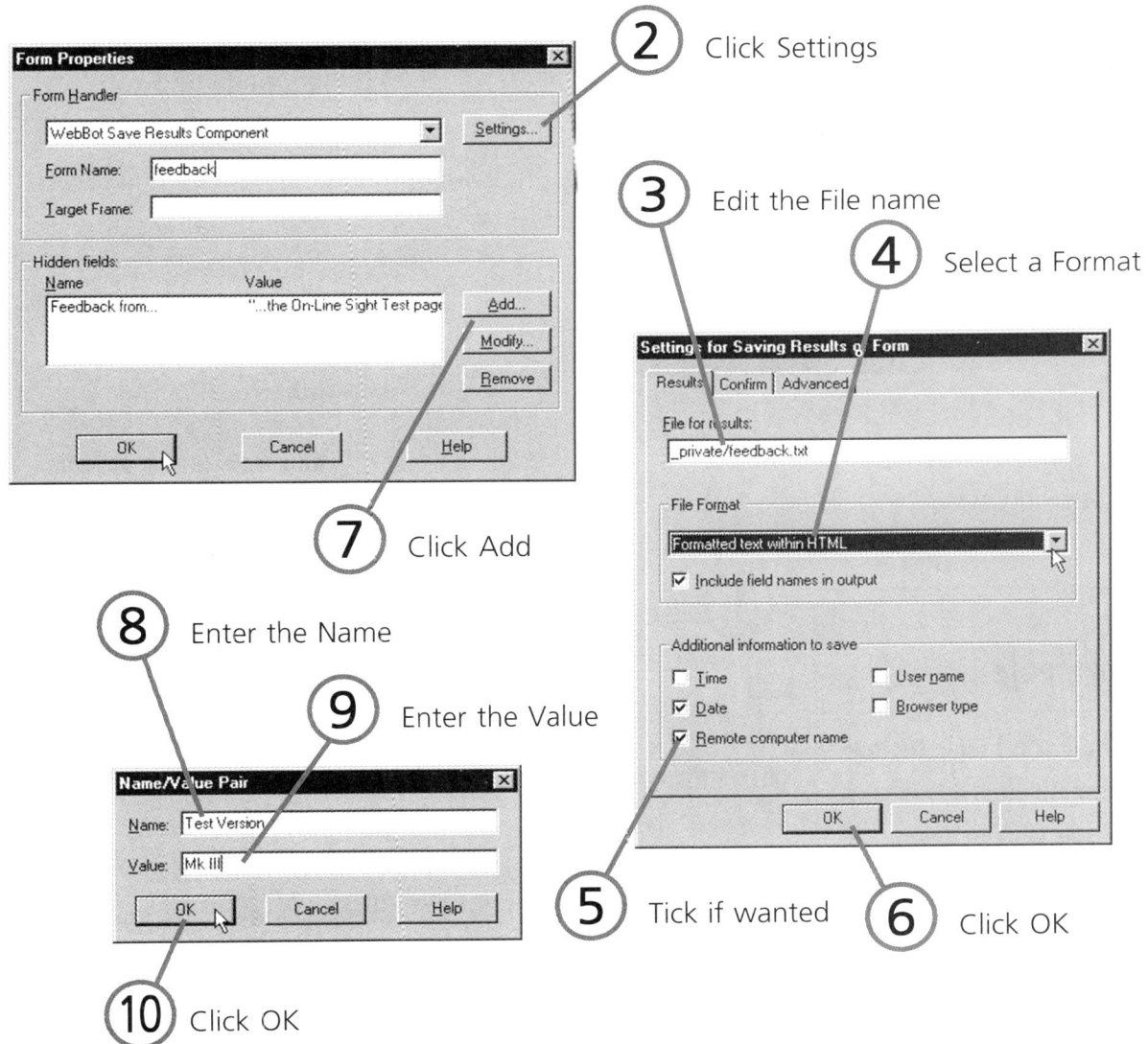

② Click Settings

③ Edit the File name

④ Select a Format

⑦ Click Add

⑧ Enter the Name

⑨ Enter the Value

⑩ Click OK

⑤ Tick if wanted

⑥ Click OK

Creating a form

When you add a form field or a button to a page, an area containing it is designated as a form. Both the form field and the form itself are inserted with standard default properties, unlike the Frames Wizard which asks you for details before creating a frame set. Once a form and its elements are on the page, you can then configure them to suit your purposes.

Using the toolbar

You can insert form elements from the menu bar, but it is easier to turn on the Forms toolbar and simply click on an icon to add a field or button.

Basic steps

1 Open the **View** menu.

2 Click on **Forms Toolbar** to turn it on.

❑ The Toolbar items on the View menu are all on/off switches – click them once to turn on, and again to turn off.

One-line Text box   Check box   Drop-down menu

Scrolling text box   Radio button   Push button

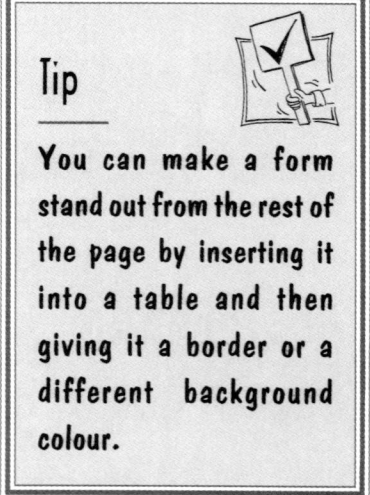

Tip

You can make a form stand out from the rest of the page by inserting it into a table and then giving it a border or a different background colour.

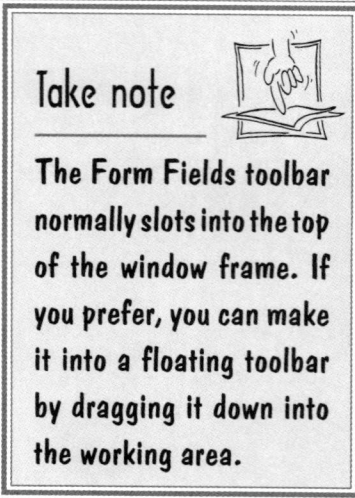

Take note

The Form Fields toolbar normally slots into the top of the window frame. If you prefer, you can make it into a floating toolbar by dragging it down into the working area.

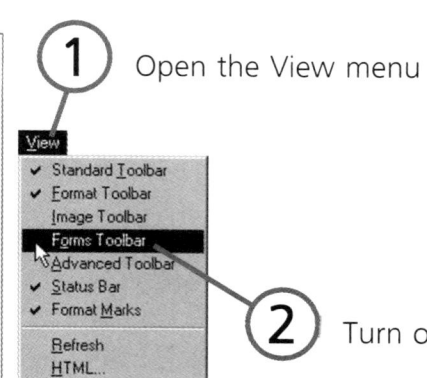

① Open the View menu

② Turn on the Forms Toolbar

Basic steps

1 Create a table with two columns and a few rows.

2 Type a prompt for information into a cell.

3 Position the cursor in the adjacent cell.

4 Click an icon on the Form Field toolbar.

5 Right-click on the form field.

6 Choose **Form Field Properties...**

7 Edit the field properties (see following pages for details of each kind).

If you want your form to look like a form, it is probably best to arrange the elements in a table so that your prompts for information are aligned comfortably with the fields for users to type into.

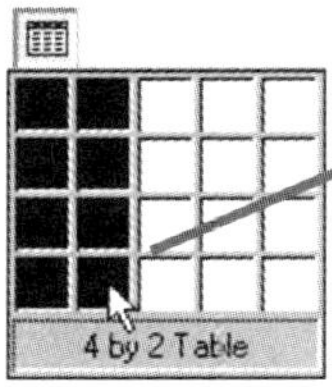

(1) Create a 2-column table

4 by 2 Table

(2) Type a prompt

(3) Click into the adjacent cell

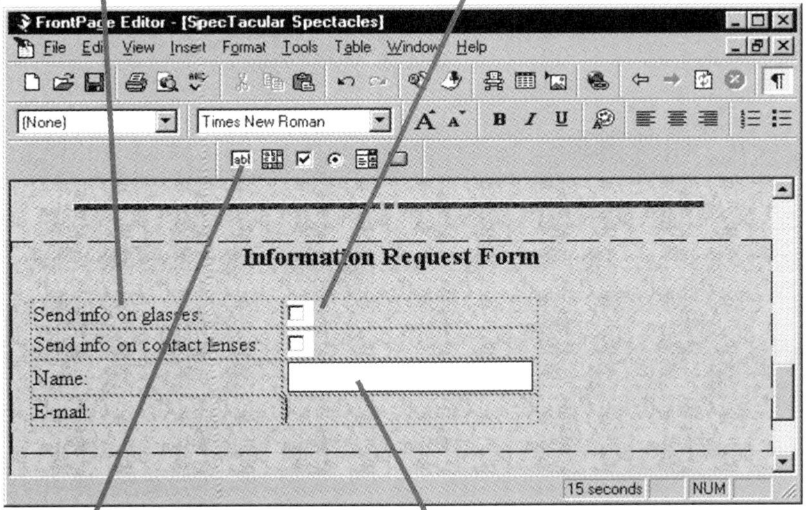

(4) Insert a Form Field

(5) Right click on a field

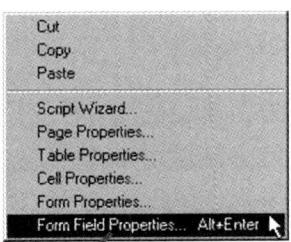

(6) Choose Form Field Properties

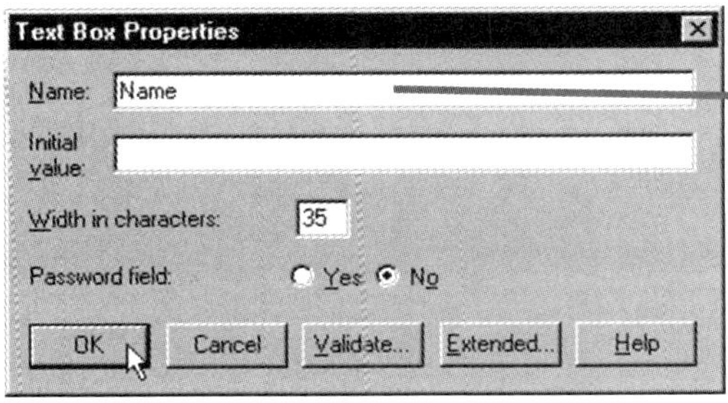

(7) Edit to define the field

Text boxes

Text boxes collect data from visitors. There are two kinds.

One-line text box

This used for entering simple information such as names, job titles, e-mail addresses, and so on. You can specify the Width, and set it as a password field, which means that any characters the visitor types are displayed as asterisks.

Scrolling text boxes

These are larger areas – addresses, questions or feedback. As for a one line text box, you can vary the width to suit its purpose, and also specify the number of lines deep it is.

Basic steps

1 Create the text box, then right-click on it for its menu and pick **Form Field Properties...**

2 Type a **Name**.

3 Set the **Width in characters**.

4 In a One-Line text box, set it as a **Password field** if it is part of an access control routine.

5 In a Scrolling text box set the **Number of lines**.

6 Click **OK**.

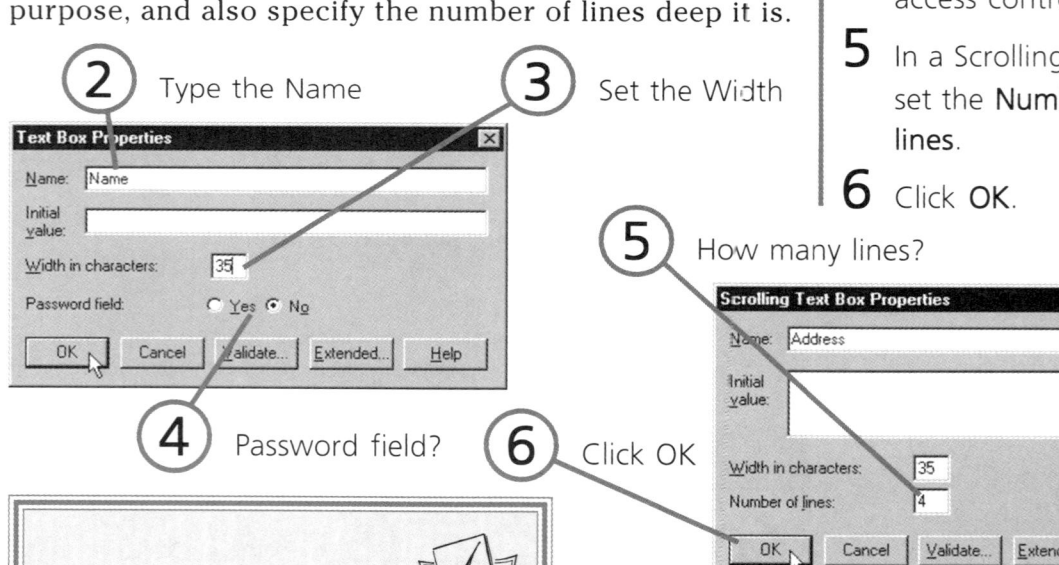

Tip

You can enter **'Initial value'** text to appear before the visitor starts typing – perhaps for a competition tie-breaker: "I like kung-fu films because..."

Take note

If you want to restrict access to your web, see the comments on page 131.

110

Text box validation

Text boxes can have certain constraints imposed on the kind of information users enter into them. This might be to stop typing mistakes slipping through – imposing an upper limit of 110 on an 'age' field, for example. It might be to ensure that the right sort of information is supplied – setting a minimum of 11 characters in a telephone field ensures that a full national code is given.

The Text box Validation dialog box gives you several ways of restricting the kind of information you are sent:

- **Data Type** - choose *Text*, *Number* or *Integer* (whole numbers only). Each type has a set of more specific restrictions:

  ○ *Text Format* – Letters, Digits, Whitespace or specified Others can be allowed or disallowed. Check the options you want to allow.

  ○ *Numeric Format* – the default is commas for grouping and full stops for decimal points (4,364.99), but you can switch to Continental-style numbering (4.364,99).

- **Data Length** – click *Required* and set a minimum and/or maximum number of characters.

- **Data Value** – using the comparisons 'greater/less than' and 'equal to', you can set upper and/or lower limits for a number entered. However, it also works on an alphabetical basis with words: 'greater than' meaning 'further towards Z than' and 'less than' meaning 'closer to A than'.

Take note

To allow characters other than letters, numerals and blank spaces in a field, you must click the Other field and type them into it. This includes all punctuation marks.

When a visitor tries to submit data which is not within the defined range, a message will tell them what is acceptable.

Netscape

⚠ JavaScript Alert:
Please enter only digit and "$" characters in the "Password" field.

[OK]

Alternatively, you can create a page to explain what sort of information is required, and set this to be displayed:

● Open the **Form properties** dialog box, click **Settings...** and then click the **Confirm** tab.

● Type the address into the **Validation failure page** field or Browse... for it.

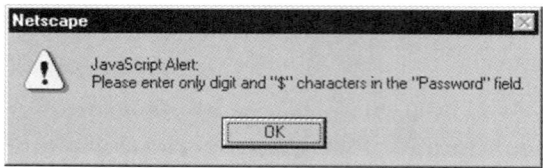

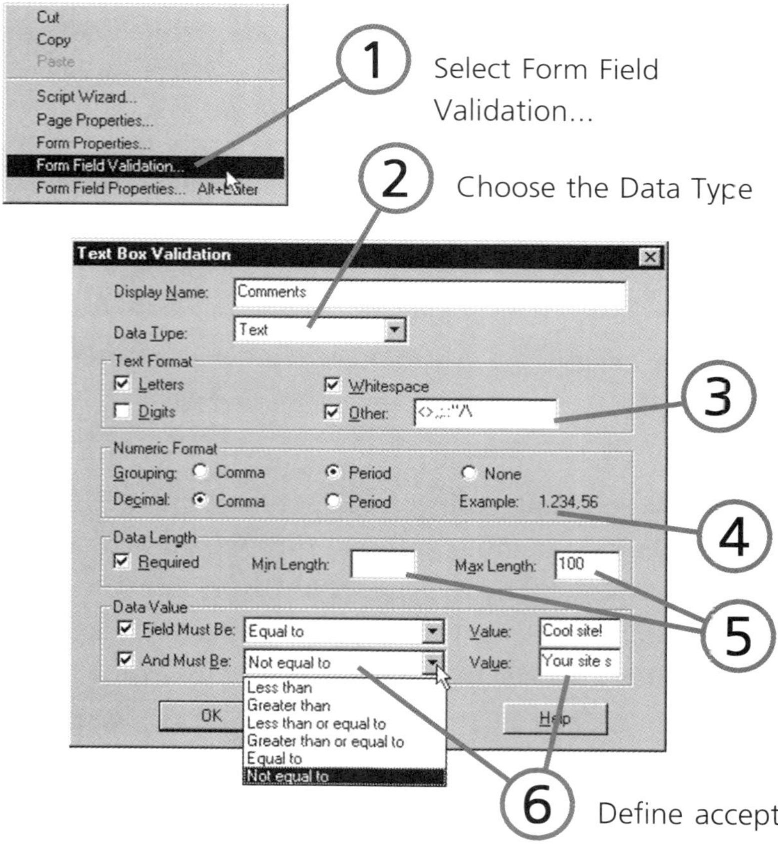

① Select Form Field Validation...

② Choose the Data Type

Text Box Validation

| Display Name: | Comments |
| Data Type: | Text |

Text Format
☑ Letters   ☑ Whitespace
☐ Digits   ☑ Other: <>.:"'\

Numeric Format
Grouping: ○ Comma   ● Period   ○ None
Decimal: ● Comma   ○ Period   Example: 1.234,56

Data Length
☑ Required   Min Length: [   ]   Max Length: [100]

Data Value
☑ Field Must Be: [Equal to ▼]   Value: [Cool site!]
☑ And Must Be: [Not equal to ▼]   Value: [Your site s]

Less than
Greater than
Less than or equal to
Greater than or equal to
Equal to
Not equal to

[OK]   [Help]

③ What characters are permitted?

④ Numeric format

⑤ Set Min and Max lengths

⑥ Define acceptable values

❑ **Validation**

1 Right-click on a text box and choose **Form Field Validation...**

2 Choose a **Data Type** to permit (*No constraints* allows any characters).

3 If you chose *Text*, click on a **Text Format** option to allow it.

4 If you chose *Number*, pick a **Numeric Format**.

5 Set upper and/or lower **Data Lengths** as required.

6 Define the **Data Values** if the data must fall within certain limits.

Basic steps

1 Click the **Push Button** button 🔲.

2 Right-click on the push button and choose **Form Field Properties...**

3 Type a **Name** for it.

4 Type the word(s) you want to appear on the button in the **Value/ Label** field.

5 Decide whether it is a **Submit**, **Reset**, or **Normal** (custom) button.

6 Click **OK**.

There are three types of Push Buttons:

● **Submit**, sends the form information to the server when clicked by the visitor.

● **Reset** clears the contents of the form, so that the visitor can start again.

● Normal buttons can be customised to perform different functions by attaching JavaScript code, or associating them with CGI scripts, but this is a little beyond the scope of this book.

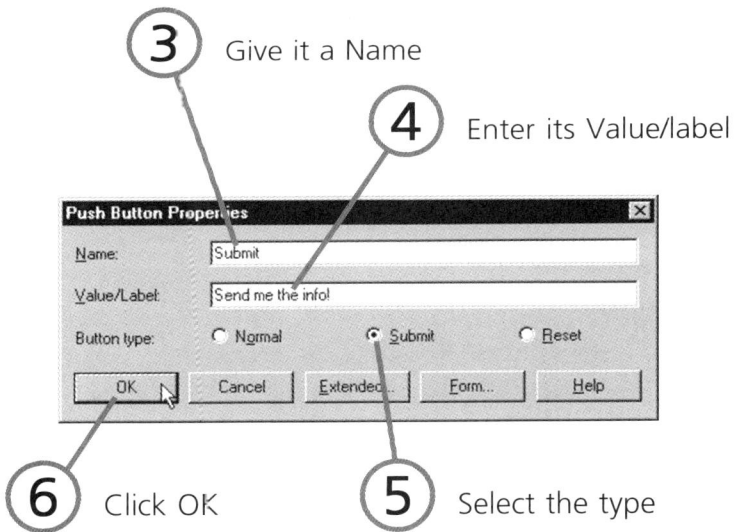

③ Give it a Name

④ Enter its Value/label

⑥ Click OK

⑤ Select the type

Tip

JavaScript and CGI scripts can both give good results for relatively little effort. If you want to learn about JavaScript, try *JavaScript Made Simple*. For information on CGI scripts, talk first to your ISP.

Radio buttons

Radio buttons are usually grouped into sets of two or more. They are used when you want visitors to select only one of a range of possibilities, because only one in a set can be on at any time.

Radio buttons are grouped by giving all members the same **Group Name**; this is returned along with the **Value** of the button which was turned on by the visitor.

Validation

You can set the **Validate...** feature to insist that at least one of a group of radio buttons be selected. In this dialog box you are prompted to supply a Display name, which is the name that visitors will see in an error message when they do not select any button. Remember to give field names which will mean something to a visitor and not just to you – see the Note opposite.

Basic steps

1 Right-click on the radio button and choose **Form Field Properties…**

2 Type the **Group name**.

3 Enter a **Value** to return if selected.

4 Decide whether this button is **Selected** or **Not** to begin with.

❑ Validation

5 Click **Validate…**

6 Type a **Display Name**.

7 Check **Data Required**.

8 Click **OK**.

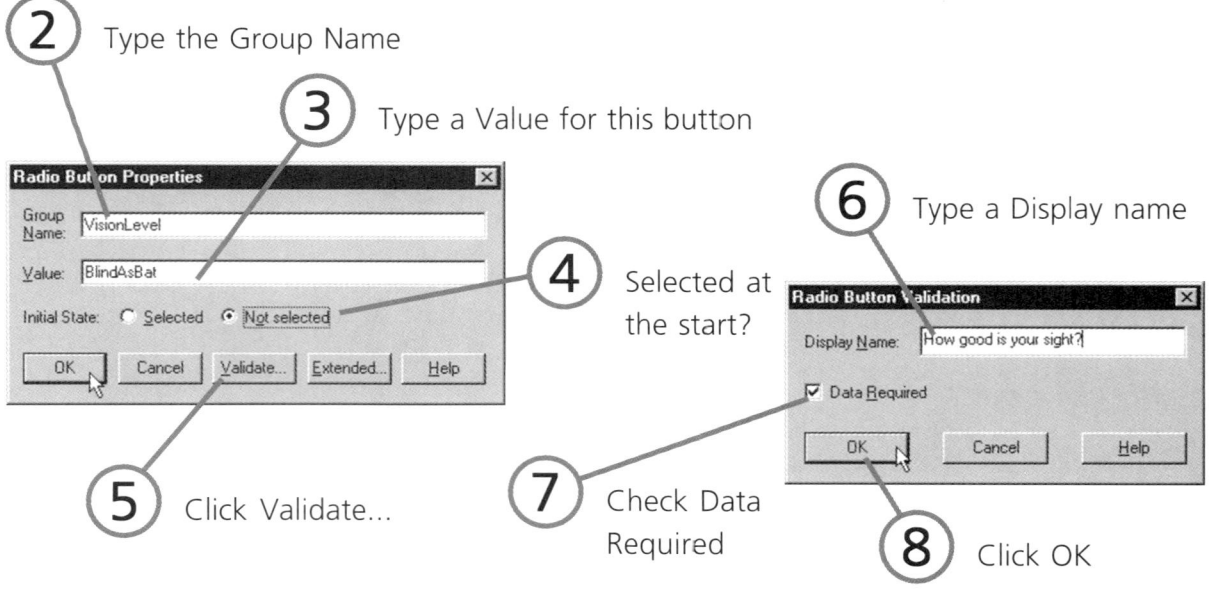

② Type the Group Name

③ Type a Value for this button

⑥ Type a Display name

④ Selected at the start?

⑤ Click Validate…

⑦ Check Data Required

⑧ Click OK

114

Basic steps

1 Type a prompt for the Check Box.

2 Click the **Check Box** button ☑.

3 Right-click on the Check Box and choose **Form Field Properties...**

4 Type a **Name** for the Check Box.

5 Enter a **Value** to be returned if checked.

6 Decide whether the box is **Checked** or Not when first loaded.

7 Click **OK**.

Check boxes

These are for simple Yes/No responses to the questions or prompts you give. The Value you specify for the field will appear alongside its Name on your results page if the box is checked; if it is left unchecked, then no value is returned. Check boxes cannot be given validation requirements.

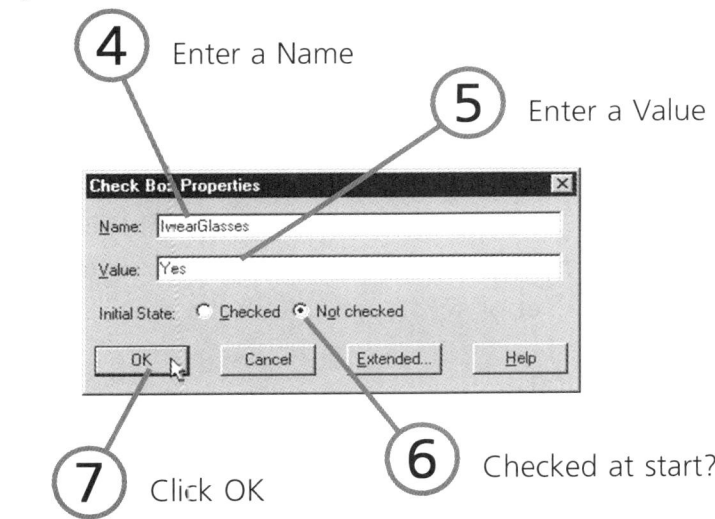

④ Enter a Name

⑤ Enter a Value

⑦ Click OK

⑥ Checked at start?

Take note

The names you have chosen for your reference may also be concise to the point of rudeness: 'VisionLevel: BlindAsBat' might be more tactfully worded, so that the prompt for the 'BlindAsBat' option reads 'Not terribly good' and the Display name for the group of radio buttons is similarly softened.

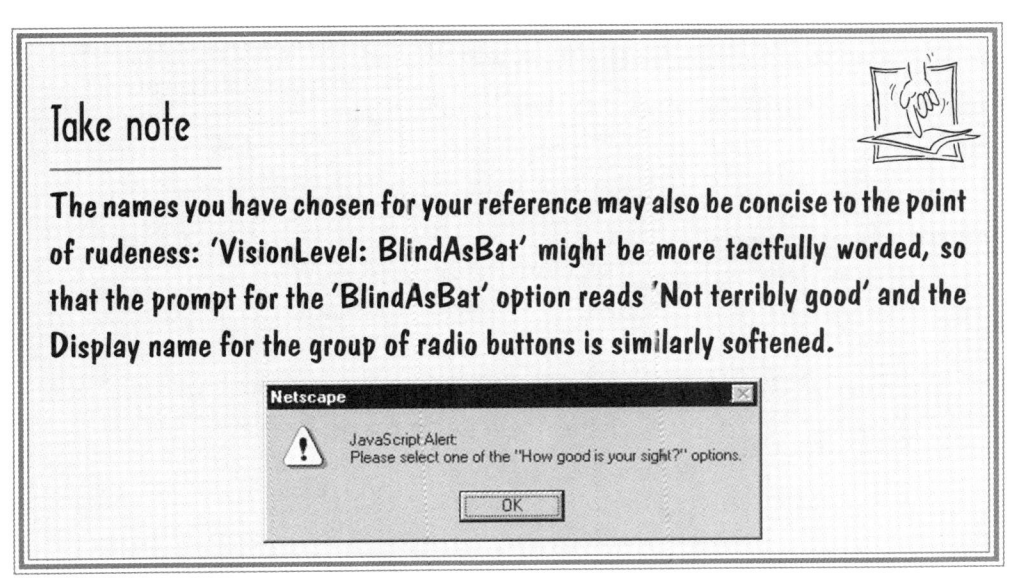

Drop-down menus

These are exactly like the menus on a toolbar, and are useful when you have a lot of options which would take up too much room to display as radio buttons or check boxes.

When a menu is first inserted, it is empty, so you will have to add the items which will appear in it, and their corresponding values, which will be returned to you in the form results file.

Height controls how the menu items are displayed. A height of 1 gives one item visible to begin with, and an arrow icon which 'drops-down' the menu. Any other height value, (e.g. 4) displays that number (4) of items in a deeper window with a set of scroll bars along the side.

Menu validation

As with other form fields, you can require that at least one item be selected from a menu before the form can be submitted. Click **Validate...** to bring up the Validation dialog box, and click **Data required**. You can also choose **Disallow first item** – this allows you to use the item which is initially visible to write a helpful prompt, such as 'Click for a list of options'.

1 Click the **Drop-Down Menu** button ▦.

2 Right-click on the menu and choose **Form Field Properties...**

3 Type a **Name** for the menu.

4 Click **Add...**

5 Type a menu item.

6 Click **Specify Value** if you want to change the suggested one.

7 Choose whether this option is **Selected** or **Not** to begin with.

8 Set a **Height** – this is the number of options showing when the menu is closed.

9 Click **OK**.

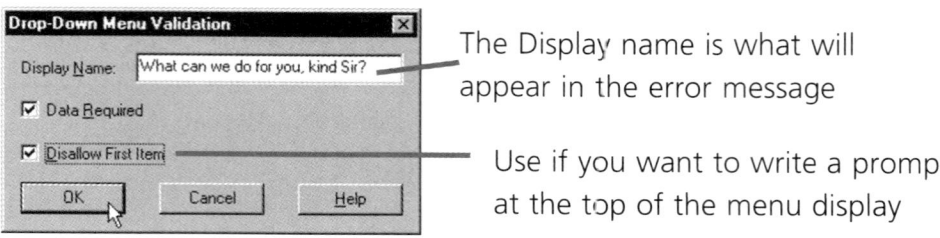

The Display name is what will appear in the error message

Use if you want to write a prompt at the top of the menu display

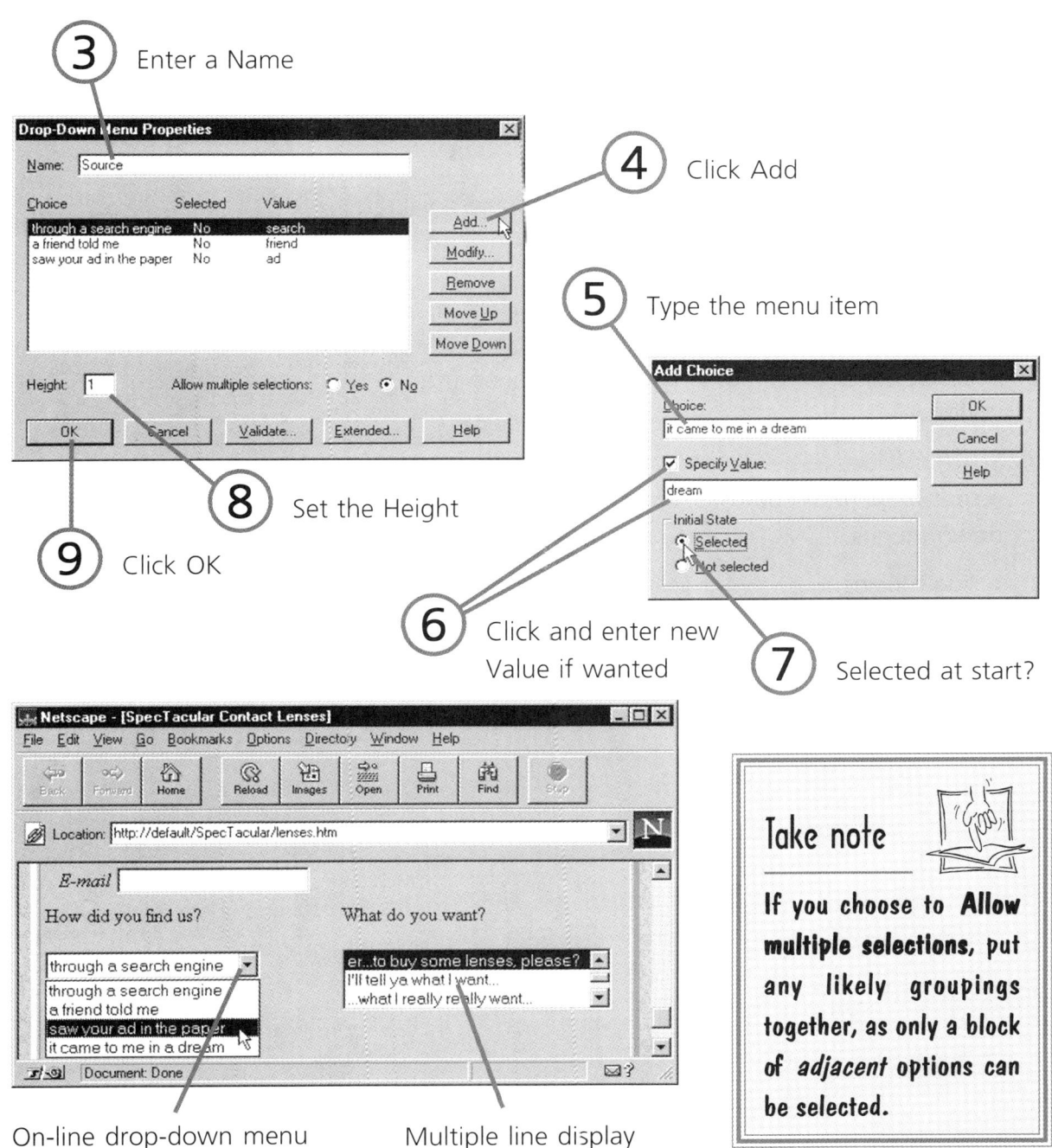

③ Enter a Name

Drop-Down Menu Properties

Name: Source

Choice	Selected	Value
through a search engine	No	search
a friend told me	No	friend
saw your ad in the paper	No	ad

Add...

Modify...

Remove

Move Up

Move Down

Height: 1   Allow multiple selections: ○ Yes ● No

OK   Cancel   Validate...   Extended...   Help

④ Click Add

⑤ Type the menu item

Add Choice

Choice:
it came to me in a dream

☑ Specify Value:
dream

Initial State
● Selected
○ Not selected

OK
Cancel
Help

⑧ Set the Height

⑨ Click OK

⑥ Click and enter new Value if wanted

⑦ Selected at start?

Netscape - [SpecTacular Contact Lenses]

File Edit View Go Bookmarks Options Directory Window Help

Back Forward Home Reload Images Open Print Find Stop

Location: http://default/SpecTacular/lenses.htm

E-mail

How did you find us?

through a search engine

through a search engine
a friend told me
saw your ad in the paper
it came to me in a dream

What do you want?

er...to buy some lenses, please?
I'll tell ya what I want...
...what I really really want...

Document: Done

On-line drop-down menu

Multiple line display

Take note

If you choose to **Allow multiple selections**, put any likely groupings together, as only a block of *adjacent* options can be selected.

117

Summary

❑ Use **forms** to collect information about visitors and to allow them to submit feedback and questions to you.

❑ Turn on the **Forms toolbar** from the **View** menu.

❑ **Create** a form by inserting any **form field**.

❑ Every form field has a **name**, to identify it, and a **value** to hold the visitor's response

❑ Use the **WebBot Save Results Component** to organise the data you receive.

❑ Use **text boxes** to ask for complex information from visitors.

❑ Specify **Values** to be returned to you as simple responses to **radio buttons, check boxes** and **drop-down menus**.

❑ **Validate** fields to ensure that the data is supplied and that it is of the right kind.

❑ **Submit** or **Reset** the form with **push buttons**.

9   WebBot Components

WebBot components 120

Table of contents 121

Substitutions 122

FrontPage Extensions 124

Scheduled components 125

Timestamps 126

Search 127

Confirmation fields 128

Further components 130

Summary 132

WebBot components

WebBot components are small program scripts which perform various functions. Some are used essentially as labour-saving devices in the construction of FrontPage webs, such as **Include**, **Table of Contents** and **Substitution**.

Include

This takes the contents of a page, such as a logo or **navigation bar** (several images next to each other, each with a hyperlink to a different page), and pastes them into other pages to save you repeating the process manually.

A page of included elements is not a web page in its own right – or rather, it is not one you want people to have access to, so save it in the *_private* folder.

Basic steps

1 Create a **New Page**.

2 Write into it the elements that you want to include on other pages.

3 Save the page in the **_private/** folder.

4 Click the **Insert WebBot Component** button 🖧.

5 Select **Include**.

6 Click **OK**.

7 **Browse...** for the page to include.

8 Click **OK**.

⑥ Click OK

⑤ Select Include

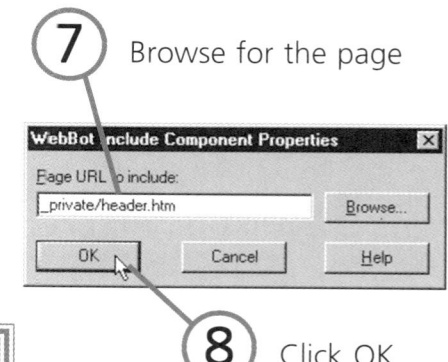

⑦ Browse for the page

⑧ Click OK

Take note

When you update or alter the contents of an 'included' page and save it to your web, all pages containing it are supplied with the new version.

Basic steps

1 Click the **Insert WebBot Component** button 🖳.

2 Choose **Table of Contents**.

3 Click **OK**.

4 **Browse…** for a starting page (usually index.htm or default.htm).

5 Set the **Heading Size**.

6 Set the options you want.

7 Click **OK**.

Creates a table of contents with hyperlinks to all the pages on your web. There are three options associated with tables of contents:

● **Show each page only once** – prevents FrontPage displaying a page every time it finds a link into it.

● **Show pages with no incoming hyperlinks** – displays pages even if they have no links from other pages to them.

● **Recompute table of contents when any other page is edited** – makes sure that it remains up to date when you edit your web.

5 Set the Heading Size 4 Browse for the page

6 Set options

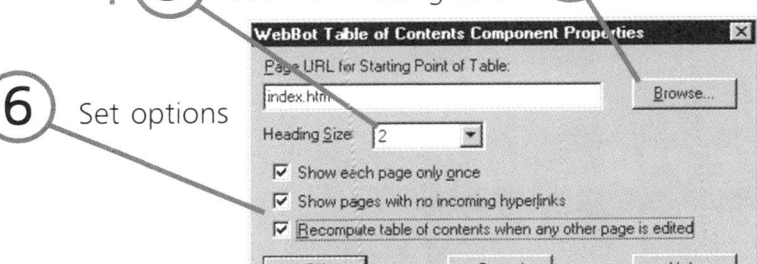

7 Click OK

The TOC page looks better in a browser!

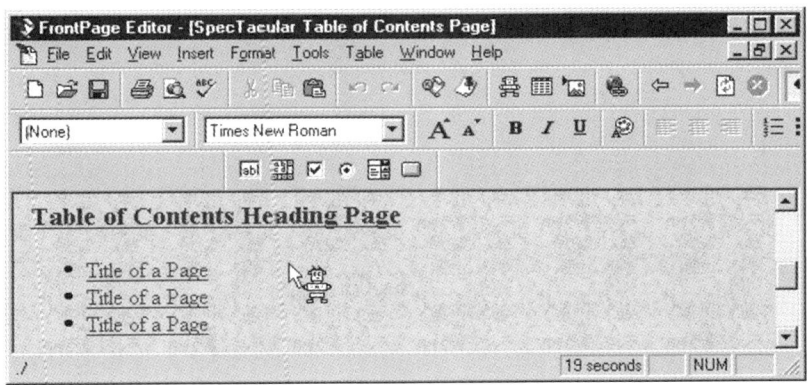

Take note

Don't worry if the table of contents appears to be stuck. It always looks the same in the Editor, but if you Preview the page in a browser, you will see how it works.

Substitutions

Names, addresses, slogans – anything which is used regularly can be assigned as a parameter, which can then be pasted into a page as a Substitution component. (They act much as AutoText in Word.)

Parameters

Parameters are set in the Explorer window, from the Web Settings dialog box.

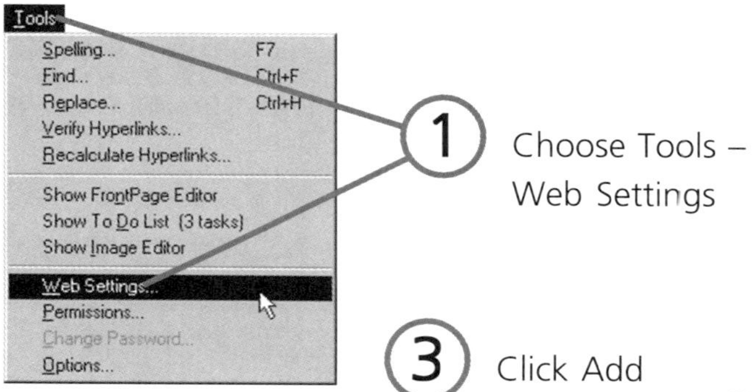

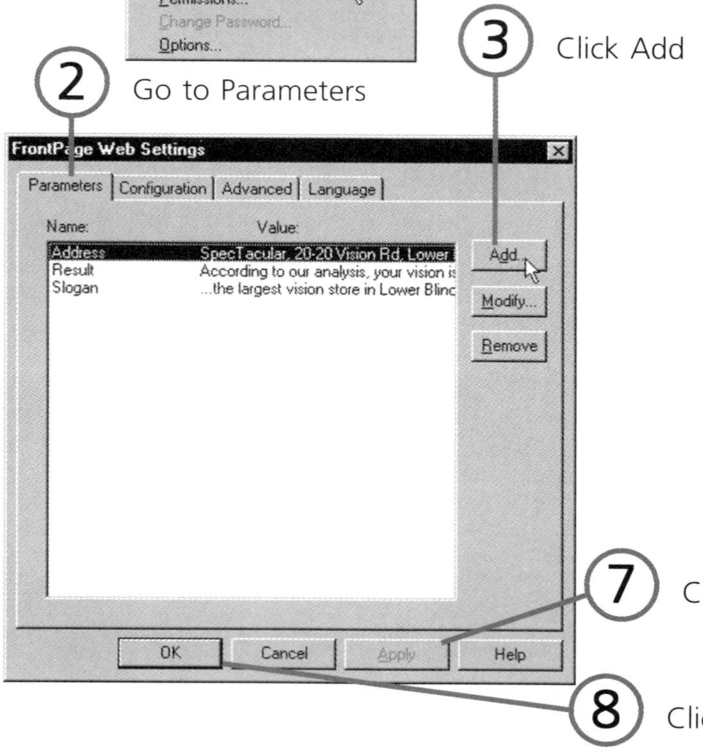

Basic steps

1 In the Explorer window, choose **Web Settings…** from the **Tools** menu.

2 Click on the **Parameters** tab.

3 Click **Add…**

4 Type a **Name** to identify the substitution.

5 Type a **Value** – the text to be substituted.

6 Click **OK**.

7 Click **Apply**.

8 Click **OK**.

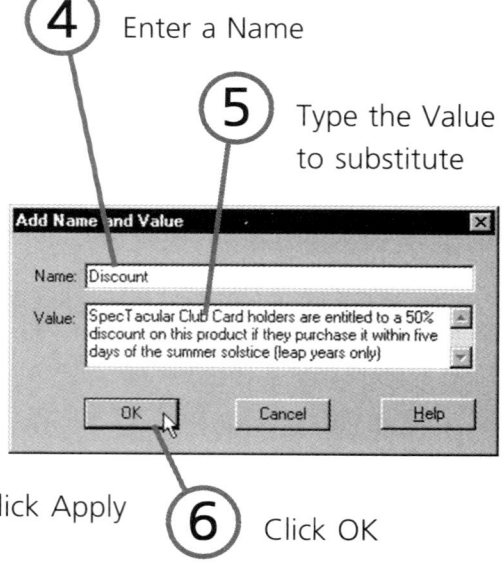

Choose Tools – Web Settings

③ Click Add

② Go to Parameters

④ Enter a Name

⑤ Type the Value to substitute

⑦ Click Apply

⑥ Click OK

⑧ Click OK

Basic steps

Using substitutions

1 In the Editor window, click the **Insert WebBot Component** button 🖧.

2 Select **Substitution**.

3 Choose a variable from the drop-down menu.

4 Click **OK**.

While the process of inserting substitutions is simple, it takes long enough to render itself rather pointless if the substituted text is only a few words – by the time you have taken your hands off the keyboard and worked through a couple of dialog boxes with the mouse, you might as well have carried on typing.

Substitutions are perhaps most useful when they are done by FrontPage – when you generate a web from a template, various details such as your name and address are made into parameters and substituted into your pages automatically.

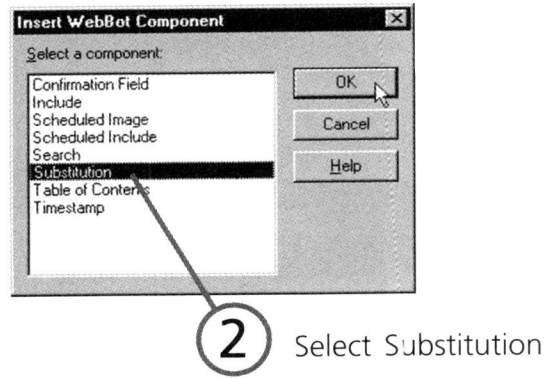

Select Substitution

③ Choose a variable name

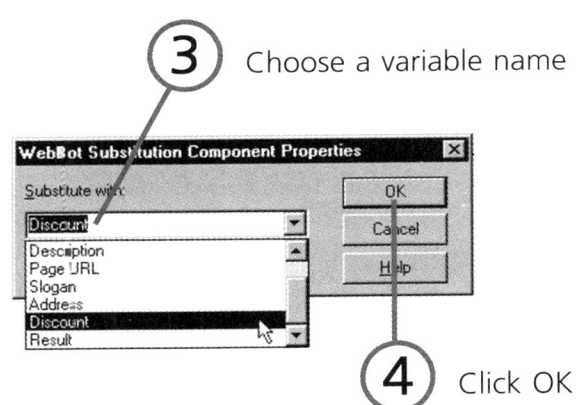

Click OK

Tip

Substitution components are not quite like Include components — they are a cut-down version, if you like, which has the disadvantage of only substituting text, not images, but the advantage of fitting anywhere. An Include component takes up the whole width of the page, whereas a substitution will slot into the middle of a sentence.

FrontPage Extensions

Other **WebBot Components** carry out functions on the World Wide Web server which hosts your web, such as stamping a date and time that the web was last updated, or organising the responses from your forms. These components require your service provider to support **FrontPage Extensions**, so you should talk to your ISP before peppering your web with clever features.

FrontPage-capable ISPs

At the time of writing, not many ISPs in the UK support FrontPage Extensions, and they are not very easy to track down – Microsoft's on-line listing only covers the USA. To find one in your area, buy a computing magazine and phone around.

Tip

If you are in London, and looking for an ISP, NetDirect is friendly, supports the Extensions and offers technical support for FrontPage. See 'Links and Resources' (page 143) for details.

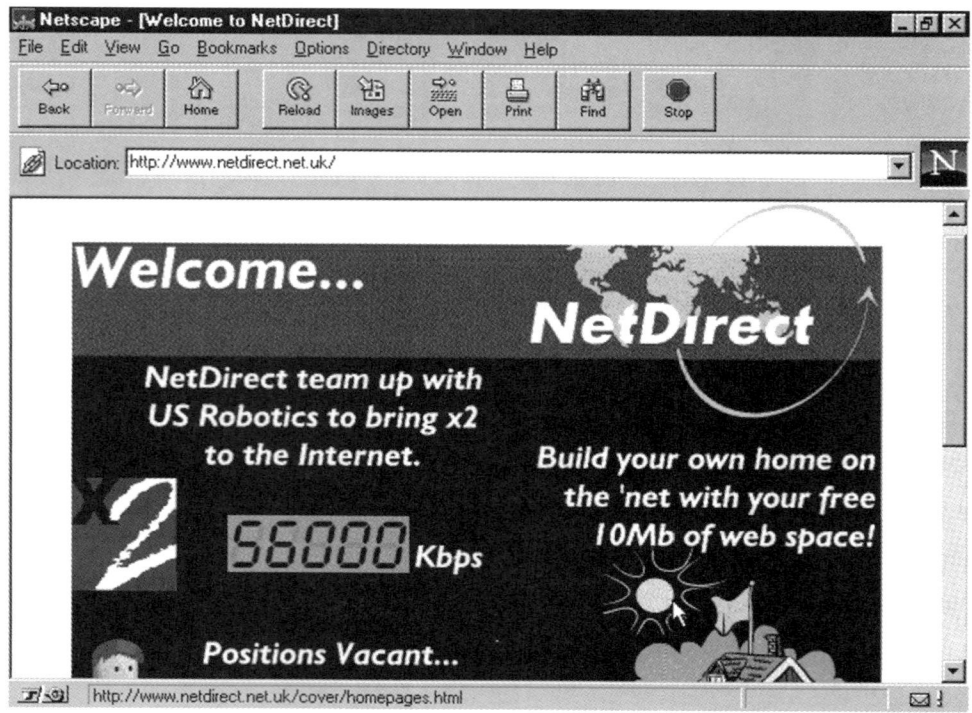

Basic steps

1 Click the **Insert WebBot Component** button 품.

2 Select **Scheduled Image** or **Include**.

3 **Browse...** for an **Image** or **Included** page URL.

4 Set a **Starting date and time**, using the drop-down menus.

5 Set an **Ending date and time**.

6 **Browse...** for an alternative image or page if you want one.

7 Click **OK**.

These display an **Image**, or the contents of an **Included** page, between certain dates and times, and not any other time. You might use these to ensure that a 'Sale Ends 6th January' sign doesn't outlive its usefulness, for instance. A scheduled component can be replaced by an alternative image or page when its time is up, or simply removed.

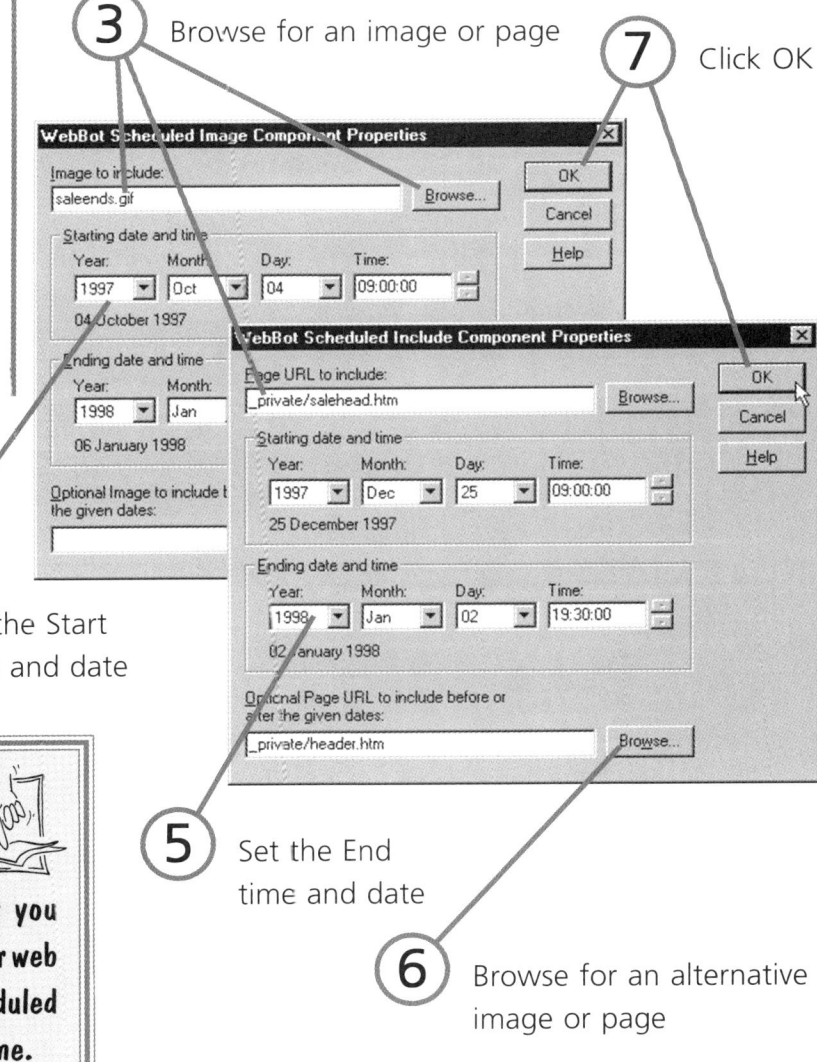

3 Browse for an image or page

7 Click OK

4 Set the Start time and date

5 Set the End time and date

6 Browse for an alternative image or page

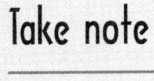

Take note

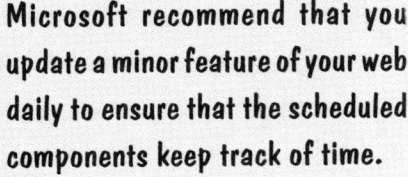

Microsoft recommend that you update a minor feature of your web daily to ensure that the scheduled components keep track of time.

Timestamps

This is a small note which states when the page was last edited (and saved to the web) or automatically updated (i.e. a change was made to another page which affects this page because a WebBot component refers to it).

However, a Timestamp only inserts a date and/or time – you will have to write some explanatory text around it, as in the example below.

1 Click the **Insert WebBot Component** button 𝄞.

2 Select **Timestamp**.

3 Set it to display when it was last **edited** or **updated** by FrontPage.

4 Choose **Date** and **Time** display formats from the drop-down menus.

❑ If you choose a time display with **TZ** after it, this shows the time zone you are in.

5 Click **OK**.

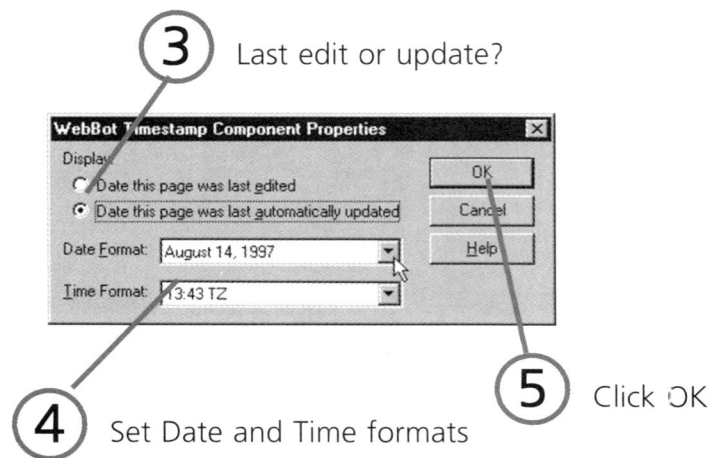

(3) Last edit or update?

(4) Set Date and Time formats

(5) Click OK

Add text around the Timestamp, and format as required

Tip

The font, size and colour of the Timestamp text can be changed in the same way as an ordinary piece of text.

Basic steps

1 Click the **Insert WebBot Component** button 🖳.

2 Select **Search**.

3 Type a prompt in the **Label for Input** field.

4 Specify the **Width** in characters of the field.

5 Type a **Label** for the **Search** button.

6 Type a **Label** for the **Clear** button.

7 Select **Additional information** to display.

8 Click **OK**.

The **Search** component creates a small form which allows visitors to search your whole web (excluding the **_private/** folder). The search returns the number of documents containing the keywords, with links to those pages. You can also choose to include extra information:

● **Score** – shows how close it matches the keywords.

● **File Date** – indicates when the page was last modified.

● **File Size** – gives the file size in kilobytes.

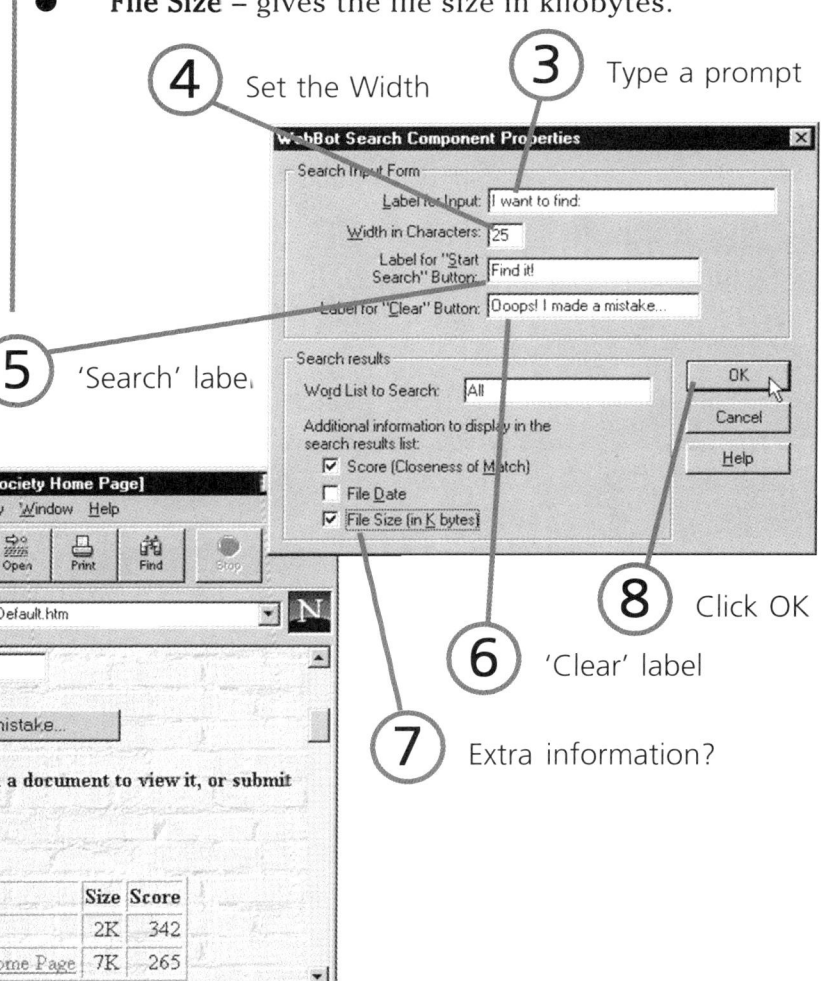

④ Set the Width ③ Type a prompt

⑤ 'Search' label

⑧ Click OK

⑥ 'Clear' label

⑦ Extra information?

Confirmation fields

When a form is submitted, you can opt to display a confirmation page, which might repeat the information for the visitor to double-check, or thank them for sending it. A confirmation field is associated with a named form field, and displays the value which the visitor has just submitted in that field. For example, where [Name] appears in the example below, the user who receives the confirmation page will read whatever he or she typed into the 'Name' field.

1 Click the **Insert WebBot Component** button 🖳.

2 Select **Confirmation field**.

3 Type the name of an existing form field.

4 Click **OK**.

5 When your confirmation page is complete, save it in the **_private/** folder.

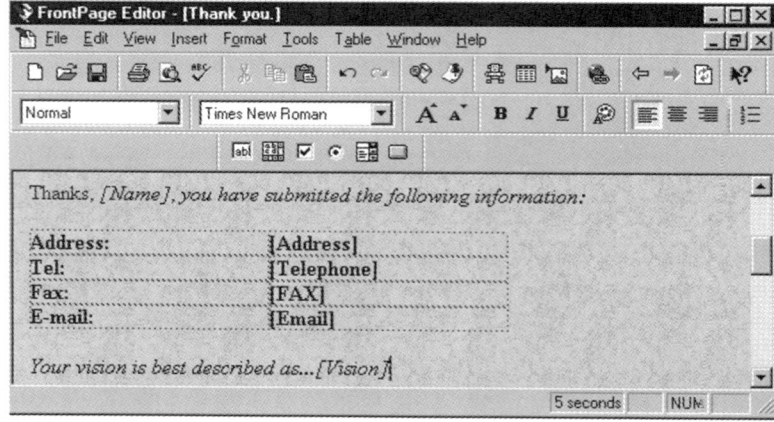

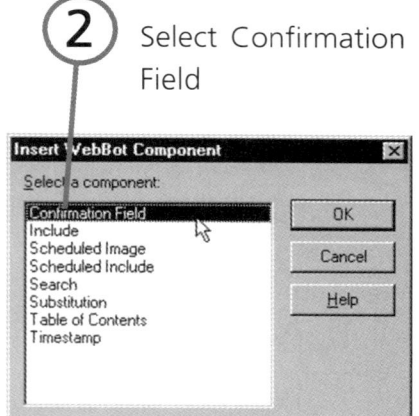

② Select Confirmation Field

③ Type the name

④ Click OK

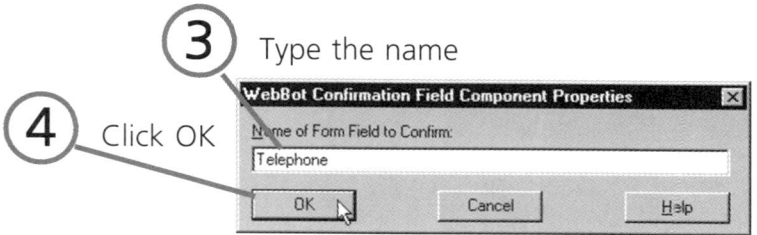

Inserting confirmation fields

Confirmation fields can be inserted wherever you want; once they are there, you can change their size, font and colour - and with them the properties of the text which the user sees on the confirmation page.

Linking it to a form

1 Right-click on the form
   for which you want a
   confirmation and
   choose **Form
   Properties...**

2 Click **Settings...**

3 On the **Confirm** panel,
   Browse... for the
   confirmation page.

4 Click **OK**.

5 Click **OK** again.

Once you have a confirmation page, you will need to edit the appropriate form to tell it to return a confirmation page to the user after they have submitted it.

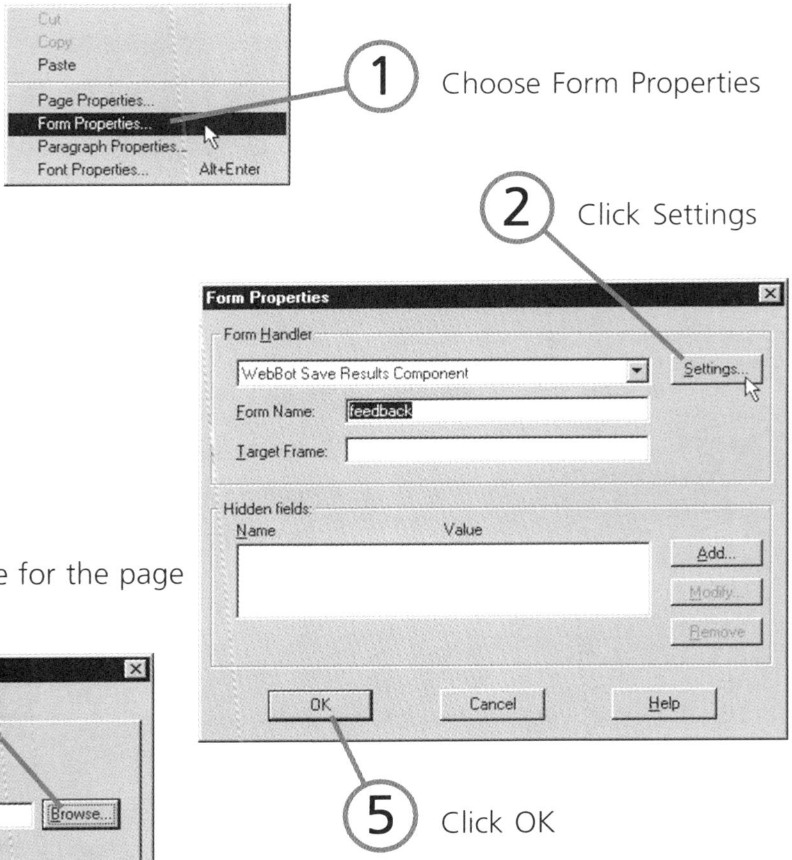

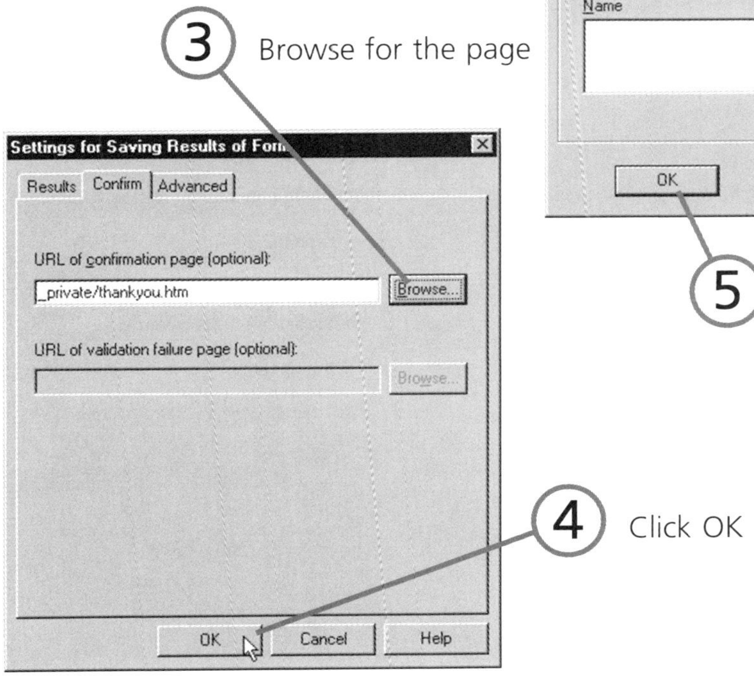

Cut
Copy
Paste

Page Properties...
Form Properties...
Paragraph Properties...
Font Properties...   Alt+Enter

(1) Choose Form Properties

(2) Click Settings

Form Properties

Form Handler

WebBot Save Results Component   Settings...

Form Name: feedback

Target Frame:

Hidden fields:
Name   Value
                                          Add...
                                          Modify...
                                          Remove

OK   Cancel   Help

(3) Browse for the page

Settings for Saving Results of Form

Results | Confirm | Advanced

URL of confirmation page (optional):

_private/thankyou.htm   Browse...

URL of validation failure page (optional):

                                    Browse...

OK   Cancel   Help

(4) Click OK

(5) Click OK

129

Further components

There are three other WebBot components which cannot be inserted into any old page; **Save Results**, **Registration** and **Discussion**. The first is the script which handles information submitted on a form, and the other two are incorporated into special template pages or webs.

Discussion webs

A discussion web allows users to post messages to a page, and to view and reply to other users' messages. The **Discussion Web Wizard** will take you through the process of constructing such a web step by step.

Basic steps

1 In the Explorer window, choose **New – FrontPage Web...** from the **File** menu.

2 Select **Discussion Web Wizard**.

3 Click **OK**.

4 Give the web a name.

5 Click **OK**.

6 Work through the wizard, selecting the options you want.

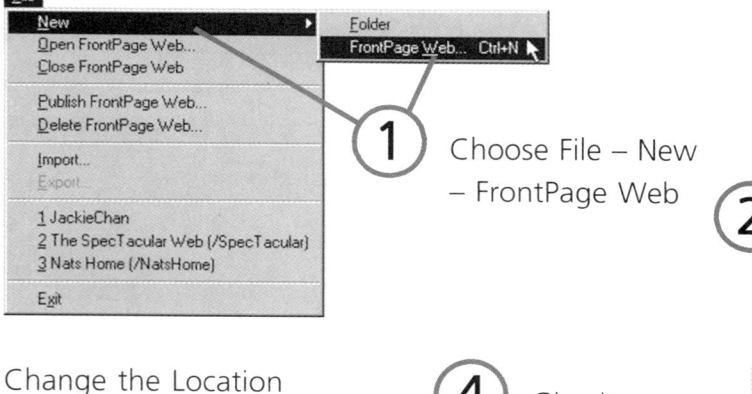

Choose File – New
– FrontPage Web

Select Discussion
Web Wizard

Click OK

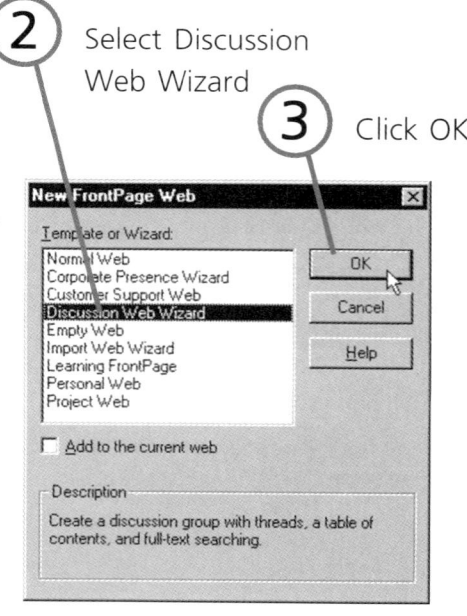

Change the Location
if necessary

Give it a name

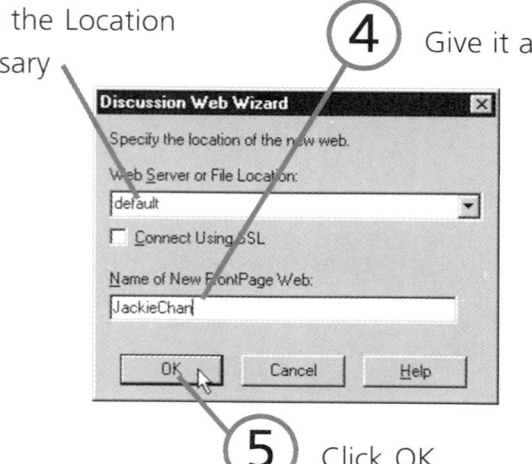

Click OK

7 Click **Next** to move onto the next page of options.

8 Click **Back** to change options you have already selected.

9 When you have answered all the questions, the **Finish** button will become active – click it to create the Discussion Web.

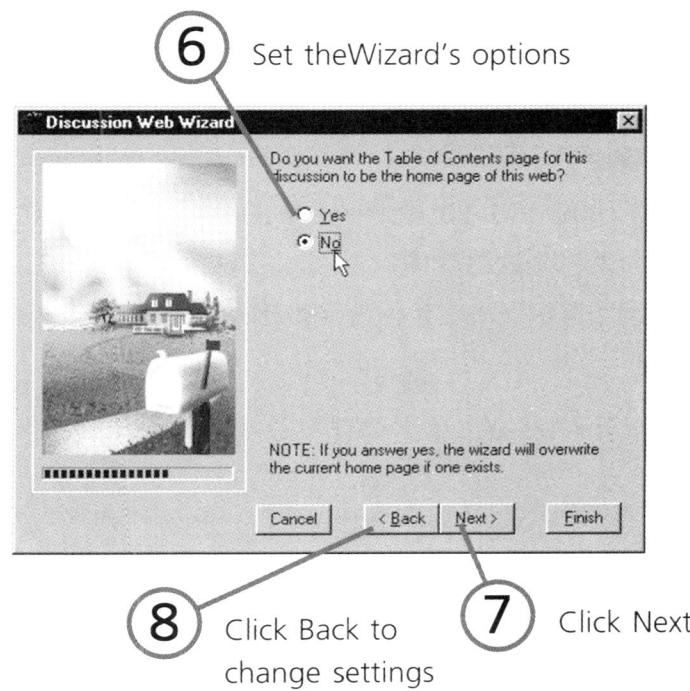

Set theWizard's options

Click Back to change settings

Click Next

User Registration

This is for use with more advanced sites which have webs within webs; using a User Registration page, access to lower-level webs can be controlled. This level of administration requires nothing like a degree in computer science, but it is a little complicated to go into here.

Tip

If you do want to set up restricted-access webs, work your way through the Help files and read the comments built into a new **User Registration** page. Your ISP may also offer FrontPage technical support.

Summary

❏ Use **Include**, **Table of Contents** and **Substitution** components to make your web-building a less tedious affair by getting FrontPage to perform routine tasks automatically.

❏ For other **WebBot** components, your ISP must support **FrontPage Extensions**.

❏ Insert **Scheduled** and **Timestamp** components to keep your web up to date.

❏ Allow visitors to find what they want in your web using a **Search** component.

❏ Confirm the information users have sent to you via a form, or personalise a 'Thank you' page using **Confirmation fields**.

❏ Create a **Discussion Web** from the Explorer window, in which users can read and reply to messages from other users.

❏ You can include a **User Registration** form in your Root Web to allow users access to other webs.

10 Publishing your web

Publishing your web 134

Updating a web 135

Network connections 136

Web Publishing Wizard 138

Troubleshooting 140

Summary 142

Publishing your web

If your connection to the Internet is with a service provider which supports FrontPage Extensions, the process is very simple. In order to use them though, you may have to obtain a **sub-domain** (Web space which has a full http address of its own, rather than the **/~username** format of personal space), so talk to your ISP even if you know that they support the Extensions.

Basic steps

1 Open a web in the Explorer window.

2 From the **File** menu, choose **Publish FrontPage Web...**

3 Type the address of the domain or sub-domain where your web will be published.

4 Enter a name for the web.

5 Make sure that the **Add to an existing FrontPage web** box is not checked.

6 Click **OK**.

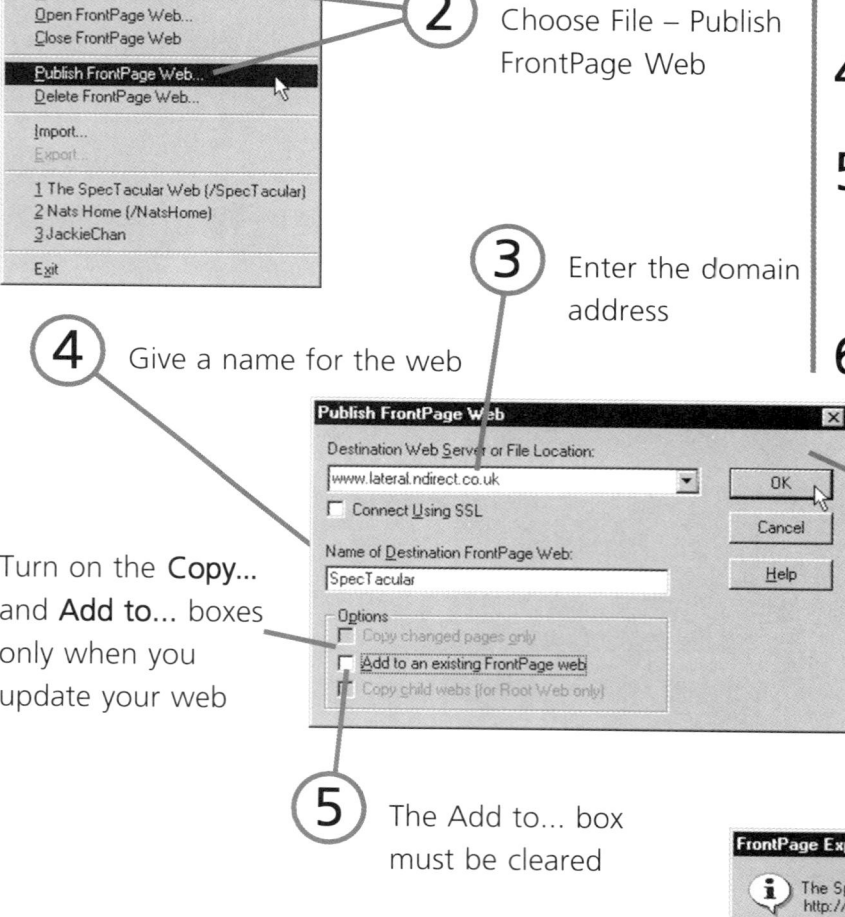

(2) Choose File – Publish FrontPage Web

(3) Enter the domain address

(4) Give a name for the web

Turn on the **Copy...** and **Add to...** boxes only when you update your web

(5) The Add to... box must be cleared

(6) Click OK

You will be told when the upload is complete

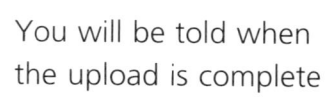

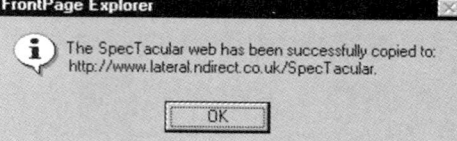

134

Updating a web

Once you have a web up on the World Wide Web, you should update it on a regular basis – the Internet is so awash with information that a static, unchanging site is unlikely to inspire visitors to return to it time and again.

There are two ways of updating your web:

- Connect to the Internet and open your web on-line from the Explorer window. Any changes you save to the web will then be effected immediately.

- Make changes on your PC and publish it as before, but this time checking the **Add to an existing FrontPage web** and **Copy changed pages only** boxes.

If you edit your web at home and then publish it, the pages you have *changed* will be updated on the World Wide Web server, but any pages you *removed* will not be altered. Obsolete pages and images will not be accessible to visitors, but will sit on the server taking up space until you get rid of them. To remove files, you will have to go on-line and make the necessary changes directly on the server.

Tip

While you are working on your web at home, it is a good idea to keep track of any files you are deleting so that you can go on-line later and remove them from your Web server.

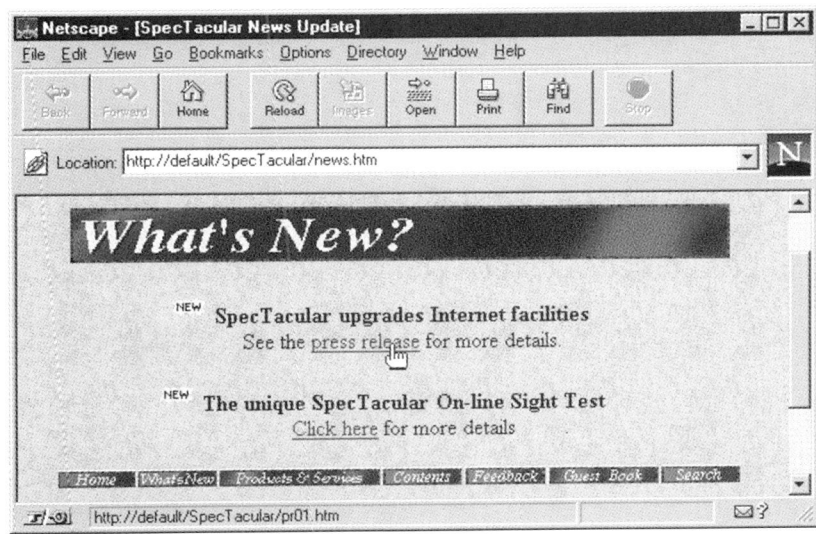

Network connections

Normally when you use the Internet, you are connected to the server's Unix network, but when you try to publish a web, you may well need to be connected to the server's Windows NT network as well. To set this up, you will need to configure your computer's **Network** properties.

The exact process will depend on what version of Windows you use and how your ISP's system works, but the Basic steps given here for Windows 95 may well be useful.

Basic steps

1 Open the **Control Panel** from the **Start** menu.

2 Double-click on the **Network** icon.

❏ If **Client for Microsoft Networks** is installed, go to step 7, otherwise:

3 Click **Add...**

4 Select **Client** and click **Add...**

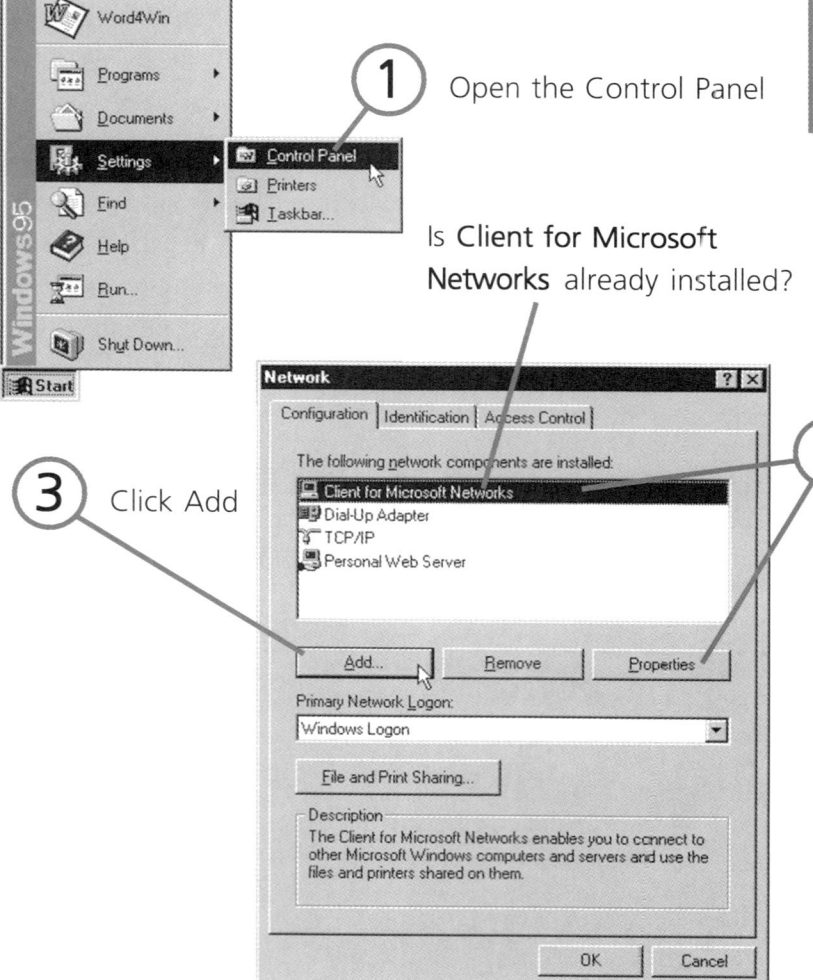

① Open the Control Panel

Is **Client for Microsoft Networks** already installed?

③ Click Add

⑦ Select Client and click Properties

Tip

If you having difficulty publishing your web, the network connections are the most likely source of the problems.

5 Select **Microsoft** in the
   Manufacturers pane,
   **Client for Microsoft
   Networks** in the
   Network Clients pane.

6 Click **OK**.

7 Highlight **Client for
   Microsoft Networks**
   and click **Properties…**

8 Turn on **Log on to
   Windows NT domain**
   and **Quick logon** (your
   ISP will tell you the
   name to enter in the
   Windows NT domain
   field).

9 Click **OK**.

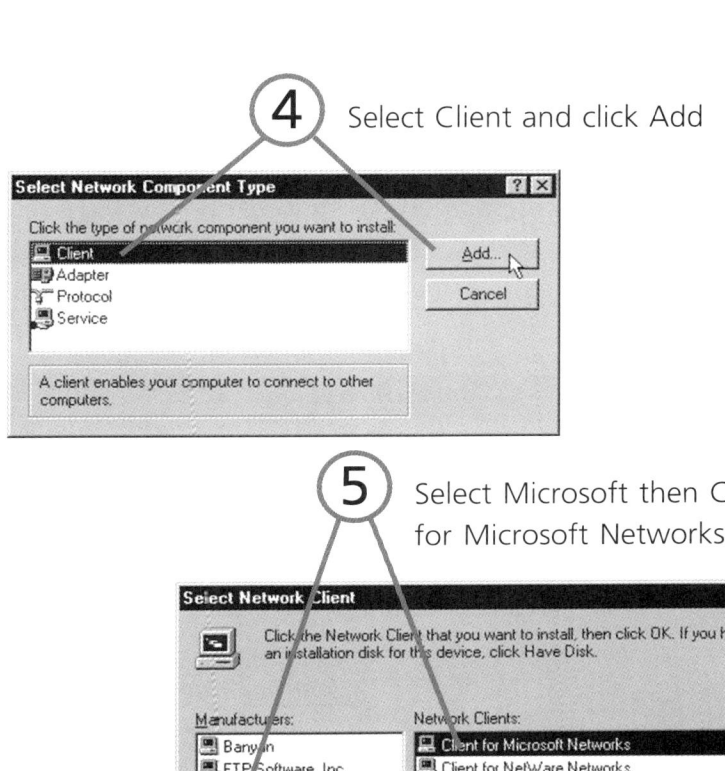

Select Client and click Add

Select Microsoft then Client
for Microsoft Networks

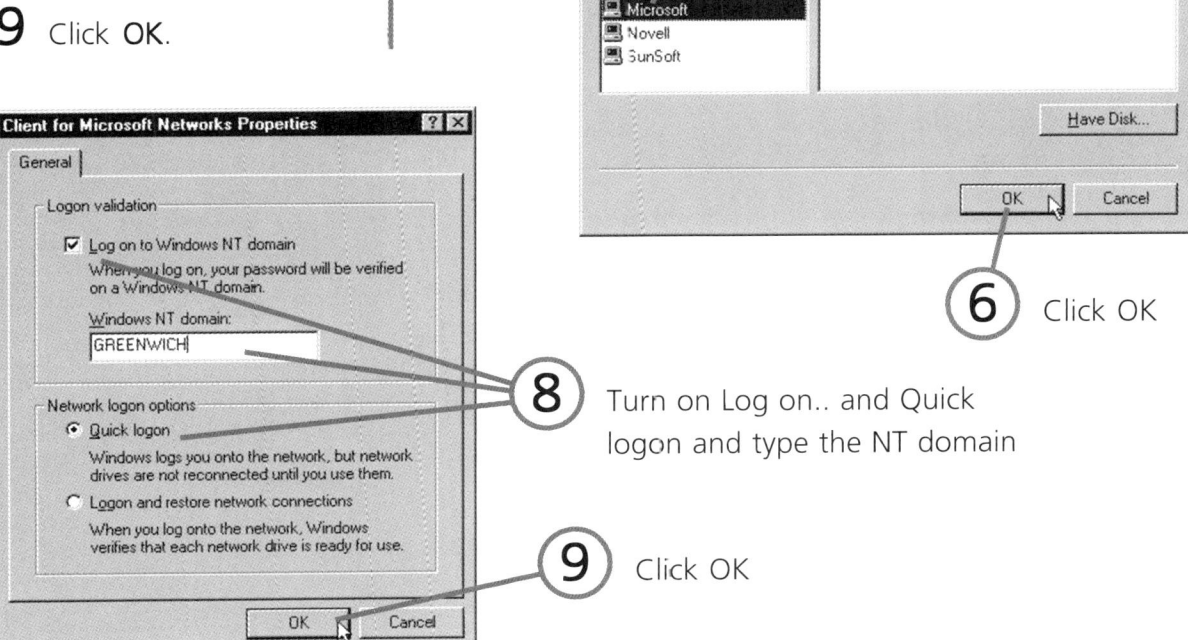

Click OK

Turn on Log on.. and Quick
logon and type the NT domain

Click OK

137

Web Publishing Wizard

There is a **Publishing Wizard** on the FrontPage CD-ROM which will guide you through the publishing process if your ISP does not support FrontPage Extensions.

If you have not already installed it, run the CD-ROM and click the **Web Publishing Wizard** icon  to install it.

1 Open the **Publishing Wizard** from the **Start** menu.

2 Follow the instructions given at each stage.

3 When you **Browse Folders…** for the web folder, it should be in **\Webshare\Wwwroot**

① Open the Publishing Wizard

Check the list – your provider might be there!

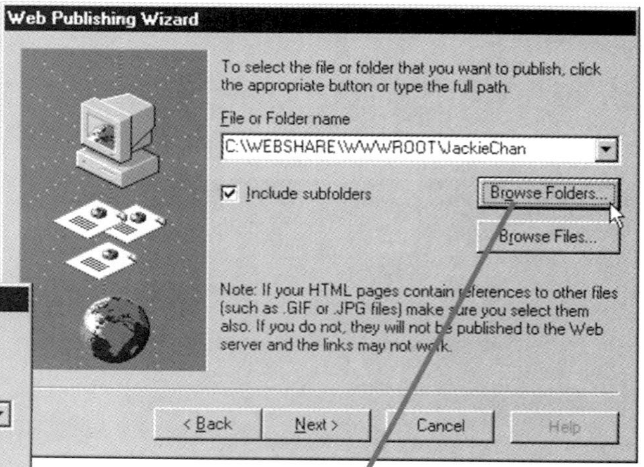

③ Browse for the web folder

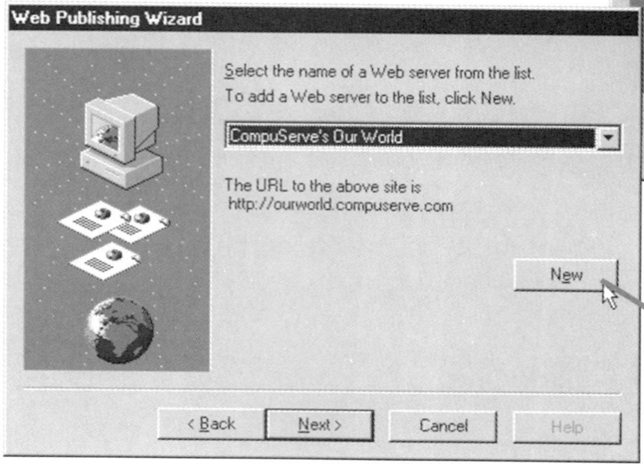

④ Click New

4 Your service provider will probably not be listed, so click **New**.

5 Type a name for your web space (this will be the same even if you have several different webs on it).

6 Enter the URL of your web space.

7 The dial-up connection to your ISP should be detected and entered automatically.

8 Click **Next** then **Finish**.

(5) Type a name for your web space

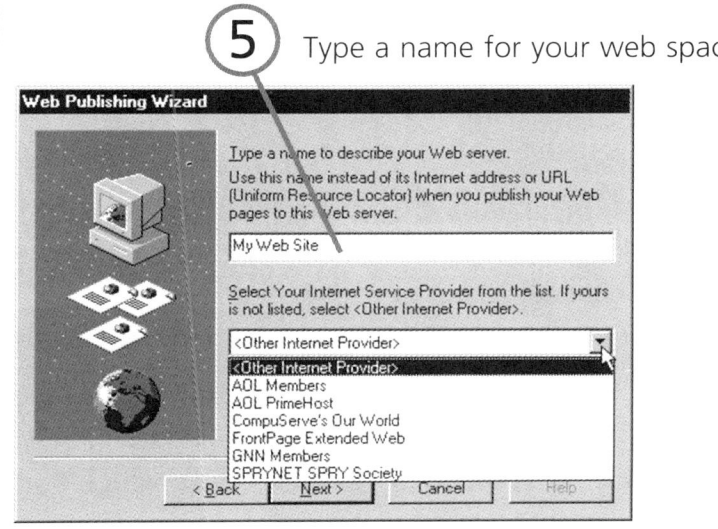

(7) Use Dial-up Networking

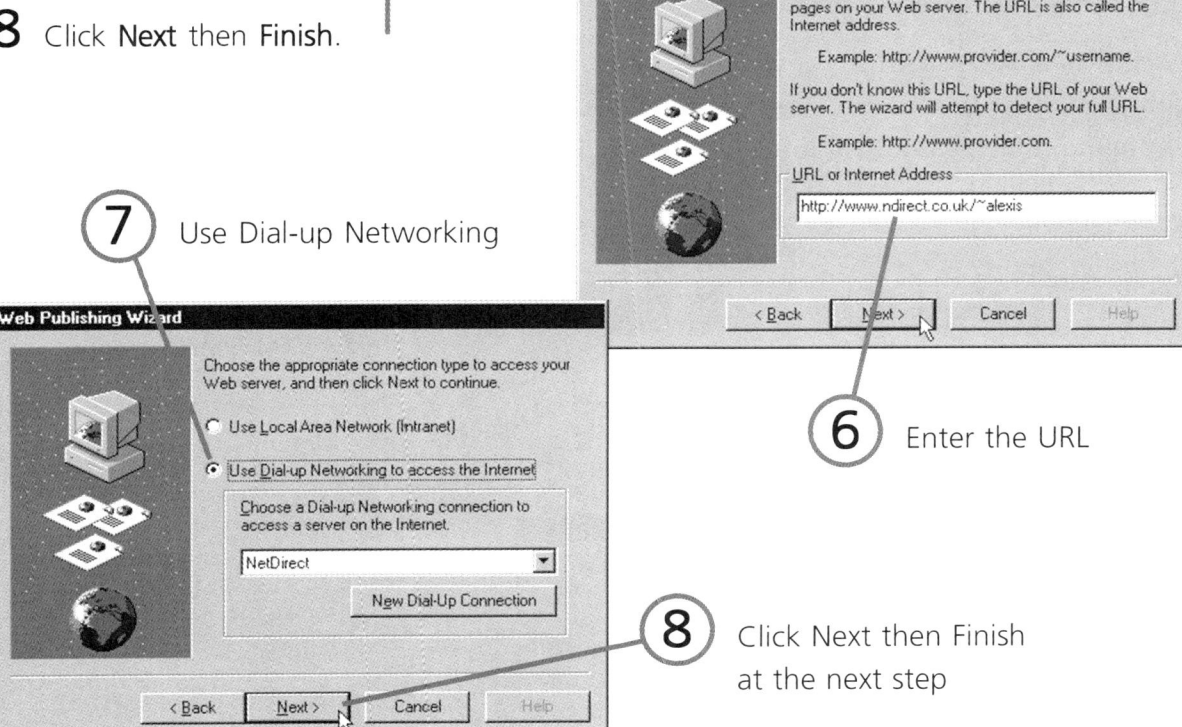

(6) Enter the URL

(8) Click Next then Finish at the next step

Troubleshooting

When the files of your web are transferred to a World Wide Web server, they are sent in a format called **File Transfer Protocol** (FTP). The information is received at the server's FTP address, which is slightly different to the http address which your browser visits to view web sites.

You may find when you try to publish your web onto your ISP's server that an error message is displayed, and a likely cause of this is that FrontPage has been unable to determine the FTP address to send files to.

To get around the problem, you will first need to find out your ISP's FTP address, and the directory to which you should publish your web. You may find this somewhere in the documentation sent to you by your ISP, or they may have a Help page on their Web site which deals with publishing or uploading problems.

If there is a section which explains how to upload your web from a DOS window, you will find two important command lines, which will look something like this:

```
Type: ftp ftp.ndirect.co.uk
```
```
Type: cd www
```
This is the ISP's FTP address

This is the directory to publish to

If you don't see anything which looks like the right information, just call your ISP and ask them.

1 Run through the **Publishing Wizard**'s steps as before.

2 When the error message appears, click **OK**.

3 Ensure that **FTP – File Transfer Protocol** is checked.

4 Make sure that your username and password are correct.

5 Enter the FTP address of your ISP.

6 Enter the correct directory (**Subfolder**).

❑ You should now get a message saying that FrontPage is ready to publish.

7 Click **Finish**.

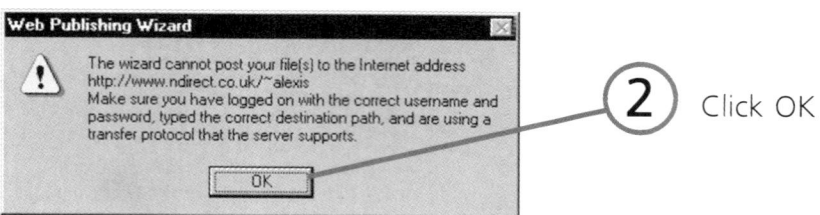

Click OK

140

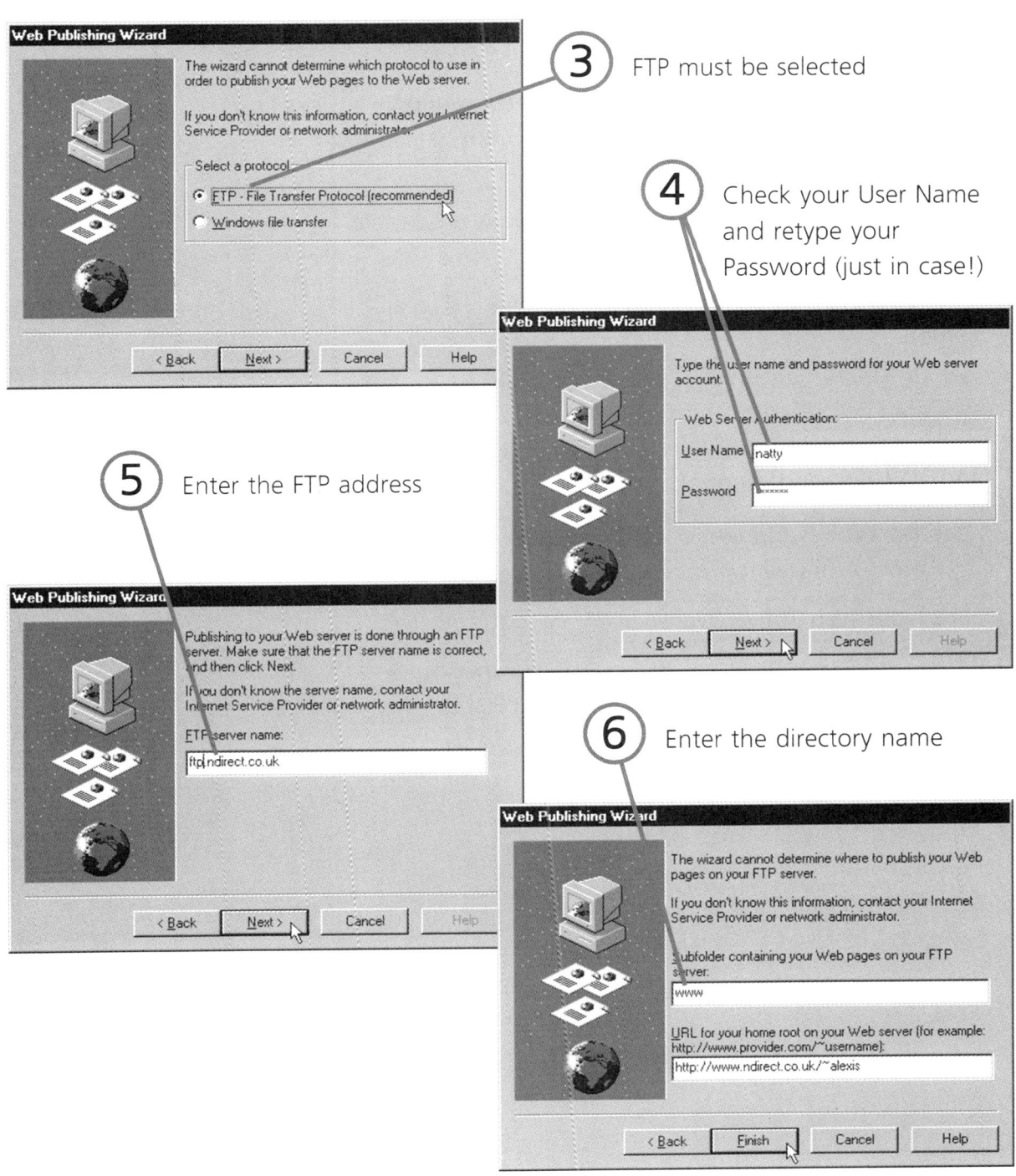

③ FTP must be selected

④ Check your User Name and retype your Password (just in case!)

⑤ Enter the FTP address

⑥ Enter the directory name

141

Summary

If your ISP supports FrontPage Extensions

❑   **Publish a FrontPage Web** from the Explorer window, ensuring that the **Add to an existing web** option is *not* checked.

❑   **Update a web** by publishing changed pages only – this time select **Add to an existing web** ...

❑   ...or **connect to the Internet** to update a web in real time.

❑   Check your **Network connections** if you are having trouble.

If your ISP does not support FrontPage Extensions

❑   Use the **Web Publishing Wizard** to guide you through the process (install it if necessary).

❑   Find your web in the **\Webshare\Wwwroot** folder.

❑   If you are having trouble, ask your ISP for their **ftp address** and the **directory** you should publish to.

❑   You may also be able to find this information from the **help pages at your ISP's Web site**.

Links and resources

www.microsoft.com/FrontPageSupport

The FrontPage section of Microsoft's home will keep you up-to-date with FrontPage development, but you will be lucky to get much help without having to pay for it.

news.microsoft.public.frontpage.client

The FrontPage newsgroup is an invaluable resource – if you have a problem, it is almost guaranteed that you will find a solution here.

www.jazzpiano.com/frontpage97

Chris Calabrese's FrontPage 97 Information Web is an unofficial FrontPage site which I have found much more useful than Microsoft.

www.ndirect.co.uk

NetDirect are one of the few ISPs to support FrontPage Extensions, and friendly to boot.

www.worldwidemart.com/scripts

Matt's Script Archive has a huge downloadable range of CGI and Perl scripts for putting various clever tricks into your web.

www.activex.com

A site dedicated to ActiveX – go to the Information Desk to find the Beginner's Guide, which is genuinely helpful.

www.xm.com/caf_/applets

The Caf_ del Sol is a site where you can download applets with clear instructions on how to use them.

Index

A

ActiveX 59
Advanced toolbar 7
Alignment 24
Animated GIFs 56
Art effects 42
AVI video clips 51
   Display options 52

B

Background image 12
Background sounds 33
Bookmarks 78
   Links to 79
   Navigating with 79

C

Cell padding 64
Cell spacing 64
Cell Span, in tables 69
Check boxes 115
Colours
   Setting 11
   Tables 65
   Transparent 32
Composer window 37
Configure Editors 36
Confirmation fields 128
Custom grids 98

D

Discussion component 130
Discussion webs 130
Drop-down menus 116
   Validation 116

E

Editing cells 69
Editor window 6
Excel spreadsheet data 70
Explorer window 4

F

Filters, Image Composer 42
Folder view 4
Font 22
   Colour 22
   Size 21
   Special styles 23
Forms 104
   Creating 108
   Data 106
   Hidden fields 107
   Layout 109
   Names and values 105
   Properties 106
Forms toolbar 7
Frame Set
   Creating 94

Frames 92
  Attributes 96
  Custom grids 98
  Editing 96
  Source URL 96
Frames Wizard 94
FrontPage Extensions 124

G

Gif Animator 57
Group Name, buttons 114

H

Header Cell, in tables 69
Headings 21
Hotspots 84
  Editing 86
HTML editors 2
Hyperlink view 4
Hyperlinks
  Checking 88
  External 83
  Following 79
  Recalculating 87

I

Images
  Alternative representations 31
  as links 84
  Background 12
  Copy and Paste 27

Drag and drop 28
Placing 26
Properties 29
Image Composer 36
Image maps 84
Image toolbar 7

J

Java 59
JavaScript 59

L

Links
  Background of image maps 86
  E-mail 81
  Editing 88
  External 89
  Reciprocal 83
  to a new page 82
  to other pages 80
  to Web pages 83
  Using images 84
Lists
  Bulleted 24
  Definition 25
  Directory 25
  Numbered 24

M

Margins 13
Marquees 54

Menu bar 6
Merging cells 66
MOV video format 53
MPEG video format 53

N

NetDirect 124
Network connections 136

O

One-line text box 110

P

Page
  Opening 8
  Saving 10
Page layout 72
Parameters 122
Preview 14
Publishing 134
  Troubleshooting 140
  without Extensions 138
Push buttons 113

R

Radio buttons 114
  Validation 114
Registration component 130

S

Save Results component 130
Saving a page 10
Scheduled components 125
Scrolling text boxes 110
Search component 127
Sounds, background 33
Sprites 38
  Erasing 46
  Extracting part 47
  Grouping and flattening 44
  Layering 41
  Patterns and Fills 45
  Shaped 40
Style pages 13
Substitutions 122

T

Tables 62
  Adjusting layout 74
  Adjusting the size 63
  and page design 71
  Borders 65
  Delete Rows or Columns 63
  Editing cells 69
  Importing data 70
  Insert Rows or Columns 63
  Merging cells 66
  Properties 64
  Splitting cells 68
  Troubleshooting 75

Text 20
Text boxes 110
  Validation 111
Text index, in Search 87
Timestamps 126
To Do List 16
Toolbars 6, 7, 108
Troubleshooting
  Publishing 140
  Tables 75

U

User Registration 131

V

Validation
  Drop-down menus 116
  Radio buttons 114
  Text box 111
Validation failure page 112

Verify Hyperlinks 88
Video formats 53

W

Warps 42
  Interactive 43
  Settings 43
Watermarks 12
Web 2
  Creating new 2
  Settings 122
  Templates 2
  Updating 135
Web Publishing Wizard 138
WebBot
  Save Results 106
WebBot components 120
Window Size, in Preview 14
Windows NT network 136
World Wide Web locations 83